CREATIVITY, IMAGINATION AND INNOVATION

Perspectives and Inspirational Stories

CREATIVITY, IMAGINATION AND INNOVATION

Perspectives and Inspirational Stories

Editor

Xavier Pavie
ESSEC Business School, Singapore

 **World Scientific**

NEW JERSEY • LONDON • SINGAPORE • BEIJING • SHANGHAI • HONG KONG • TAIPEI • CHENNAI • TOKYO

Published by

World Scientific Publishing Co. Pte. Ltd.

5 Toh Tuck Link, Singapore 596224

USA office: 27 Warren Street, Suite 401-402, Hackensack, NJ 07601

UK office: 57 Shelton Street, Covent Garden, London WC2H 9HE

British Library Cataloguing-in-Publication Data

A catalogue record for this book is available from the British Library.

The original title of the Work (Le goût d'imaginer sa vie) is Copyright © Société d'Édition Les Belles Lettres, 2018. Translation by Roisein Kelly.

CREATIVITY, IMAGINATION AND INNOVATION
Perspectives and Inspirational Stories

ISBN 978-981-3272-99-6

For any available supplementary material, please visit
https://www.worldscientific.com/worldscibooks/10.1142/11063#t=suppl

Desk Editors: Sandhya Venkatesh/Daniele Lee

Typeset by Stallion Press
Email: enquiries@stallionpress.com

Printed in Singapore

INTRODUCTION: HAVING THE TASTE FOR IMAGINING ONE'S LIFE

Prof. Xavier Pavie

Director of iMagination Centre
ESSEC Business School

Taste is chemistry, an experience which involves mixing a large number of elements, creating a sensation as much as trying to explain it. Like touch and smell, sight and hearing, taste is, in the first instance, subjective and our attempts to objectify it through explanation and justification come later. If it can be said that taste is chemistry, this is the case because it involves mixture and combination, and, like chemistry, it assembles and associates. Chemistry addresses the composition, reactions and properties of materials by examining atoms and their interactions. Taste does the same, using the eyes, nose, tongue and the rest of the body to analyze what is presented to it in order to accept, reject, love, benefit from, enjoy or push it away. Our taste is constantly on the alert, in response to a piece of music or a painting, food or a smell. It remains on the alert and protects us, teaches us and makes us grow. Taste gives meaning to the senses, because it builds us up and makes us who we are. Always under construction, always learning, taste is the essence and the driving force behind living beings, especially for those who want to remain alive. Because taste can fade, be reduced to what it already knows, lose its capacity for further learning and no longer be confronted in order to remain in a state of constant development. Taste is alive if it is considered as such. The life of a living being resonates to the same extent because it is an alchemy: physical, intellectual and spiritual. And it must be fueled perpetually and be constantly challenged by experiences and confrontations, discoveries and trials. It is the vivaciousness of life that makes it worth living. It learns by doing, develops by choosing, grows through its development and only achieves fulfillment through being lived. The activity of living is not a matter of course and living a conformist, traditional life without taking the trouble to live to the full is not only possible but very often becomes the normal, not to say trivial, course of events. Only a minority of individuals seek to invent their lives and to break free from conformity, for the simple reason that singularity often requires effort, time, failure and disillusionment. To design, imagine and have a taste for imagining one's life is to choose to exist via a long, winding path that is complex and loaded with obstacles, but which leads to wisdom and knowledge, the pillars of humanity. In the 1970s and early 1980s, Michel Foucault gave this quest and need to build one's life the name "the aesthetics of existence."

IMAGINING THE AESTHETICS OF EXISTENCE

Michel Foucault uses this expression "aesthetics of existence" to describe life attitudes and behaviors: "I would like to show how, in classical Antiquity, sexual activity and sexual pleasures were problematized through practices of the self, bringing into play the criteria of an aesthetics of existence."[1] More specifically, it is defined as the practice of the art of living, the art of existence, an ethical practice consisting of freely imposing on one's way of life an individual form and style that give birth to a "way of life whose moral value does not depend either on one's being in conformity with a code of behaviour, or on an effort of purification, but on certain formal principles in the use of pleasures, in the distribution that is made of them, in the limits we observe, in the hierarchy we respect."[2] This aesthetics of existence does not cover merely a dimension related to pleasure or an individual dimension, and this is understandable when we describe it in contemporary philosophy and more broadly in contemporary thought through modernity. Foucault returns to the notion of modernity in the work What is the Enlightenment?[3] drawing on Baudelaire in his book "The

---

[1] Cf. the question of the bivum in Antiquity, Xavier Pavie, Le choix d'exister, Les Belles Lettres 2015, pp. 35–45; Michel Foucault, "Usage des plaisirs, techniques de soi" in Dits et écrits II, op. cit, p. 1365.

[2] Michel Foucault, Histoire de la sexualité II, L'usage des plaisirs, op. cit, pp. 120–121.

[3] Michel Foucault, "Qu'est-ce que les Lumières", in Dits et écrits II, op. cit, p. 1381.

Painter of Modern Life?" Modernity is not simply a form of relationship with the present, it is also a way of establishing oneself.[4] That is why modernity is in strong correlation with asceticism, because accepting oneself in a life lived in the present would not be enough to be modern, since it means considering oneself as a specific object of construction, which Baudelaire calls "dandyism." Foucault takes time to comment on Baudelaire's work, which depicts the asceticism of the dandy who uses his body, his desires and his behavior to make his existence "*a work of art*".[5] For Baudelaire, Foucault recalls, "*the modern man is not the one who sets out to discover himself, his secrets, and his hidden truth: he is the one who seeks to invent himself. Modernity does not liberate man in his own being, it compels him to face the task of producing himself*".[6] It should be noted that for Baudelaire, this self-production and self-invention can only take place exclusively in art and not in society. This position is not adopted by Foucault, for whom art is not the only possible place for self-development.

Modernity has to do with the stylization of oneself, like the creation of a work of art. A form of stylization exists in the sense of a work done on oneself, a self to which one has to give a form: a form of self and a form of existence. For neither the self nor existence are in any way preformed, and something has to be made of them. Work is required on an aesthetics of existence, and that is what the dandy does.[7] We must be careful to work, train and stylize this self and this existence. This stylization is put into practice by the ancient Greek model, which demanded self-control in relation to one's own body but also to women, boys and the truth. Baudelaire's dandyism is a new aesthetic shaping that has become disciplined. Standing paradoxically against Greek conventions and moderation, dandyism implies no less for Baudelaire himself the "*rigorous laws to which all its subjects are rigorously submitted*".[8] Foucault's reference to Baudelaire's work, "*The Painter of Modern Life*" is famous for the defense and updating of this notion of the aesthetics of existence. The dandy is, in a way, the figurehead of this Foucauldian concept, with a modern application.

---

[4] *Ibid.,* p. 1389.

[5] *Ibid.,* p. 1390.

[6] *Ibid.,* p. 1390. Cf. Baudelaire, "Le peintre de la vie modern", in *Critique d'art*, Gallimard, "Folio", 1992, p. 345, 350–351, 369–372.

[7] Frédéric Gros, "Le souci de soi chez Michel Foucault", *op. cit.,* p. 26.

[8] Charles Baudelaire, "Le peintre de la vie moderni", *op. cit.,* p. 369.

Dandyism for Baudelaire is a "*vague institution*"[9] outside the realm of law, produced by the independent character of individuals whose only perspective is that of "*cultivating the idea of beauty in their own persons, satisfying their passions, feeling and thinking*".[10] Baudelaire, in these few words, which begin the chapter "The dandy", both shows the idea of making oneself a work of art and at the same time develops the concept of resistance, as Foucault would seek to establish it with regard to the issue of power, even if this resistance is only an indirect consequence of the desire to make oneself a work of art. In other words, one can wonder whether Foucault, from one and the same idea in Baudelaire's works, which is to make oneself a work of art with the effect of being outside the realm of law, does not bring out two ideas — firstly, resistance to power outside the realm of law, preserving one's independence and secondly, the idea of making oneself a work of art. All the more so since the very concept of resistance in Foucault is at least two-fold: on the one hand, the idea of protest and rejection of power, on the other hand a positive process of creation.[11]

Although Foucault has shown how he brings this notion of a work of art closer to an aesthetics of modern existence, the notion of resistance does not appear as clearly in Baudelaire's writings. In fact, the resistance that can be read in Baudelaire's works is, on the one hand, the composing of the dandy as a work of art outside the realm of law but, on the other hand, as the poet shows, the notion that "*dandyism appears especially during transitional periods when democracy is only partially faltering and debased*".[12] In the confusion of these periods, when individuals are "*downgraded, disgusted and idle*"[13] dandyism comes along, somehow proposing a way of life, a method "*that work and money cannot confer*".[14] Of course, this is not exactly the same resistance to power relations that Foucault seeks to develop, and that is probably why he does not refer to it, because, for Baudelaire, the dandy turns to a preferable form of aristocracy, almost

---

[9] *Ibid*, p. 370.
[10] *Idem.*
[11] Michel Foucault, "Michel Foucault, une interview : sexe, pouvoir et la politique de l'identité", in *Dits et écrits II, op. cit*, p. 1560.
[12] Charles Baudelaire, "Le peintre de la vie moderne", *op. cit*, p. 371.
[13] *Idem.*
[14] *Idem.*

castigating democracy," *which invades everything and levels everything.*"[15] One can cannot help but see the connection with Tocqueville, who could be described as a dandy, at least from a political perspective. Nevertheless, although, fundamentally, Foucault's political perspective departs from that of dandyism, this does not prevent dandyism from being a form of resistance through a life proposal directly opposed to what is traditional.

IMAGINING ONESELF AS A WORK OF ART

The issue of creating lifestyles arises in Foucault's writings, as he studies the way we are produced as subjected individuals and on the means of escaping from this subjugation.[16] At this point, Foucault is focusing on Greece as part of his *History of Sexuality*. Ancient philosophers interest him because they show that one can shape one's own subjectivity by working on oneself. These different lifestyles in the Hellenistic epoch inspired him in his attempt to get rid of both the ways of being and also the thoughts handed down by History and imposed by social structures and traditions. The consequence must be the reinvention of oneself, a new original creation of oneself.

This self-creation, like that of our ancestors during Antiquity, calls for a set of elaborate, rigorous practices whose aim is to inflict on the self the control and examination of oneself, both from the point of view of behavior and that of regime, body and mind. The challenge is to rediscover the spirit of a certain type of self-control and self-sufficiency with the expectation of happiness, which existed in ancient times. This means stylizing oneself, perfecting oneself by oneself, which is the source of pleasure as well as happiness. The famous "stylization" of the ancient philosophers, which Foucault emphasizes, is the process of what one submits to in order

---

[15] *Ibid.*, p. 372.

[16] It should also be noted that Foucault obtained the model for the idea of an aesthetics of existence, of the creation of oneself by oneself that he would seek out in Greek writings, in the United States during the period when he taught in Berkeley and New York during the 1970s. During this time, he discovered the gay communities and the practices of subjectivation, self-creation and new models between individuals and new ways of life. He became aware of the stylization of existence, self-practices and collective experiences, all of which related to his work, at the time, on Greek and Roman Antiquity. Cf. Didier Eribon, *L'infréquentable Michel Foucault. Renewals of critical thought* (dir.), Actes du colloque du centre Georges-Pompidou, 21–22 June 2000, EPEL, 2001. Quoted in *Hérésie*, Fayard, 2003, pp. 35–64.

to achieve these challenges. As summarized by David Halperin, "*self-cultivation then produces a self that can offer the same type of pleasure to its owner as a beautiful physique or a work of art.*"[17] Thus, in Foucault's works, this ancient self-culture, in its subjectivity, helps an individual to control himself and to stylize his existence according to his own definition of the most "beautiful" and "pleasant" way of life.

It is in this context that Foucault expresses regret that society is interested in art only through objects and not individuals,[18] clarifying that he is astonished that art is a field of specialists where the experts are the artists. He wonders why life cannot be a work of art: "*What surprises me is the fact that in our society art has become something that only relates to objects and has no relation with individuals or with life, and also that art is a specialized field of experts who are artists. Could not the life of any individual be a work of art? Are a painting or a house objects of art, but not our life?*"[19] To this question, Foucault answers that the use of *bios* as material for a work of art should be considered, stating: "*I think that there is only one practical outworking to this idea of the self which is not a given fact [...], we must make ourselves a work of art.*"[20]

If Foucault suggests making oneself a work of art, with the intention of constituting an aesthetics of existence as he applies it to himself, this is not with a view to dissemination, exhibition or artistic exhibition. The project is to make one's life a work of art without going as far as to say that being a "work of art" is the final goal. Aestheticism is no longer simply understood as aesthetic dandyism, but above all as a transformation of oneself by oneself[21]: "*My problem is my own transformation. This transformation of oneself by one's own knowledge is, I believe, something quite close to the aesthetic experience. Why would a painter work if he is not transformed by his painting?*"[22]

17 David Halperin, *Saint Foucault, op. cit.*, p. 84.

18 Michel Foucault, "On a genealogy of ethics", in *Dits et écrits II, op. cit.*, p. 1436.

19 *Ibid.*, p. 1211 et 1436 (slightly modified).

20 *Idem.*

21 Michel Foucault, "An interview with Michel Foucault by Stephen Riggins", in *Dits et écrits II, op. cit.*, p. 1354. "For me intellectual work is connected with what you would define as a form of aesthetics — by which I mean self-transformation."

22 *Ibid.*, p. 1355.

In addition, and this is in line with the notions of change, transformation and innovation, which are important for Foucault,[23] the execution of a work of art has a strong unknown dimension at the beginning of its creation. What will this work of art ultimately be? What will it look like? When will it be completed, if it can be? This is the paradox of the project to make his life a work of art without saying what this work of art will be, or even exhibit it as such in the usual places of art.

In fact, this "aesthetic remodeling"[24] is carried out from a meliorist perspective. It is only this search for improvement that drives the creation of this work of art, "*to train, surpass oneself and control the appetites that might carry you away.*"[25] It consists firstly of working on oneself, on who one is, what one wants to be and secondly of training, exercise and effective practice; what is required is "*to give one's life a style through patient exercise and daily work*",[26] as Foucault goes on to say, quoting a statement by Nietzsche here. As is the case for artistic work, thoroughness, rigor, exercise and practice are needed. It is this repetitive, daily work on oneself, on one's style of being and life that demonstrates the analogy with art. With Foucault, there is a desire for permanent work on oneself because: "*The main interest of life and work is that they allow you to become someone different from who you were at the beginning.*"[27] This is the principle of all art, the blank canvas on which a painting will be created, a piece of music paper where the notes will be placed, or a block of stone from which a shape emerges. There are as many ways to build art as there are multiple ways to build oneself.

Foucauldian *subjectivation* is an unlimited gesture in terms of time as well as methods. It is up to each individual and each group to invent the form that suits them and to continue working constantly to reinvent themselves. This invention of life forms is both unknown and mysterious

---

[23] Michel Foucault, *Le Courage de la vérité, Le gouvernement de soi et des autres II, op. cit.*, p. 228. Cf. Michel Foucault, "Le triomphe social du plaisir sexuel: une conversation avec Michel Foucaul", *in Dits et écrits II, op. cit.*, pp. 1127–1133.

[24] Richard Shusterman, *Vivre la philosophie — Pragmatisme et art de vivre*, trad. Christian Fournier et Jean-Pierre Cometti, Klincksieck, 2001, p. 57.

[25] Michel Foucault, "L'éthique du souci de soi comme pratique de la liberté", *in Dits et écrits II, op. cit.*, p. 1531.

[26] Michel Foucault, "À propos de la généalogie de l'éthique", *in Dits et écrits II, op. cit.*, p. 1437.

[27] Michel Foucault, "Vérité, pouvoir et soi", *in Dits et écrits II, op. cit.*, p. 1596.

but, for Foucault, this game of life and self-construction "*is worth it only to the extent that we do not know how it will end.*"[28] *Subjectivation* is the permanent reinvention of oneself that takes on existence only in multiplicity and plurality. What matters is that the individual invents himself for his own good; that he lets himself be carried away by the idea of another life whose boundaries we do not necessarily know, but which will lead to his well-being.

Richard Rorty specifies that what Foucault wanted was the good of his fellows and, at the same time, an identity different from theirs, "*he wanted to help them, while inventing a self that had nothing in common with theirs.*"[29]

This ability to make oneself a work of art is also for Foucault a contemporary way of actualizing cynical philosophy. And it is in art that we are still able to find aspects of cynicism: "*Art is capable of giving existence a form that breaks with all others, the form of real life.*"[30] Going for "real life" is one of the most fundamental issues facing cynics. Foucault associates art directly with the cynical attitude: "I therefore believe that this idea of the artist's life as a condition of artistic work, the authentication of artistic work, the work of art itself, is a way to resume, in a different light, with another profile and of course another form, this cynical principle of life as a manifestation of scandalous rupture, by which the truth is revealed, manifested and given form."[31] What Foucault is seeking to show is that modern art establishes a relationship which is not of the order of imitation, of ornamentation. On the contrary, it lays bare, it decodes, it brings back to basics. At elementary level, it is true that modern art proceeds from the laying bare of existence, "*this is cynicism in culture, the cynicism of culture turned against itself.*"[32]

For Foucault, cynicism is present in contemporary philosophy, as it seems to have always been present. One could thus, through the centuries, create a history of cynicism that would extend from Antiquity to the

---

[28] *Idem.*
[29] Richard Rorty, "Identité morale et autonomie privée", *in Michel Foucault philosophe. Rencontre internationale Paris, 9, 10, 11 janvier 1988, op. cit.*, p. 388.
[30] Michel Foucault, *Le Courage de la vérité, op. cit.*, p. 173.
[31] *Idem.*
[32] *Idem.*

present day,[33] with German authors such as Nietzsche, Tillich, Heinrich, Gehlen or Sloterdijk.[34] One might wonder if Foucault himself would not be included in this enumeration of thinkers who actualize cynicism, which ceaselessly mixes the concern for the aesthetics of existence with *parrhesia*[35] — fundamental for the cynics — this may involve politics, but also madness and power.

Foucault's intention to make his life a work of art often seems precursory. He is not, however, the initiator of this metaphor in contemporary philosophy. Strangely enough, here again, he never refers to Anglo-Saxon thought, a whole current of thought from Walter Pater to Oscar Wilde, which expressly puts forward the idea of making one's life a work of art. The latter expresses in fact that *"to become a work of art is the object of life"*,[36] since for him life itself is a work of art. The work and life of Wilde are composed in this way, the latter referring, like Foucault, to the Hellenistic period to create an aesthetic of oneself.[37] In *"Pen, Pencil and Poison"*, Wilde clearly expands the dimensions of an aesthetics of existence through Wainewright. Wilde says of him that *"as an art critic, he is particularly interested in the complex impressions produced by a work of art, and to be aware of the impressions one feels is surely the first step in aesthetic criticism."*[38] One's first understanding of this could be that it is a simple feeling about art but, as Wilde continues, Wainewright *"considered that life in itself is an art, that it possesses its stylistic processes in the same way as the arts that seek to express it."*[39]

If we were to look into the distant past for a reference to this metaphor, we might, of course, quote Emerson, who explicitly announces that *"one*

---

[33] *Ibid.*, p. 164.

[34] *Ibid.*, pp. 164–165.

[35] Cf. Michel Foucault, *L'Herméneutique du sujet, op. cit.*, p. 131. Xavier Pavie, *Exercices spirituels, leçons de la philosophie antique, op. cit.*, p. 130.

[36] "To become a work of art is the object of living"; quoted by Richard Ellmann, *Oscar Wilde*, Penguin, 1988, p. 292. Oscar Wilde, *The Works of Oscar Wilde*, New York, Dutton, 1954, p. 934. Cf. Didier Éribon, *Réflexions sur la question gay*, Fayard, 1999, p. 347.

[37] Oscar Wilde, *The Soul of Man under Socialism*, in *The Complete Works, op. cit.*, pp. 1174–1197. Cf. Didier Éribon, *Réflexions sur la question gay*, Fayard, 1999, p. 348.

[38] Oscar Wilde, *La plume, le crayon, le poison*, in *Œuvres*, trad. D. Jean, Gallimard, "Bibliothèque de la Pléiade", 1996, p. 812.

[39] *Ibid.*, p. 810.

must live one's life as a work of art",[40] and also Nietzsche[41] but, especially in Antiquity, Epicrates, praised by Pseudo-Demosthenes. Pseudo-Demosthenes does, indeed, show that the boy's life, his *bios*, must be a "common" work and, as if it were a work of art to perfect, he calls all those who know Epicrates to give this figure to come "*as much lustre as possible.*"[42]

The connection between Wilde and Foucault is interesting because, although there is a clear distance between the eras and societies of the two protagonists, they clearly come together on the dimension of the aestheticizing of existence.[43] Wilde sought to constitute a role, a position and an attitude to facilitate a creation of oneself where prevailing norms are excluded. Foucault encourages the invention of new relationships between individuals, new ways of life, the purpose of which is, in particular, resistance to power on the one hand and the reformulation of oneself on the other.[44]

LEARNING HOW TO MAKE ONE'S LIFE A WORK OF ART USING A TRANS-DISCIPLINARY APPROACH

Imagining one's life can be found throughout all ages, in all eras, in different schools of thought, and there is general agreement that the aesthetics of existence is a construction and that making one's life a work of art is done on the basis of what happens to us in life, what we choose to experience, the people we meet and the unique experiences we face. It cannot be decreed spontaneously, and it comes from a slow process of transformation, understanding and learning. In other words, the aesthetics of existence emerge only through a phase of discovery, research, analysis, observation and even astonishment.

Aristotle tells us that the primary quality of a philosopher is his ability to be astonished, because this quality is fundamental for whoever wants to design his existence and direct it toward wisdom. The ability to open up

---

[40] C. Jon Delogu, *Ralph Waldo Emerson, une introduction, op. cit.*, p. 78.

[41] Dans *La Naissance de la tragédie*, Nietzsche expose que sous le charme de Dionysos l'homme n'est plus artiste, il est devenu œuvre d'art. Cf. Nietzsche, *La Naissance de la tragédie*, trad. Jean-louis Backès, Gallimard, "Folio", 1995, pp. 289–310.

[42] Michel Foucault, *Histoire de la sexualité II, L'usage des plaisirs, op. cit.*, p. 277.

[43] Cf. Didier Éribon, *Réflexions sur la question gay, op. cit.*, p. 348.

[44] *Idem.*

to the world, to be astonished by what it offers and to observe it with an ever-new eye helps to change our vision, modifying the prism that we look through, steeped in certainty and habit. A young child is easily amazed, whereas a baby is seldom surprised, but he quickly acquires a curiosity that develops throughout his days, discovering a balloon, an animal, a fruit, music, etc. His imagination develops alongside this curiosity and he imagines himself going into the toy that he is enjoying playing with, he is ready to swallow a raw vegetable although it needs to be cooked and his parents' double bed is sometimes an ocean or from time to time a trampoline.[45] In the school system, the objects that provoke his curiosity are numerous: disciplines, teachers and classmates. However, the method of schooling is unfavorable to the imagination, since it involves sitting on a chair for several hours a day, trying to digest subjects through words and texts. Here, we are already starting to kill both imagination and curiosity, creativity and dreams. High school and college are not places where imagination can flourish spontaneously, and higher education is not better suited to it. Study Law, Philosophy, Management or Mathematics, and you will be guided by the Professor's words, books, and other exercises. The student's imagination is constantly pushed back into its rightful place: nowhere. No imagination, no curiosity (apart from where it is necessary in the discipline), no creativity: cramming and other types of learning by heart are the recurring figures in education.

A transdisciplinary approach seems to be the way to recover imagination, creativity and curiosity. This transdisciplinary approach does not claim to be a discipline but rather seeks to connect all disciplines. Unlike the multidisciplinary approach (juxtaposition of different expert viewpoints) and the interdisciplinary approach (dialogue between disciplines), a transdisciplinary perspective seeks to produce its output from its ecosystem. The Manifesto of transdisciplinarity indicates that, as the prefix "trans" shows, it is at one and the same time between disciplines, across disciplines and beyond any discipline. Its purpose is the understanding of the world in its current state, whose imperatives include the unity of knowledge.

This Manifesto of transdisciplinarity explains why we have all been trained by disciplines, and that in classical thought there is nothing, strictly

---

[45] *Cf. Michel* Foucault, Le corps utopique, Lignes, 2009.

nothing that is cross-disciplinary and beyond any discipline. This forces us to think in terms of several levels of reality, all independent of each other, neglecting the spaces between disciplines.

Disciplinary research involves, at most, one and the same level of reality and in most cases it involves only fragments of one and the same level of reality. By contrast, transdisciplinary thought focuses on the dynamics generated by action at several levels of reality at the same time. The discovery of this dynamic necessarily involves disciplinary knowledge. Transdisciplinary thought, whilst not a new discipline or a new hyper-discipline, feeds on disciplinary research, which is, in turn, enlightened in a new and fruitful way by transdisciplinary knowledge. In this sense, disciplinary and transdisciplinary research are not antagonistic but complementary.

The three pillars of the transdisciplinary approach are the levels of reality, the logic of the included third and complexity. They are the basis for defining transdisciplinary research methodology. Although obviously this is only possible with just a hint of indiscipline.

More than 20 years ago, the Charter of transdisciplinarity was established alongside the Manifesto of transdisciplinarity. This Charter was established at the first World Congress on the subject in Portugal, where one of the spokespersons was Edgar Morin. This Charter emphasizes a very large number of values such as rigor, respect and tolerance and constantly ensures recognition of the different realities that open up to us, obliging us, in a way, to start the dialogue between science, art, literature, poetry and inner experience.

It advocates the dignity of the human being as a citizen of the world and considers education as the authentic way to develop intuition, imagination and physical sensitivity. Finally, this Charter is forged on a solid ethic, which postulates that the economy must serve humanity, rather than the latter serving the former.

Whether we are students, teachers, creators, innovators, intellectuals or craftsmen, we must be heirs of this charter of transdisciplinarity to make it alive and practical. Tomorrow's world cannot be built by yesterday's brains using training methods that have had their day. And although we have all been educated with disciplines, we must rethink the

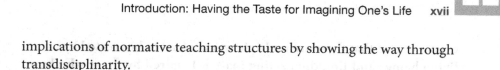

implications of normative teaching structures by showing the way through transdisciplinarity.

IMAGINE, INSPIRE, CREATE

For several years, ESSEC *Business School* has led a transdisciplinary initiative entitled *iMagination Week*. This week encourages students to imagine a long-term view of the world in different areas: politics, health, entrepreneurship, lifestyles, education, etc. In addition to the educational path that leads them to formulate concrete answers about the world as they believe it should be, the students are, in parallel, confronted with transdisciplinary experts: palaeontologists and astrophysicists, punk singers and chocolate or jam craftsmen. When the students see a cyborg man, they stir up their imagination; when they listen to a Fields medalist, they immerse themselves in the most captivating of mathematical adventures; when they watch an artist perform before their very eyes, they become like children, amazed by what they see and eager to express themselves; when they listen to an astronaut, their eyes, brain and heart overflow with ideas. Thanks to this confrontation with all these actors, disciplines, sciences and arts, the students become curious again, learn to ask questions again, and start to experience wonder, so dear to Aristote, again.

The many speakers at iMagination Week, each of them as prestigious as the next, have agreed to contribute to this book. Each of them, in their respective fields, have drawn up an aesthetics of existence and they have all decided to make their lives a work of art. Paying the price of suffering, doubts and effort, they have nevertheless accomplished a great work, that of having singularly imagined their lives. Driven by deep motivation and carried along by extraordinary strength, some have accomplished unique feats, others have developed a singular school of thought. Some have sought to understand, with rigor and determination, how the world is built, and others have taken care to build it through art, science, activism and personal conviction.

Here, they offer us their vision of the imagination, through their life-path and experience. Rather than offering us a pre-set path, they show us that paths exist. **The inspiration we can draw from this must resonate in us to help us understand that there is not a single form of aesthetics of**

existence and that there are multiple works of art to be created by us, as living beings and thinking, acting matter. Inspired by those who have had a taste for imagining their lives, let us be careful to have the taste for imagining ours. This is perhaps the first lesson that we remember when we read about these experiences, and which resonates quite naturally with us: no one, apart from ourselves, can create our existence or imagine our life for us.

ACKNOWLEDGMENTS

We would like to thank all the speakers who took part in iMagination Weeks between 2012 and 2016 in France and Singapore:

Jacques Attali, Alan Chong, Jean-Loup Chrétien, Gilles Descôtes, Christian Duquenois, Jacques Genin, Liu Jianjun, Idriss Aberkane, Laurent Alexandre, Henri Atlan, Marie-Paule Cani, Yip Yew Chong, Yves Coppens, Gaspard Delanoë, Jean-Louis Étienne, Christine Ferber, Neil Harbisson, Nicolas Huchet, Alexandra Ivanovitch, Alexandre Jardin, Nathalie Joffre, Jean Jouzel, Etienne Klein, Desmond Kuek, Kathrine Larsen, Michael Lonsdale, Pierre Marcolini, Dominique Méda, Éric Michel, Fabrice Midal, Olivier Morandais, Pascal Picq, Bridget Polk, Pierre Rabhi, Hubert Reeves, Patrick Roger, Joël de Rosnay, François Salque, Zacharie Saal, Alain Simon, Pierre Tarraquois, François Taddei, Alvin Tan, Jacques Testart, Nadia Thalmann, Hervé This, Cédric Villani, Laurent Villemur, Bertrand Vingère, Didier Wampas, Kevin Warwick and Mike Wood.

We would also like to thank the patrons of each edition of the seminar: Geoffroy Roux de Bézieux (E84), Nicolas Bordas (E82), Véronique Bourrez (E85), Vincent Grimond (E78), Olivier Mégean (BBA91), Bénédicte Richard (E82) and Corinne Vigreux (BBA87).

Finally, we would like to warmly thank all the people involved in making iMagination Week a collective success:

Dalila Abina, Luce Abrate, Jose Aliel, Dany Allaoui, Elise Aubry, Khadija Ben Ahmed, Laurence Bouchayer, Kentia Boulay, Martine Bronner, Isabelle Bui, Daphné Carthy, Gilles Cieza, Pierre Clause, Sophie Cohendet, Béatrice Collet, Cédric Defay, Philippe-Pierre Dornier, Martin Duval, Valérie Fournier, Mitsuru Furata, Nicolas Glady, Valérie Hitier-Lallement, Sophie Jacolin, Thomas Jeanjean, Thierry Jonquois, Roisein Kelly, Yann Kerninon, Natalie Kettner, Marie-Noëlle Koebel, Sarah Lasquibar, Sébastien Lecordier, Kok Fann Leong, Hughes Levecq, Noëlle Loo, Gabrielle Luypaerts, Sophie

Magnanou, Olivier Massiot, Cristobel Morison, Hélène Mugnier, Emily Mah Ping Ong, Peter O'Connor, Michaël Oualid, Anne-Claire Pache, Félix Papier, Laura Patanella, Chloé Renault, Françoise Rey, Florian Rouain, Maïka Seng, Mélanie Teillet, Valérie Wasson, Nicolas Wauquiez, Kevyn Yong, et certainement de très nombreux autres...

A special mention must be made for Jean-Michel Blanquer, Hughes Levecq, Peter O'Connor, Anne-Claire Pache, Françoise Rey and Vincenzo Vinzi for their unfailing support to this unique experience, which received the Daniel Tixier Award for Academic Excellence in 2014 by the ESSEC Foundation. and was honored within the framework of the *Innovations That Inspire* initiative by the AACSB International.

CONTENTS

THE ORIGINS OF THE UNIVERSE

Yves Coppens
Paleontologist, College de France

TRANSFORMISM: FROM INERT MATTER TO LIVING MATTER

Talking about transformation when discussing evolution is very appropriate because before it was coined as "evolution", it was called "transformism." Evolution, as we call it today, is in fact, the quintessence of transformation, imagination and creativity.

Einstein once said "*Imagination is more important than knowledge. For knowledge is limited to all we now know and understand, while imagination embraces the entire world, and all there ever will be to know and understand.*" Other scientists, on the other hand, argue that in order to be thorough, science requires imagination. This is very interesting because science is quintessentially thorough, and yet it needs to be nurtured and fueled by our imagination, which is what gives us drive to explore new lines of research, as well as providing the tools we need to posit theories.

Human beings belong to the history of life, which in turn belongs to the history of earth, which belongs to the history of a galaxy, which belongs to the history of a universe. So when discussing the origins of humankind, to what exactly are we referring? The origin of human life? The origin of mammals, animals, the living world? Earth? The Solar system? The universe?

John C. Mather was able to date the origin of the universe back to somewhere between 13.9 and 13.5 billion years ago, leading to an average of 13.7 billion years ago. That is when the first traces of matter were detected, and from that point forward, everything was transformation. First came unstable matter, which was very warm, dense, particularly bright, and most importantly changing, or transforming if you will. This matter presents a unique specificity: as soon as it exists, it transforms, in order to become increasingly complex and increasingly organized. This is all the more interesting in that it took place in a universe determined by stable physical rules. Had it been otherwise, we would not have been able to understand it, or identify these transformations. The physical laws of our world have not changed for the last 14 billion years, and yet its matter has continued to transform and evolve toward increasingly complex and better organized forms.

The history of the universe begins with matter, somewhat inappropriately called inert matter, which progressively went from quarks to nucleons (particles), then to atoms and molecules, each of which is more complex than the other. Our world is characterized by an obsession for change. As soon as the sufficient conditions are present, the transformation occurs. Matter first appeared in large "pancake" structures, which then divided into galaxies, which in turn divided into stars. The dust from stars which was not able to agglomerate led to the formation of comets, asteroids and planets. And so, Earth is only one small planet, dust, which was not linked to the Sun, and was formed at the same time as the solar system, i.e. some 4.6 billion years ago. In the beginning, Earth was not protected, and thus was bombarded by objects from the sky: meteorites, comets, etc. Comets brought water, and other objects brought gas. As Earth also produces gas, this created an atmosphere, and over time, the water became oceans. Both the oceans and the atmosphere were trapped on Earth due to gravitational forces of mass and distance between our planet and the sun. This is the reason our planet has water, a protective atmosphere, and what makes it so specific. To date, we have not found anything similar, although we probably will someday.

Starting 4.6 billion years ago, and from the moment oceans were generated, which took some 500 million years, the same obsession for transformation continued in the water and on Earth. And so, molecules became increasingly complex and organized, to become cells: clusters of molecules with a membrane which, for the first time ever, presented a wonderful, more complex and organized characteristic: they were able to reproduce. This transition from inert matter to living matter led to a paradox: inert cells became increasingly organized, leading to living matter which is increasingly diversified, and yet increasingly controlled.

KINGDOM ANIMALIA

Living matter began on Earth 4 billion years ago in water, with unicellular organisms. Around 2 million years later, these had evolved to multicellular organisms, later diversifying into animals and plants, approximately 1 billion years ago. Around 5.35 million years later, vertebrates, i.e. beings with a spine, developed underwater. These living beings, initially referred to as chordates, represent a form of progress because the spine is an internal skeleton, thereby more flexible, and acts both as a spring and a shock absorber. This means that life existed and evolved under water for 3.5 billion years, only emerging some 500 million years ago.

Life left water, or more accurately, water left live. Because of gravitation, water underwent regressions, and so animals who were in the water were exposed to air, and either died or adapted. In adapting, fundamental changes occurred. Vertebrates, for example, developed lungs in addition to gills in order to survive in this new environment. These amphibian beings marked the beginning of the life of terrestrial vertebrates on Earth. Over time, some of these became reptiles, and some of these reptiles became mammalian reptiles, i.e. mammal-like reptiles. Around 200 million years ago, they became oviparous mammals, and 100 million years later they became placental, viviparous mammals, thereby ensuring greater protection of their progeny. This reflects the notion of progress which is inherent to transformism, and is the driving force of the transformations undergone by these beings. Life, nature, the universe, present an obsession for change. Change does not always occur because all the conditions are not met, but as soon as the conditions are met, transformations occur to preserve life. The same can be applied to plants. They started by reproducing through spores, which were very fragile and sensitive to humidity. Some 400 million years ago, these spores became seeds, which are more resistant to humidity. Here, we observe nature's obsession to preserve the species. Of course, some species do not succeed in their transformation and become extinct.

Life continued its evolution, and led to the emergence of primates. This category encompasses humans, pre-humans, great apes and monkeys. Primates are placental mammals, whose first traces date back to 70 million years ago. One of the key components of transformation is adaptation: the ability to adapt to new, changing conditions. A living being can only live within a given environment. The first primates were insectivores, but they found an ecological niche, or in other words, a part of the environment which was available to them. This environment comprised the first flower trees, and therefore the first fruit trees. So, these placental mammals adapted to arboreal life, and as a result of this adaptation, they adapted to the combined consumption of flies, as they had done in the past, and of plants, brought to them by this new environment. This marked the origin of the primates from which we descend. Among other things, this also led to the development of the opposable thumb, and therefore the ability to grasp, and their eyes became more centered in order to gain depth perception and see in three dimensions, a vital skill when living in trees and jumping from one tree to another. In order to facilitate tree-climbing, what used to be claws became nails, and the pectoral girdle was developed. The structure of the eye socket also evolved in such a way that they developed the necessary cell layer to see colors, which they needed to eat fruit.

These primates evolved throughout the world in different ways in Africa, Asia and America, and among these primates, some 10million years ago, new primates appeared: hominidae, the last common ancestor of chimpanzees and humans. Of course, this means that from an anatomical, physiological, ecological, ethological and genetic point of view, chimpanzees are the closest beings to us. From an evolutionary viewpoint, the descendants of these common ancestors lived in different environments. Some lived in a dense, rainforest environment; and others in a much more uncovered environment, made of less dense forests and prairies; the former being more humid, and the latter dryer. The root causes of transformism are often environmental, and that is probably why pre-chimp and chimp descendants developed in ways that corresponded to adaptation to the forest. Contrary to common belief, it is not that chimps did not evolve and that humans did. It is simply that they did so in different ways, based on their environment. Pre-humans, living in a more open, aerated spaces, with a greater variety of grasses, in which pastures started appearing, reacted and adapted to their environment by standing up. This is both extraordinary and extravagant. Other animals, such as monkeys or bears, for example, are able to stand for a short period of time to defend themselves, to see further or to carry what they need, but such a behavior is exceptional and temporary. Pre-humans on the other hand walked all the time, became bipedal and continued to climb. We were able to identify and analyze this evolution thanks to "Lucy." The analysis of her remains revealed there was a transition phase from the common ancestor and first pre-humans which were fully bipedal and climbed. This meant that in the history of evolution after insects, primates adapted to a diet of insects and fruit, and then, pre-humans adapted to fruit and roots.

Between 3 and 2 million years ago, a new climate change occurred. The land became increasingly dry. The drought was so significant that the animals from these ecosystems were forced to find alternative solutions to adapt to these new conditions. Trees and pollen progressively disappeared, going from a ratio of 0.4 at 3 million years to 0.01 at 2 million years, with trees surviving only in valleys which were more humid. In order to adapt to this state of things, nature, with its obsession with for preserving its species, transformed and adapted.

It may seem surprising that all these evolutions were successful, and evolved in the "right" direction. In fact, geneticists explain that when a crisis occurs, rather than triggering one mutation in an attempt to adapt, there are 100 or 200 mutations at the same time, in order to guarantee greater success at survival. Some animals transformed successfully, and others — mastodons, for example, despite many evolutions — did not. Hominids found five solutions, each of which was adapted to a specific ecological niches. At the time, there were five large bio-geographical regions, which differed slightly from one another. In the Afar region, i.e. North-Eastern Ethiopia, at the crossroads between Ethiopia, Somalia, Eritrea and Djibouti, they developed stronger skulls and teeth to adapt to their new vegetarian diet. In Eastern Africa, i.e. southern Ethiopia, Kenya, Tanzania and Malawi, this evolution was two-fold. They became more powerful and stronger, in order to be more physically dissuasive because they were more vulnerable and more exposed; and at the same time, they developed a very large dentition to eat plants which had not existed before, or at least not in abundance. In Southern Africa, the solution is similar to that of Eastern Africa but not identical. In the rest of southern Africa, the Gracile solution is observed, with the emergence of Australopithecus Africanus and Australopithecus sediba: they were still characterized by a small brain, and were good climbers and walkers. The fifth solution, found in Eastern Africa, is human beings. They were bipedal, better walkers and runners, they stopped climbing, simply because there were fewer trees, and their dentition transformed in order to adapt to an omnivorous diet, which they were forced to adopt due to the lack of plants. This, in turn, had a positive impact on our evolution, as it provided necessary proteins for the development of the brain, which became larger, more complex, and better organized. As the brain grew, the distribution of the lobes changed. Since there was not enough room for the brain to continue expanding, the brain started creasing. This meant it was better irrigated, and helped enhance the brains processes.

What the study of evolution has taught us is that human beings were born from a need to adapt to a climatic change. It is as simple as that. Just like horses, giraffes, dogs or elephants, we came into being arising from a natural need to transform with the obsession of ensuring the survival of the species. This development led the human brain to go over a threshold which had never been attained before, and by corollary, the brain reached a level of reflection never attained before.

CULTURAL EVOLUTION

When life appeared, molecules went from being inert matter to living matter, and with more cerebral matter, we went from being living matter to thinking matter, which changed things dramatically. For the first time, human beings were able to reflect on what they knew, they became aware of their own knowledge. This meant they were able to anticipate, think ahead, and to have an impact on their environment. For example, using two natural shapes, they were able to create a third shape, thereby making the first deliberate tool ever made, and for the first time, human beings could have a voluntary impact on their environment.

Of course, this ability to reflect on knowledge, ourselves and our environment also meant we became aware of our mortality, which immediately led to the exponential development of our intellectual, ethical, esthetic, cognitive and spiritual abilities. This means that within a natural environment, which had existed for 14 billion years, a new, cultural, environment emerged and would, ultimately, have a retroactive effect on our natural environment. For example, in Melka Kunture, a site in the upper Awash valley near Addis Ababa, a series of human habitations were found, which were home to Homo Habilis, Homo Erectus and Homo Sapiens successively. Put in schematic terms, the analysis of the successive layers of the land unveiled that an initial group "A", which can be dated back to 1.5 million years, produced a "Culture A." The subsequent group, "B", i.e. the product of a biological transformation, continued to make tools "A." This demonstrates that our cultural environment was born, but that it developed at a slower rate than that of natural evolution. Gradually, Group "B" produced a culture "B." This was followed by a group "C", which produced a culture "B", followed by another group "C" with a culture "C", then a group "C" with a culture "D" and a culture "E", and so on and so forth, thereby indicating that while biological evolution continued at a steady pace, cultural evolution grew insidiously, and as natural evolution stagnated, cultural evolution evolved exponentially. Now, we are able to stop natural evolution in its tracks, thanks to our cultural evolutions. For example, doctors and medications mean we are able to postpone our natural evolution and prolong our natural life.

All these scientific observations were discovered through the impetus of imagination. In order to grapple with the world we live in today and imagine the future which awaits us, it is important we understand some key elements. Over billions of years, we went from being inert matter to being living matter; we are descendants of the living world, which is 4 billion years old; we came from water some 500 million years ago. We belong to the reign of animals, are very close to apes and are still subject to the laws of biology. The transformations in our brains and thought processes are the product of natural transformations triggered by nature's obsession for the conservation of species, and the individual, which is the specificity of the thinking world. This means: we are a small, average sized-mammal, on a small, average-size planet around an average-size star, in an average-size galaxy among billions of galaxies and suns. However, in this immensity, to our knowledge, we are the carriers of the most complex part and element of matter produced over the last 14 billion years. So, we are nothing and yet important, until one day, our imagination leads us to discover something bigger or smaller.

HOW IMAGINATION CAN SHAPE THE WORLD

Etienne Klein
Physicist, Director of Research at the CEA
(Alternative Energies and Atomic Energy Commission)

THE BIRTH OF MODERN PHYSICS

What exactly is physics? Physics is not the mere "bureaucracy" of what can be observed. Neither is it the mere observation of visible phenomena in everyday life in order to identify the physical laws which underlie them. Physics is not the "plagiarism" of reality. One can infer physical principles from an observation of real-life phenomena which seem to explain them, but which always prove to be false when tested. This means that researchers in physics need imagination skills more than they do acute observation skills. Science philosopher Alexandre Koyré explained that the challenge of modern physics is to "explain reality by the impossible." Indeed, from the early days of modern physics, i.e. since Galileo, the laws of physics always disprove observation, or at the very least, provide sufficient evidence to force us to question what we observed. The first to understand a phenomenon with which everybody is familiar, The Motion of Falling Objects, was Galileo. As Aristotle had observed, and still can be observed today, heavy objects fall faster than lighter objects. Therefore, based on observation, Aristotle came to the logical conclusion that heavier bodies fall faster than lighter ones. This idea was accepted by all and was not questioned because it was consistent with what could be observed. However, in 1604, Galileo Galilei simply wondered if this law was true. The legend says that he climbed to the top of the Tower of Pisa, to drop two different size objects. Of course, this is not what he did. Had he done that, he would only have been able to prove that heavier objects fall faster than lighter ones. This was only invented after the fact, in order to "win over" the last bastion of Aristotelians that there were experiments which could back his theory.

How then, did Galileo, proceed? He invented what is today referred to as a "thought experiment." Contrary to what the name seems to indicate, this is not a mental exercise in reasoning. It consists in taking a law or theory, and prolonging it in a sort of "theoretical space" to see how far it can go. I suppose a law is true, I imagine a given situation, and I identify — based on the principles dictated by the law under analysis — what would happen in this situation which I can imagine but cannot implement. He considered the law was true, and imagined a situation whereby two objects, one light and one heavier, a bullet and a heavy cannonball, for example, were connected to each other by a string, and then he imagined dropping this system of objects. If we assume heavier objects do indeed fall faster than lighter ones, the string will soon pull taut as the lighter object slows down the fall of the heavier object. But the system considered as a whole is heavier than the heavy object alone, and therefore should fall faster. The same law leads to two contradicting results. How then can this contradiction be resolved? Simply by concluding that both objects fall at exactly the same speed, which is not what can be observed. Therefore, the very first law of modern physics is a law which contradicts observation.

Without going into the technicalities of relativity and quantum mechanics, it is even worse! Modern Physics, particle physics, cosmology, to name but a few, offer physical constructs, based on statements which, when heard for the first time, seem completely nonsensical. What I want to demonstrate with this is that those who discovered these laws are people who imagined things they had never seen. This then calls for verifying whether what we imagine is true. Physics then, is not only an exercise of the imagination, it also requires experiments, reasoning, testing ideas created by our imagination. This also raises the question of whether what is true can be imagined: are we capable of imagining what is, can we transcend our senses, through our intellect or intuitions. Physics, therefore, offers a constant dialectic relationship between what is real and what is imagined, which is tested through theorization and experimentation.

THE POWER OF THOUGHT EXPERIMENTS

At the age of 15, Einstein decided to quit school. He renounced his German citizenship, and went to join his parents in Italy. For a year, he was unschooled, and used this time to go on long walks in the mountains. After a couple of months, he sent a letter to one of his uncles, in which he explained the subjects to which he wanted to dedicate his life. All these issues focused on light: what is light? How does it travel? Is it independent or does it need a medium? Is it a physical object or the vibration of a physical object? He asked questions nobody had even contemplated until then. For example, he wondered whether light emits light, and if so, at what speed this emitted light travels. Does the second light go at the speed of light plus the speed of light? If this second light also emits light, at what speed does this other light travel? And so on and so forth. He concluded that if light emits light, even though speed of light is inherently finite, it can become infinite through a chain of successive emissions.

One year later, he was in Aarau in Switzerland, in an attempt to join the Polytechnic Institute of Zurich. He devised another thought experiment, only this time staging his own body. He wondered what would happen if he were to chase a beam of light. At the time, light was described as being made up of electromagnetic waves. If you are "riding" a light beam, this means you are also riding an electromagnetic wave, much in the way of a surfer who is riding an actual wave. While riding the light beam, the light should appear at rest, just as a surfer is at rest on top of the wave. We should observe such a beam of light as an electromagnetic field at rest. And yet, this is surprising because there is no such thing, neither on the basis of experience nor according to Maxwell's Equations. This means that in this situation, we are faced with a paradox that equations and electromagnetism neither see nor account for.

Ten years later, in 1905, he finally found the answer to this question, which he defined through the special theory of relativity. This theory provided the answers to the two questions he formulated. With this theory, he found that if light emits light, the latter will always go at the speed of light. This means that the speed of light is constant, regardless of the speed of the source, and irrespective of who is measuring the speed of light. This means that if a light bulb is coming toward you at a speed which is close to the speed of light, light will not be traveling at the speed of light plus the speed of the bulb, it will only be at the speed of light. If you run behind a photon which is traveling at the speed of light, and you reach a speed which is close to the speed of light, you cannot simply go a little faster to catch up with it. Whatever speed you are traveling at, the photon will always travel at the speed of light from you. As for his second question, i.e. on the possibility of riding a light beam, he concluded that it was not possible because light has a constant speed with regards to us, and therefore cannot be stationary with regards to light. He published these conclusions on June 30, 1905, in an article which laid out the founding principles of the special theory of relativity.

What is interesting is that this theory takes up Galileo's principle of relativity. Einstein did not invent anything; these principles had already existed for four centuries. This principle sets out that "motion is like nothing", which means that when you are in motion, everything happens as if you were not. This is what enables us to actually be in motion, provided the motion is steady or uniform, i.e. is linked to a Galilean reference frame. In other words, the laws of physics do not change depending on whether you are in motion or still. The second thing he says is that stillness is a shared movement. I am still relative to you, but that does not mean that we are still. Earth turns around the sun at 29 km/s. Relative to the sun, we are going extremely fast, and yet have the impression we are still relative to others, because we share the same reference frame. What relativity says, then, is that there is a democracy of reference frames, i.e. all reference frames you can imagine are equal to one another, in the sense that the physical phenomena which take place within them will develop in the exact same way.

He later understood the implications of this: $E = mc^2$. If we suppose that the speed of light is constant, then every object must have a mass–energy. As long as an object has a mass, then it has tremendous energy simply because it has a mass; and in the formula, it is the speed of light which changes status, it becomes a constant of physics, and this is true even when there is no light involved in the process whereby an object will lose energy. In other words, the status of the speed of light changes. It is no longer simply the speed of a given object in motion, it is a much more fundamental structure which can be found everywhere, even in space time.

Part of Einstein's genius was his ability to look at ordinary things from a whole new perspective and logically follow through on the consequence of the insights he gained from his new perspective. Take, for example, Einstein's platform thought experiment. If a train arrives at station A at 7 o'clock, the pointing of the hour hand to seven and the arrival of the train are simultaneous. What does this entail? How does this compare to the arrival of a train at station B at 7 o' clock and my looking at my watch in station A? How can I know in station A that a train is arriving at station B? I need a signal. Will this signal and the arrival of the train be simultaneous? To this question, he posited it was not possible. Light travels at a finite speed, which means I will receive the signal after the train has already arrived. What would happen, then, if a train arrives at 7 o' clock at station A, and that I am running on the train as the train enters a platform of station A? That is a question nobody had ever asked, because everybody was sure that there was only one unique time frame, Newtonian time, i.e. absolute time, which is the time of the universe: if two elements are simultaneous in space, they must be simultaneous for observers. Whatever this movement may be. With a simple question, Einstein challenged an entire frame of reference.

VISIONARY IMAGINATION

By 1905, he had already published five brilliant papers, each of which could have earned him a Nobel Prize. Despite this, he was struggling to find a position at a university. Two years later, while working at the Federal Intellectual Property office in Bern, sitting at his desk after lunch, in a semi dreamlike state, a process by which he made a conscious effort to subject his imagination to his will, he made what he referred to as the "the happiest thought of [his] life." This idea was an idea anybody could have had, and yet nobody had ever consciously formalized it. If we accept that all objects fall at the same speed, regardless of their weight, then if I fall off the side of a building, my weight is the force that pulls me down in my fall. If, as I am falling, I were to drop an object, this object would fall at the same speed. This means that in my fall, I would be able to look at this object and yet not see its movement, as it would become weightless in relation to me. This would mean that weight produces an effect which cancels out the cause, therefore, how can I fall? Einstein did not "invent" anything original *per se* with this thought experiment. However, he analyzed the implications of Newton's law in a remarkably original way. This led him to postulate the Principle of Equivalence, which states that "the inertial and gravitational masses are identical." In other words, gravitation and acceleration are equivalent, i.e. the acceleration of the fall "transforms away" gravity. He then wondered if this was also true the other way round: could an acceleration mimic gravity? He posited that it could. Let us take, for example, an air-tight elevator. If a physicist drops a ball in this elevator, since he is in a gravitational field, then this ball will accelerate toward the floor. Let us now imagine the elevator is placed away from any gravity field, therefore, in an area in space where there is zero gravity. If the elevator were then to accelerate upwards, with an acceleration equal to that of Earth's gravity, then a ball released in this elevator would also accelerate toward the floor. This means it is impossible to distinguish between a gravitational field and an equivalent uniform acceleration, i.e. the physicist in the elevator would not be able to tell whether his weight is due to gravity or acceleration.

Two years later, he was in Prague, teaching at a university, and was completely obsessed with elevators. He then designed a new thought experiment: if a beam of light were to shine horizontally across the elevator toward the far wall of the elevator, and if the elevator was at rest, then you would see the beam of light travel in a straight horizontal line. Because the speed of light is not infinite, it therefore needs a certain amount of time to travel to the far end of the cabin. If the elevator is accelerating upward, then as the light beam travels sideways, the cabin accelerates upward, which means the beam will follow a curved path downward relative to you. But if the beam of light curves in the accelerating elevator, the equivalence principle then states that the beam of light should also follow a curved path in a gravitational field. Light, therefore, has no mass but is curved by gravitation. He published a paper explaining that the ending of light could be tested during a total solar eclipse, i.e. when the light of the sun is hidden, we are not blinded by its light, so that the stars near the sun can be observed. The light of the stars is deflected by gravitation, namely the gravitational effect of the sun. The position of these stars when the sun is between us and them will not be the same as when there is no sun.

In 1914, there was a solar eclipse visible from Crimea. German astronomer Erwin Freundlich then mounted an expedition to verify this principle.

Unfortunately, as WW1 broke out, Freundlich and his team were arrested, and all of the expedition's equipment was confiscated. Some weeks later, the members of the expedition were exchanged for Russian prisoners. In a way, this was "fortunate" for Einstein's theory, because it was not correct. Had Freundlich been able to take the intended measurements, he would have disproved Einstein's theory. In 1915, Einstein corrected his calculations and defined the equations of the general theory of relativity: everything we had previously learned about gravitation was wrong. Gravitation is not a force; it is simply that objects which are subject to gravitation experience inertial motion. Objects travel along a straight line in curved space time. In other words, gravity is due to a space–time curvature. This was a veritable revolution, and gravitation became a whole new concept. It is a geometric deformation of space–time and not a force which attracts objects. By corollary, objects are not subject to any gravitational force. In fact, there is no such thing as weight, only mass. In today's society, this can only come as good news. No need to go on a diet!

In May 1919, a team led by the British astronomer Arthur Stanley Eddington set out to confirm Einstein's theory. In the inanity of the post-war world, he wanted to demonstrate that he, an Englishman, could prove the theories of a German. He wanted to prove that science could transcend nationalism, the "ultimate pestilence".[1] He was able to confirm Einstein's prediction of gravitational deflection of starlight by the Sun with two simultaneous expeditions. This happened at the end of WW1; people needed a distraction, and so the press coverage of the event was unprecedented, turning Einstein into a worldwide "star", no pun intended. This theory demonstrated that the links that were believed to be definitive in space, time, matter, and energy were forever changed. This gave rise to hope that a new world could be built, maybe one that would not lead to a war.

A BRAVE NEW WORLD

In 1916, an ill and malnourished Einstein started working on gravitational waves. Just as accelerated electric charges emit electromagnetic waves, he

---

[1] *The World of Yesterday*, Stefan Zweig.

wondered if an accelerated mass could emit gravitational waves, which would create ripples in the fabric of space–time. This means that as a gravitational wave passes through space, the distance between two points will be modified, not because they move closer to one another, but because the space between the two spots contracts, thereby reducing the distance between the two points. In other words, two spots which are immobile in space will be drawn closer to each other through the contraction of space. In the 1920s, scientists were able to observe the corollary of this, i.e. the expansion of the universe. American astronomer Edwen Hubble saw that the further galaxies are from us, the faster they recede from us. In other words, the greater the separation between them and us, the more they move away from us. At the time, the conclusion was that galaxies are moving away from each other, and therefore that the universe is expanding. However, interpreted in the light of Einstein's relativity theory, this led to the conclusion that it was not that the galaxy was expanding, but rather that this happened because the space–time is expanding. Therefore, galaxies do not move through space, they move in space, because space is also moving. This proves the extent to which something can change depending on how it is interpreted. This proves that facts can be misinterpreted, and that the interpretation of a fact depends on the theory which is employed.

At the beginning of the 1920s, scientists discovered what is now referred to as the expansion of the universe. A gravitational wave is simply a continuous disruption of space–time by ripples radiating from a source, which modifies the distance between objects and causes slight timing changes. On February 11, 2016, scientists were able to observe a very fast variation of the distance between two points (10 ms). Years prior, scientists, using general relativity, had already been able to calculate the amount of energy which would be given off as gravitational waves in the event that a pair of black holes were to merge. Two parameters had been factored in: the mass of the first black hole, and the mass of the second black hole. These calculations were extremely precise and detailed. In September 2015, such a wave passed through an American detector only days after it was put in operation. This was incredible luck: this wave had traveled 1.7 billion years, and it passed through earth precisely when the detector was put in operation. It is all the more incredible considering that the European detector, in Italy, had been temporarily shut down. The results of the calculations and the results of this observation were compared, and they aligned perfectly. This confirmed that the mass of black holes was equivalent to approximately 30 solar masses. We were even able to calculate that the black hole resulting from the merger of the initial two black holes, emitted the equivalent of 3 solar masses' worth of gravitational radiation. As a rough order of magnitude, the atomic bomb only converted 1 gram of matter into energy.

Einstein worked on gravitational waves relentlessly for 16 years! What this life story tells us is that anything is possible. Einstein started off with a simple idea, never gave up, and worked toward it tirelessly, slowly but surely, never losing sight of the question, and always considering the implications of the responses. This, I believe, is something we can all learn from.

MY LIFE AS A MATHEMATICIAN

Cédric Villani

Mathématicien
Professor at the University of Lyon
Head of the Henri Poincaré Institute
Fields Medal Winner in 2010

"Work to live; live to work": the topic of this iMagination Week is the perfect topic for a philosophical dissertation. And so, I will attempt to follow the codes of such an exercise, using examples drawn from my life as a mathematician.

WHAT IS 'TO LIVE'?

As required in any dissertation, we should begin by defining the terms of this topic: life and work. "To Live" can mean attempting to survive or, on the contrary, leading a comfortable life; having a short existence or enjoying our golden years; feeling weighed down or feeling happy; leaving descendants who will prolong our presence on Earth or having no progeny. Nowadays, when we say we want to live "full" lives, this means experiencing many things, traveling all over the world, etc.

In the life to which we aspire, some of our desires are contradictory. Those who want to protect themselves from potential suffering must refrain from falling in love, thereby missing out on one of the experiences which is the essence of life. Those who want to travel the world will sometimes put their lives at risk in so doing, but then again, staying at home means missing out on wonderful experiences. Arbitration is inevitable.

The tyranny of numbers to which we are subject today, whereby each aspect of our existence is rated and quantified, often means that the richness of a life is measured against the wealth a person's salary lets them amass. Fortunately, some warning voices condemn the vanity of such a perception, and there are business leaders who turn down highly-paid, and highly-stressful, jobs, choosing instead to dedicate their life to other activities. Albeit on my small, individual scale, I am one of those who turned down "big bucks." As a mathematician, I could easily have tripled or quadrupled my salary by crossing the Atlantic to teach in an affluent American university. I chose not to because I wanted to stay in an environment which is dear to me, to enjoy what I view as a better quality of life, but also because I feel I have more to accomplish here than there.

How would I describe my life? In many ways, I am not very different from anybody else: I am married, I have children, I enjoy listening to music and reading books... Other aspects however are specific to my life as a mathematician, the first of which is my many trips and exchanges. I have traveled to over 50 countries to give conferences and meet people. My son has been to nine different schools, following me to Lyon, Princeton, London, Berkeley, Paris, etc.

A mathematician's life is predominantly made up of three activities: listening, speaking and understanding. Each of these is an opportunity for privileged moments, which give me a real sense of fulfillment.

The Moments which Make Up a Life

If I were to mention the milestones which marked my career, I would start by an event which occurred at the end of my PhD. The PhD in itself was already a crucial step in my career as a mathematician. For the first time, I was allowed to carry out research as an adult, to find novel solutions to a problem, to meet researchers throughout the world to build my own answers. At that time, I wanted to be an independent mathematician. My PhD focused on statistical physics, particularly in the field of stability — for example, how can statistics help define the way in which the particles which make up a gas organize themselves spontaneously through collisions? This led me to Probability theory, or Gaussian distribution. One day, I was reading a very specialized book on statistical theory which established a relationship between geometry and probabilities, a book recommended to me by a member of my thesis jury based in Atlanta. As I read, I could see similarities between the demonstration I was discovering and a conference by German mathematician Felix Otto which I had attended some weeks prior. He was trying to solve nonlinear diffusion equations with tools borrowed from probability theory. I felt that I could solve the problem from the book I was reading borrowing from other methods, namely those used by Felix Otto. At first I failed, but with perseverance, I finally succeeded. This marked the beginning of a new era in my career. I started exploring how different fields intersected: the theory of partial differential equations from statistical physics on the one hand, and a combination between theories of geometry and probability, linked to the issue of optimal transport.

This research was published in an article written in collaboration with Felix Otto. It was only a couple of weeks work, but this discovery had a very significant impact. To date, this is still my most-quoted article. This illustrates a well-known phenomenon in the scientific world: the impact of research is not the sole result of the amount of work poured into it. Often, a breakthrough is a matter of being at the right place at the right time. If I had not attended the conference by Felix Otto, and if I had not read the book recommended to me by a member of my jury, I would not have been able to connect them. I was lucky in identifying a possible link between both approaches, and this discovery took me in a new direction. This is very typical of the life of a mathematician.

Mathematician, but also Manager, Writer, Volunteer …

Let us now look at other aspects of this life of mine. As the Head of an Institute, I manage a team which, as with any human society, is often crisscrossed with drama. I have had to learn to navigate relational issues. I also have to seek funding, build partnerships, manage a budget of several million Euros. As interesting as this is, it is very different from the typical life of a mathematician.

In a way, I also lead the life of a writer: I publish books, promote them, I attend fairs and take part in television programs. I have learned that books are the best vector for reaching individuals, and conveying subtle messages.

I also take on the role of a public figure, giving conferences throughout the world for researchers, associations or schools, on topics as varied as the kinetic theory of gases, astronomy, the life of illustrious mathematicians, great scientific controversies, the age of the planet. Society is so avid for knowledge that this takes up a large part of my life. For example, my last trip was to South America. Over a period of 10 days, I gave six public conferences in Uruguay, Chile and Mexico.

Another aspect of my life is my role as President of the association Musaïques, which supports the creation of electroacoustic musical instruments from which innovative research, artistic and pedagogical projects are being launched, focusing primarily on people with disabilities. This position requires defining a clear strategy, coordinating events, finding partners, funding. I am also a member of several scientific committees, namely for Orange, and a newly-created entity of the European Commission, and I also strive to develop partnerships with Africa. Every year, I spend about a fortnight on the African continent to teach and to work hand in hand with different governments or institutes. I have also been invited to take part in activities which are quite novel for a mathematician, such as being on the jury of a film festival or a gastronomic contest. Everything is an opportunity for learning!

The Perpetual Work of the Mind

Do not be mistaken, the work of a mathematician is not always as easy as the experience I shared earlier. Take, for example, another event in my life, which required much more arduous work. In 2009, I had been invited to spend a semester at the Institute for Advanced Study of Princeton, in New Jersey. Princeton is one of the most-renowned places for mathematics, almost mythical. Along with the Parisian École Normale Supérieure, it is one of the institutions which trains most Fields Medal winners. Albert Einstein and other great mathematicians spent some time there.

At Princeton, I worked relentlessly to prove a phenomenon called Landau Damping, which is specific to plasma physics. A plasma is a gas in which electrons can move freely. Unlike other gases, they are a sort of ideal world, devoid of friction or collision. Despite this form of perfection, spontaneous relaxation, "landings" or disruptions are experienced. When you excite plasma, the excitement decreases spontaneously as opposed to being maintained.

I was exploring this phenomenon with one of my former students based in Paris, with whom I was in constant contact. I embarked on this project thinking it would be a simple exercise. However, I soon found out it was a very large, complex problem, which would probably lead to a veritable mathematical discovery. However, our first demonstration (aiming to prove the relevance of our approach to our peers) was over 100 pages long, and was unsuccessful. I had stated some months earlier that I would solve this problem, so I was under a considerable amount of pressure. I was working day and night to reach the goals I had set myself, but faced insurmountable obstacles. After an all-nighter, I went to bed, discouraged by these failures. When I woke up the next morning, this nagging voice in my head kept on saying "the second term has to be moved and completely transformed." This unlocked the solution: the terms of the equation had to be shifted around. And so, I got back to work. This proves that even when you think you have explored all possible options, even when you are exhausted and at a dead end, if you give your mind a rest, it will keep on working for you. It is able to deliver a revelation to you when you wake up.

WHAT IS 'TO WORK'?

The etymological roots of the French word come from the Latin, *tripalum*. which refers to an instrument of torture. A rather bleak vision… The English language is more optimistic. In English, it has the same etymological root as the word '*ergon*', which we find in 'ergonomic', that is, in the ability to design easy-to-use objects. In fact, work can cover each of these aspects: it can be a cause of suffering, a servitude we are forced to obey in order to ensure sustenance, but it can also be an exciting activity, a purpose for which we would be ready to sacrifice our life: creating a *work of art*, being involved in a collective project, preparing for a sports competition. This involves effort, but devoid of any negative connotation.

Work as a Mission

Work can take another, third dimension and refer to the mission which we give ourselves, the contribution we want to make to the planet. For some people, such a mission is a means to self-fulfillment. Others, however, believe this is the mission entrusted to them by a higher power.

In the scientific field, the discovery of the meter is a beautiful example of this "missionary" dimension. The meter was born in the aftermath of the French Revolution. It emerged from the desire to define a universal unit of measurement which could be shared by humanity as a whole. Scientists of the time considered that Earth was the only object shared by all people, and a universal unit of measurement should then use the dimensions of Earth as a reference. Today, such units are defined by the laws of physics, and shared not only by humans but by the universe as a whole. Two French scientists, Méchain and Delambre, were commissioned by the state to measure Earth with the greatest precision possible. They dedicated years of their life to this task, traveling through war-ridden countries and exposing themselves to, and contracting, serious diseases. One of them thought he had made a mistake in one of his initial measurements in Spain, but he could not go back to correct it because the country was at war. This supposed mistake haunted him for the rest of his life. These two scientists had the strong belief that they had been invested with a sacred mission which they had to complete at all cost, regardless of the hardships and suffering they were to endure, a mission for which they were ready to give their life.

When Pleasure and Weariness Come Together at Work

The three dimensions of work — the work we are obliged to undertake in order to survive, the work we do out of pleasure, and the work in which we see a mission — can be combined or overlap in a number of ways. Recreational work can thus become distressing. At first, I thought that being an examiner for the entrance exam for the École Normale Supérieure would be very exciting: it would be the opportunity to identify the great mathematicians of the future, to spot talent. But when you see applicants one after the other, non-stop, it actually becomes a very tiresome. I no longer did this activity out of pleasure but out of obligation.

It is the same when you are on the editorial committee of a journal. What could be more stimulating than contributing to the genesis and dissemination of scientific articles? However, there are so many texts to coordinate and authors to manage that it is difficult not to go crazy.

At first, I took great pleasure in providing tours of the Institute, to show where Albert Einstein discovered the theory of relativity and where the very first great seminar on mathematics was held. But by the 100th time, trying to attract potential partners, it becomes a real bind.

The first time I was interviewed on radio, it was very overwhelming. Thousands of people were about to listen to my ideas, the slightest mistake would haunt me for years! It was a moment of great emotion. Today, after having taken part in a number of shows, it has become routine. All activities, even the most pleasant ones, can become trying when repeated over and over again.

Why do We Need to Work?

In recent years, on a number of occasions, I have felt I was going to die of exhaustion, quite literally. My friend Philippe Chaffanjon, former Director of France Info, died of a sudden heart attack when he was only 50 years old. Olivier Ferrand, a promising young politician who was at the head of the Terra Nova *think tank*, and had very strong sense of ethics and the common good, died at the age of 43. Pierre Berger, the CEO of Eiffage, passed away at the age of 47. They all succumbed to professional burnout. Where do you draw the line between dedicating energy to an activity you are passionate about and putting your health in jeopardy?

The propensity to work is something shared by humanity as a whole: we need to keep busy. Idleness often goes hand-in-hand with depression. It is through work that civilizations were built, but it is also these civilizations which created work. Our prehistoric, hunter-gatherer ancestors worked very little, maybe 15 hours a week. As agriculture developed and the population grew, it was imperative to ensure the sustenance of an ever-growing number of individuals. We are made in such a way that we give ourselves work.

The equation "work to live and live to work" affects us as individuals as much as it affects humanity as a whole. Even today, the most ambitious projects, those which spark dreams by the technological prospects they offer, require a tremendous amount of work. They are conducted by entrepreneurs who work like madmen, bringing in their wake partners who devote the same energy and dedication to the project. It is through the feeling of being entrusted with a mission that men and women can actually get through such an overwhelming amount of work.

Besides, people always tend to push the possibilities given to them to the limit. If a source of energy is discovered, it will be exploited; if a society generates wealth, it will be reinvested in the development of new activities; if a technology can be used to move faster, people will use it to travel further.

The phrase "work to live and live to work" also has a geographical dimension to it. An exhibition which is currently showing at the Palais de Tokyo titled *Exit* illustrates this beautifully. It offers representations of the movements of capital and people throughout the planet. It explains how 12 so-called rich countries generate wealth for 60 "poor" countries thanks to the money immigrants transfer back home. These exchanges of funds are three times greater than the total amount of international cooperation. These men and women work, often in strenuous and difficult conditions, to provide basic subsistence for their families back home. This exhibition also presents another aspect of "work to live": the fruits of work protect us from the consequences of disasters and epidemics. Depending on whether a disaster takes place in the northern hemisphere, i.e. in developed countries, or the southern hemisphere, i.e. poor countries, the consequences of a same natural disaster on populations will be drastically different. The number of displaced persons can be 1000 times greater in the south than in the north. Therefore, all work carried out in order to create adequate infrastructures and to control nature leads to greater stability in the lives of individuals worldwide.

We are unable to stay idle, even when we have provided sufficient work to satisfy our primary needs and to ensure our safety. Whenever we have free time, we often use it to work on something. Some explain this the following manner: at the origins of human societies, only a few men went hunting to feed the tribe, but they did not accept that others remained inactive during their absence, and so, they put them to work. Schumpeter theorized a similar idea demonstrating that when a new technology arises and takes charge of tasks which, until then, had been carried out by people, society always invents new activities for the latter. In the future, most of today's professional actions will be carried out by machines. But we will always find replacement occupations.

In 1933, economist John Maynard Keynes predicted that in few decades, the time would come when men would be freed from work thanks to machines. He further stated that before the total disappearance of work, people would live through a transitional period in which they would work 15 hours a week, i.e. three hours a day. This would be more than enough to meet all their needs. The economist saw this as a rather bleak prospect for those who do not have the talent to keep themselves entertained: *"Yet I think with dread of the readjustment of the habits and instincts of the ordinary man, bred into him for countless generations, which he may be asked to discard within a few decades. To use the language of to-day — must we not expect a general 'nervous breakdown'?"*[1]

This opinion is quite widely shared. Churchill also anticipated that men would work less in the future. However, it seems this is not the case: technologies designed to simplify our lives and replace our workforce are in fact driving us to work more. One would have thought that such a fast and convenient tool as e-mail would be liberating. And yet, we spend hours every day replying to messages. Every year, I send approximately 13,000 e-mails! We have become slaves to this tool which we thought we could control.

Working to Live Your Passion

Famous entrepreneur Elon Musc, CEO of Tesla, once stated that in order to come up with an innovation, one had to work at least 60 hours a week. I myself have, on occasion, dedicated much more than 60 hours a week to my research. I found it stimulating, and it pushed me to always do more and go further. When undertaking any scientific research, the initial goal — solving a problem — gradually fades away, and research becomes an activity *per se*: you publish article after article, you always want to go further, to go deeper. It is unavoidable. However, this does not necessarily have to be a bad thing.

Between 2005 and 2008, I dedicated approximately 4,000 hours of work to the book *Optimal transport, old and new* in which I explore the issue of optimal transport as it was developed from the 18th century onwards.

---

[1] Keynes J.-M. (1930), *Essays in Persuasion. Economic Possibilities for our Grandchildren*, By John Maynard Keynes, Elizabeth Johnson and Donald Moggridge, Royal Economic Society.

Writing this book was a very enriching process. It could have been much shorter. What was initially meant to be a booklet of reading notes became a thousand-page volume. Why did I do it? Because I felt that was my mission, and it was a fascinating and an exalting experience for me. In this type of project, there comes a moment when a book becomes your master: it needs you to continue. You give yourself to it day and night, to the point where it becomes an obsession and you even forget to eat. One day, I was on a plane to a conference, and to my dismay, I suddenly realized I hadn't saved my manuscript, which I had with me. If we were to crash, all my work would have been in vain! I was more concerned about the legacy of my work than my own life! When you are involved in such an all-encompassing work, you temporarily lose your sense of reality. You no longer feel effort or pain: work becomes a drug. The project to which you dedicate your life will be fulfilling in the most literal meaning of the word. Once I was working on this book on the train, and my computer battery died. I spent the rest of my journey working in the toilet, using the power outlet for shavers. It was just unthinkable for me to take a break, even if it was only the time of the train journey.

Art history provides many wonderful examples of compulsive work. The most emblematic might be the Ideal Palace by Ferdinand Cheval, a building which required 93,000 hours of work from someone considered a madman by his village. His work, today, is recognized as a masterpiece of Naïve art.

Valuable Work

All of this inspires three thoughts. First, work can be a value in itself. The fable by Jean de La Fontaine titled *The Ploughman and His Sons*, tells the story of a rich farmer, who, nearing death, tells his sons that a treasure is hidden in the land he is leaving them: all they have to do is dig it over, carefully, to discover it. His sons worked relentlessly, and yet they found nothing. However, the crops flourished more than ever that year. "Though hidden money found they none, Yet had their father wisely done, To show by such a measure, That toil itself is treasure."[2] concludes the fable. This is particularly true for intellectual work: we need to

---

[2] Translation is our own.

stimulate our mind in order to push our intellect further, whatever the subject of such a reflection may be. And so, education is not so much a matter of teaching knowledge that can be useful, but rather of training our mind in the exercise of thinking.

Work is then invested with a near religious dimension. It is interesting to see that Rule of Saint Benedict *"laborare et orare"*, work and pray, has become *"laborare est orare"*, to work is to pray. Work is so precious to some that they worship it.

What is worthy of note, is that all great discoveries required a colossal amount of work whereas, nowadays, faced with the same issues, we would have the means to reach the same results much faster. Let us take, for example, the discovery of elliptical motion by Kepler. This discovery was the fruit of immense calculations done manually. With today's technology, this would take no more than a couple of minutes. Similarly, Neptune and Uranus were discovered indirectly, by observing the irregularity of the trajectory of other planets, through much hard work. It would have been so much easier nowadays! And yet, that is not how things happen: discoveries always come about as a result of disproportionate efforts.

WORKING TO LIVE TOGETHER

All these notions can easily be transposed from an individual level to the level of organizations or companies. Just like people, companies work to live and live to work. They assign missions, but must also comply with other tasks in order to ensure their sustainability. The ultimate goal of Google was to create search engines which could revolutionize the way we use the Internet. Today, however, it has become the world's largest advertising platform. The revenue it derives from advertising enables it to finance its technological developments. A virtuous circle is set in motion whereby the intensification of work leads to an intensification of human activity, which in turn involves more work, and so on and so forth.

In conclusion, could we not work together to live together, and live together to work together? No activity other than collective work weaves as strong a relationship between individuals, even though in doing so it also heightens tensions. For example, for a couple, the work of raising a child can reinforce their bonds of marriage, just as it can stress them and drive them apart.

Nevertheless, working together is something which is highly emotional on a social level. I experienced this in all my activities. I conducted most of my research in the framework of collaborations, the first of which was my work on the Landau landing with Clément Mouhot. We exchanged hundreds of emails, so much so that we became two parts of the same brain, he in Paris and I in Princeton. This happened again while working on a comic book with artist Baudouin.[3] For 18 months, we talked on a daily basis. Undertaking joint projects is to forge indestructible bonds with others. From that point of view, science has the wonderful advantage of being a collective enterprise directed towards a common goal: overcoming the unknown. Scientific communities are extremely closely knit. I can go to any university in the world and be warmly welcomed by scientists who will not see me as a competitor or a threat, but rather as a colleague and friend: they know that we are driven by the same passion.

---

[3] *Les rêveurs lunaires, quatre génies qui ont changé l'histoire,* Cédric Villani and Edmond Baudoin, Gallimard-Grasset, 2015.

INSPIRATION: CREATIVITY AND CONTEXT

Mike Wood
Architect, Grant Associates

BEING A LANDSCAPE ARCHITECT

For landscape architects, the design process typically includes a spark of creativity, which is a response to a challenge that generates an idea. This is then refined through a logical sequence and design process. As landscape architects, much of what we do is not only about creating and imagining but also about pragmatic problem solving, responding to particular site constraints, complying with local statutory requirements and, perhaps most important to many of our clients, it is about being achievable. This includes responding to the challenges of budget, timing, and availability of plants and materials and ongoing maintenance. Landscape architecture is not only about the planting *per se*. It involves the collaboration of a variety of specialists including ecologists who determine the types of plants we should use and how to best nurture them, structural and civil engineers, lighting consultant and art curators. Gardens by the Bay is a good example of the success of this collaborative process; however, it is generally a standard approach for all of our projects.

Landscape architects are passionate about making meaningful experiences to a broad range of intended users. This often includes engaging and interactive experiences through exciting ways of combining landscape and sustainable technologies to get people up close and personal to a wide range of plants and natural systems. Inspiration often comes from a blend of creativity and context. We try to embed our projects into the identity of the place, to be complimentary to its character and to express a particular identity that we can use throughout the design.

GARDENS BY THE BAY

The story with the Gardens by the Bay started in 2006. Grant Associates were one of the few companies selected to submit proposals for an international design competition. Our brief was to create the most amazing tropical gardens in the world, incorporating cutting-edge environmental design and sustainable development principles. We had to factor in the challenges of both the Singaporean climate and working on a reclaimed waterfront. We wanted to capture people's relationship with nature and use innovative technology to create rich educational and recreational experiences for both local residents of Singapore and visitors from around the world. All these elements informed the vision and creation of the gardens. The first stage of the Gardens by the Bay, Bay South, was completed in 2012.

The general structure of the Gardens can be broken down into three different sections that explore the relationship between plants and people. The first section focuses on People and Plants. This provides opportunities to showcase how we could express plants we use in our everyday life, and how we could use them to explore the challenges inherent to urban growth. The second is a reflection on Nature's Balance. It focuses on planting merging with technology. The last space is dedicated to the Fragile Forest.

The whole project is about plants. Specifically, to allow the full appreciation of their forms, colours, textures, functions and, ultimately, their importance to us as humans in the 21st century. NParks have sourced plants from across the planet to create a unique botanical reservoir and a visual and sensory spectacle. At this moment, this incredible collection of botanical diversity is just taking root and hinting at the magnificence to come over the next 100 years and more.

In addition to permanent planting displays and collections of rare species, the gardens will feature temporary displays. Maintenance is an essential part of the garden story and is implicit in the client's desire to explore new boundaries in horticulture. Nevertheless, the whole aspect of environmental sustainability has been a central theme of the design evolution including going to considerable lengths to ensure an efficient energy strategy for the cooled conservatories and the creation of a unique reservoir of Southeast Asian Rainforest species.

THE ORCHID CONCEPT

At the competition stage, we looked for an idea that somehow captured the spirit and ambition of Singapore. The orchid became our metaphor for the project. It is the national flower of Singapore, and whilst its flowers are recognised for their exotic beauty, it also possesses a remarkable physiology that allows it to thrive in quite hostile environments. This intelligent environmental infrastructure alongside natural beauty became the twin threads of our approach. We also enjoyed the idea that the orchid is perhaps the most cosmopolitan of species in the world which allowed us to speak about Singapore as a global hub.

THE COOLED CONSERVATORIES

The Cooled Conservatories, designed by Wilkinson Eyre Architects, are home to two glass biomes — the Flower Dome (cool dry biome) and Cloud Forest (cool moist biome). They are an iconic feature of the Gardens that showcase the application of sustainable energy solutions and tell the story of plants and their intimate relationships with man and the ecosystem. At the same time they offer a spectacular visual and spatial experience for the visitors.

The Flower Dome replicates the cool, dry climate of Mediterranean as well as that of semi-arid sub-tropical regions like South Africa and parts of Europe like Spain and Italy. The Cloud Dome replicates a cool, moist climate found in Tropical Montane regions between 1,000 and 3,500 metres above sea level, such as Mt. Kinabalu in Sabah, Malaysia, and high elevation areas in South America.

About 226,000 plants from every continent except Antarctica expect to be featured in the conservatories. Many of these species face the threats of climate change and habitat loss brought about by human activities. It is hoped that displaying them in the conservatories will help to promote awareness of the wonders of nature and the value of plants to Man and the Environment.

THE SUPERTREES

One of the most iconic and memorable features of Bay South are the Supertrees. They were developed to provide an immediate balance to some of the iconic existing, and future, buildings around Marina Bay. There are 18 Supertrees in total, and they are an integral part of the overall site environmental systems. In addition to the creation of habitat and shaded spaces through the use of vertical planting, some will have photovoltaic cells to harvest solar energy, others include rainwater harvesting and some will be integrated with the Cooled Conservatories and energy centre to serve as air exhausts. Through the development of the trees in this concept, the Supertrees became a true expression of the coming together of natural and technological systems.

THE THEMED GARDENS

The Theme Gardens showcase the best of tropical horticulture and garden artistry. Together with mass flowering and coloured foliage landscape, they form a spectacle of colour, texture and fragrance, providing a mesmerising experience for visitors. The Themed Gardens feature two spectacular collections, one focused on 'Plants and People', the other on 'Plants and Planet'.

Heritage Gardens — 'Plants and People'

The four Heritage Gardens reflect Singapore's four main ethnic groups as well as the city-state's colonial heritage. Each garden explores the rich cultural significance of different plant species:

- Malay Garden — the story of life in a traditional village
- Indian Garden — inspired by a traditional lotus flower motif
- Chinese Garden — inspirational places for writers, poets and artists
- Colonial Garden — the story of crops, spices and plants as 'Engines of Empire'

The World of Plants — 'Plants and Planet'

The World of Plants forms the second collection of Gardens and is based on the theme 'Plants and Planet', showcasing the biodiversity of plant life on our planet:

- Secret Life of Trees — functions, evolution and role of trees in the rainforest
- World of Palms — celebrating the rich diversity and shapes of tropical palms
- Understorey — stories about plants of the forest floor and their roots
- Fruits and Flowers — exploring the amazing forms and functions of different species
- Discovery Garden — plant evolution through ancient groups of plants
- Web of Life — the interrelationship between rainforest flora with fauna.

5

INTERCULTURALITY AND TRANSDISCIPLINARITY

Alvin Than

Founder and Artistic Director of the Necessary Stage

The name of our company is *The Necessary Stage*. I formed this company in 1987 while still at university, as a non-profit theatre company. Our mission is to create original indigenous and innovative theatre. Over the years, we have developed a collaborative method. We try not to have too much hierarchy in our working processes. Instead, playwright and directors work together as collaborators. Something that is important to us is to use our stage to represent the different cultures which make up Singaporean society. We always try to work with actors from different nationalities, who speak different languages, to explore issues of cultural identity. This is what we refer to as interculturalism. We have rejected the notion of "multiculturalism" because we feel it has been tested and failed. Multiculturalism is simply different cultures co-existing in one country. What concerns us is how different cultures, be they Malay, Chinese, Eurasian, Peranakan, or Indian interact and how they can come together. I am Peranakan, my family came from China and settled in South East Asia. My sister married into a Malay family, and so my family is already a mix, and is the expression of a new form of ethnicity which emerged from these cultural encounters, which is the product of interculturality, ethnic hybridity. Singapore is unlike any other Asian country. Traditionally, Asian countries have a strong mother culture, which is the case in Korea, Japan, Malaysia or India. Singapore, however, has been known to be a "cultural oven." We do not have our own culture because our culture is what has emerged from all our migrant cultures coming together. The strength we have resides in how we blend those cultures together and how they interact with one another. Singapore has become an example of a veritable global village. This aspect of our community is something we wanted to explore from the outset. Neither I nor the playwright we work with studied drama *per se*, simply because there was no such major at that time, 1989. We both studied litera- ture; I also took sociology and he took languages. Our theatre making is, in fact, the coming together of these three disciplines. Sociology plays a very strong part in what we do; this involves a lot of field work, research and interviews. That is what makes our theatre socially engaged.

The theme of this week is "work to live and live to work." That is what we are interested in. Our work is called socially-engaged theatre. In the past, socially-engaged theatre was looked down upon as not being artistic enough. But in the 1990s, playwrights tried to re-imagine this discipline, by avoiding prescribing any solutions while still rooting their work in social conditions. This type of socially-engaged theatre often offers a vari- ety of points of views and different perspectives, but no solution is offered in the end. A playwright once said "today's solutions become tomorrow's problems." I like this idea, and that is what we strive for in our work. We are not so presumptuous as to prescribe a solution, we promote no utopia. Our goal is simply to show what we have observed in life, spark a discussion and provoke thought.

This is precisely what we did with *Off Centre*, a play which focused on mental illness. We went to a psychiatric institution to interview patients, and it was a real eye-opening experience for us. Before that, we had written plays that were close to our hearts; our first play was about us graduating and joining the workforce. A lot of our early plays reflected on direct needs and concerns. We simply had to interview each other or search within ourselves. When we chose to explore issues of mental illness, however, we had to meet and interview people suffering from mental health problems, those who were actually in a hospital, those who were in a halfway house and those who were in after-care services. As artists, this process was very interesting because we had to really look at, interview and understand peo- ple and realities that were foreign to us. For example, we interviewed a student who fell into the spiral of mental illness because he was obsessed with succeeding at school. At first, he did not want to talk to us. When he eventually started talking to us, he did not want to let us go. When we asked him where was working now, he suddenly became withdrawn again. His social worker explained that in Singapore, when applying for a job you must declare whether or not you have or have had mental illness problems. If you check that box, you either do not get the job or are paid half as much as other candidates, which is nothing less than discrimination. This was very interesting for us, because in our research we had gathered a lot of material on foreign contexts, but with these interviews we began to understand the issue from a local point of view, and so make our theatre more engaged, more relevant. *Off Centre* was initially commissioned by the Singapore Ministry of Health in 1993 for an amount of $30,000. However, the things we unveiled in the play were deemed unsettling by the Ministry and it no longer wanted to support the play. We told them we wanted to return the money and go on with the play anyway because so much work had gone into it. It was a tremendous success and was critically acclaimed. The government launched an investigation into us because they were suspicious, and wondered where we got the money from. The investigation found there was nothing to find, other than the fact that we were passionate! It was very difficult at the time to convey this passion to the government, to get them to understand why people still wanted to be involved in the project without receiving any money.

Later, our company faced further turmoil because we chose to explore Forum Theatre. This is a Marxist form in which there is a 15-minute play which ends in a tragedy, after which the audience is invited to replace the protagonist and change the outcome of the play. This art form, first created by Marxist practitioner Augusto Boal, was banned, and our company was nearly closed down by the authorities in 1994 for using it. Fortunately, the National Arts Council came to our rescue, and decided that while the form should be banned, our company would not. This definitely raises questions on the issues of "living to work and working to live." This is a question we often ask ourselves in the arts: how do we create an art that reflects life? When does our work become dangerous?

Because Singapore is such a young nation, we do not have a strong cultural voice. We do not have that extensive body of literature other cultures have. We studied Shakespeare and other great playwrights, reading all the footnotes to fully understand the cultural implications of what we were reading. What we wanted to do with the *Necessary Stage* was explore and share our own culture, our own sensibilities. How else can anybody from outside ever understand us? It can be challenging to focus on a country which is so small, and to gain cultural confidence when your country is easily ignored by the world. Our play *Best Of* focuses on a Malay woman trying to get divorced. She cannot get divorced because she must first consult the Syariah Court and obtain permission from her husband. The play is written in Singapore Standard English, but the voice of the character switches to English words with a Malay syntax. This is another form of English, but audiences who can speak English can understand it. We brought this play to New York and were asked why we had not standardized it so that it was understandable by foreign audiences. I told them since we had struggled with Shakespeare's plays, *Trainspotting* and other international films, I think it is only fair you meet us halfway. That is what interculturalism is: it is all about how we can meet half way.

When I look at the world today, I see politicians focusing on issues of national security and economic success, experts focusing on business models and economics, and yet no-one is focusing on cultural differences. We do not have the vocabulary or the toolset to settle cultural differences. That is why the whole world is plagued with problems today: we have become a global village and we all live together, but instead of greater understanding there is no understanding. I think that this is the very role of culture. Culture is the place where we can actually try to bridge these differences. Today, however, culture is still greatly underestimated, particularly so in Asia.

Recently, I was invited to speak at the ASEAN Summit. The opening consisted of a dance display, representing different national traditions and folklore, after which the economists and politicians began their discussions. Culture in Asia is never taken seriously, it is used merely as a seat warmer, as a means of entertainment. What people fail to see is that the arts and culture constitute a soft power which can reach people and bring us closer. Through our theatre making, we try to bridge this disconnect.

Another aspect of the differences we explore in our work is transdisciplinarity, i.e., exploring different art forms and working with different artists, be they dancers, graphic artists or multimedia artists. This is what we did with *Frozen Angels*, for example. It was commissioned by the Singapore Biomedical Advisory Committee. As the world advances its research on life sciences, stem cells and artificial intelligence, they were concerned the population might not be ready for such advances. They asked us to do a short 45-minute play for schools so they could explore these issues and engage the younger generations in the discussion. In order to explore such a future and what it entailed for us from a social viewpoint, we wrote three short plays. The first one is about designer babies, the ability to design genes. The next is about a mother who works in an organ transplant shop, which are everywhere in the future depicted in the play. One day she discovers her daughter has kidney failure and so she asks her employers for help, but they refuse and demand $35,000 for a new kidney. Despite all the wonderful scientific achievements, money still rules the world. What good can scientific progress bring if we, as individuals and if society, cannot benefit from it? The third and last play focuses on a couple celebrating their 200th anniversary. The wife tells her husband that she wants to stop taking their longevity serum because she wants to die. This play questions whether the social standards we have today are compatible with the lives scientific progress will bring us. For this play, we combined digital media and theatrical performance.

When we do interdisciplinary work, or intermedia work, we can use multimedia as a means to express what is not spoken. When we started, we used multimedia to circumvent censorship. We had to submit our work to get a license and we were obliged to submit a script, we used multimedia to get across the sensitive things we wanted, without having to submit it to censors.

Mobile 2: Flat Cities, was designed to engage a dialog with young Singaporeans and young Japanese. The younger Japanese generations are not aware of the atrocities Japan committed in South East Asia during World War II. They all know about Nagasaki and Hiroshima, but the role of their country is generally left out of their textbooks. A former Japanese soldier turned actor now lives in Malaysia, and he was surprised that he was only ever cast for roles depicting a cruel Japanese soldier, and could not understand the origin of this stereotype. He started researching, and this was the starting point of our play. Thanks to jumps through space and time, the play explores stories of personal and social tensions across Asian cultures. Two characters from different eras are confronted, one, a deceased Japanese officer from World War II with strong nationalistic views, the other a young, modern, Japanese man about to marry a Malay woman. The officer does not understand how the young man can betray his nation by marrying a foreigner, and states that his patriotic sentiment was rewarded with a shrine. The young man then informs him that he is buried in the Japanese Cemetery Park, a cemetery initially founded by brothel-keepers as a burial ground for the Japanese woman brought to Singapore for prostitution. It was very interesting for us to get South East Asia and Japan to look into the past, to reconfigure the present in order to look to the future. It was very interesting because when the Koreans watched it they felt we were too lenient, because they have a different relationship with Japan.

Our play was not intended to represent South East Asia as a whole, but rather to engage a discussion between our local reality, and that of Japan. Singapore was only occupied for 2 years and does not have the same angst as other countries do. Young Singaporeans have no memory of the war. The play we offered explores our ties with this part of our history, and cannot, nor does it intend to, represent South East Asia as a whole. In this particular play, the use of multimedia became a tool for us to bring up the war and those things that are absent in Japanese history. So in that sense, multimedia plays a vital role, it is not used merely to be decorative or to create visual impact. It is used as an actor, which contributes to the meaning of the story we are trying to tell. This is what we refer to as intertextual meaning, or a collage. You can collage the world on stage!

In our latest play, *Road Rage*, we explored the role of social media. Singaporeans have become very angry as of late and there is an increasing number of incidents. Before the audience attends the play, they can friend one of the characters on Facebook. Onstage, they see how one character provokes a girl and pushes her to her limits. This character records the whole scene and uploads it online. The video, of course, does not show the whole truth, and all you see is how exasperated this young woman is, and in the video she is the only one using vulgarities. The editing of the video paints her as sexist, racist and very angry, but does not inform the viewers in any way how she was provoked. The audience in the theatre can see the difference between what happened and what was uploaded. Social media, thus, is a wonderful platform for experiments on our responsibility as viewers, and how we interpret things we come across on social media.

This is the core of what we do: interculturality and interdisciplinary, both of which are concerned with the "other", be it another ethnicity, another art form, another discipline. Working with others is no easy task. Many tensions underlie the process of trying to understand the other side, trying to empathize. A lot of what we do involves negotiations, and this is something that needs to take place for real interculturality to emerge. By engaging in interdisciplinary and intercultural projects, we put ourselves in a position where we have to collaborate, work together and not compete. To live to work and work to live is connected to that, in that we are trying, through our work, to improve the way we live and to create opportunities for social transformation. Rather than just thinking about what you do in life, and what changes need to be made to society, you must constantly question how you actualize the changes you want to bring about in the work you do and the way you work.

6

ENGAGING OUR INTELLIGENCE TO SAVE LIFE ON EARTH

Hubert Reeves

Astrophysicist, Montreal University

How can we put into perspective our collective presence on Earth with the universe in its entirety? I invite you today on this journey between infinitesimally small and infinitely large.

Now more than ever, we are inundated by information. Some positive — about scientific discoveries, for example — some terrifying — lately the news has been flooded by the latter. In order to map out the path of our existence, we need to synthesize this information. I will endeavor to do so by telling you a beautiful story. The story of our birth, but also another story, the grimmer story of the devastating effects that human activity imposes on the planet.

THE BEAUTIFUL STORY OF THE WORLD: THE BIRTH OF LIFE AND OF THE UNIVERSE

Fundamental discoveries made during the course of the 20th century have deeply influenced our understanding of the formation of the universe.

A Huge Universe in Motion

Man has long believed, following Aristotle, that the universe had always existed as he knew it, fixed and immutable. That certainty was only shaken at the start of the 1920s, thanks to the discoveries of Edwin Hubble.

This great American astronomer was the first to observe the universe in its largest dimensions with the help of the most powerful telescope of his time, the Hooker. His work is fundamental to our understanding of the universe on several counts, starting with the discovery of its vastness.

Edwin Hubble observed galaxies, those celestial bodies that can include up to hundreds of billions of stars and which make up the building blocks of the universe. Up until then, we thought that the universe was smaller, hardly more than a few stars, the sun and the moon. Thanks to Hubble, we know that as far as we can observe, the universe is comprised on the contrary of hundreds of billions of galaxies, which in turn include hundreds of billions of stars. The universe is thus profusely organized into structures of all kinds. On the wider scale there are galaxies and stars, while on the smaller scale dozens of millions of species inhabit the earth, from bacteria to elephants. On a smaller scale still, our universe is composed of molecules, of sugar or water for example, and then of nuclei and atoms.

Edwin Hubble is also responsible for another discovery: galaxies are not static but draw continuously away from each other. This is what we call the expansion of the universe. This expansive motion follows a certain set of rules, with the nearest galaxies pulling away more slowly — which is to say at over 60 miles per second — than the more distant ones. This means that in the past, galaxies were closer to each other, but also that the universe is not the static environment which Aristotle was talking about. It changes as time goes by, and therefore has its own history.

On the basis of these discoveries, scientists, astrophysicists or nuclear physicists, assigned themselves the task of reconstituting the history of the cosmos with their respective means, be it CERN's particle accelerator in Geneva for nuclear physics, or telescopes for astrophysics.

Mankind, a Chapter in the History of the Universe

In 1965, another fortuitous but fundamental discovery took place, adding to our understanding of the history of our universe. Arno Allan Penzias and Robert Woodrow Wilson, two engineers from the Bell Telephone Company who were working at NASA, "captured" the layout of the cosmos at its very beginnings by chance, using radio telescopes. Thanks to them we possess a snapshot of sorts of the sky around the time of the Big Bang. This picture, by giving us the means of comparing the universe in its current configuration with what it was in its beginnings, is of incredible value for piecing together the history of the cosmos. It offers a wealth of lessons from which to learn.

First of all, it shows that contrary to our current rich and structured universe, the universe used to be structureless. There is no galaxy, star, planet or living being to be observed, much less giant molecules such as DNA, simple molecules, atoms, carbon, nitrogen or oxygen, or even atomic nuclei. On the contrary, we see the emergence of a kind of incandescent magma brought to extreme temperatures, made up of what we in physics call elementary particles, objects without structure such as electrons, light photons and quarks.

As a result, the reconstitution of the history of the universe amounts to considering a history of matter organizing and structuring itself, which is to say, conceiving of the increasingly complex association of particles into atomic nuclei and finally into atoms and molecules, as well as the parallel formation of stars and galaxies. This also enables us to trace the first living beings on Earth to the primitive ocean, first as small cells or plankton, which initiated the biological evolutionary chain.

Human beings, each of us, are nothing more than a component in the history of the cosmos. The atoms we are made of were produced by stars, while our molecules were formed in interstellar space. Such is our relation with the universe: we are the products of nature. Our existence is a chapter in the life of the universe.

Nature's Creative and Playful Methods

Science helps us better understand the playful and creative methods of nature, which is structured like an alphabet with atoms for letters. Among these methods, we find two fundamental elements at every level of natural organization: creative confluences and emergent properties. In the first, individual systems converge and combine into new ones, while in the second, the new systems created possess new properties not present in the original systems.

Take water for example, a molecule made up of an atom of oxygen and two atoms of hydrogen. This water, which is a solvent, possesses properties that are different from those of the atoms of which it is composed: the oxygen that we breathe in the air, or the hydrogen, plentiful in interstellar space but nowhere to be found in its natural state. It so happens that the constitution of the water molecule in interstellar space, thanks to the atoms created by the stars, presents the emergent properties of a solvent.

The principle of creative confluence and emerging properties is abundantly illustrated by the evolution of species from the molecules of life, such as DNA and chlorophyll, from which appeared the human species, consciousness and intelligence. As Albert Jacquard liked to say, this history makes of us "nameless wonders."

I propose you to accomplish one of the greatest feats ever achieved in the universe: it involves shutting your eyes and telling yourself "I am, and the world is around me." This simple moment requires the rallying of 1029 electrons and quarks, combined into molecules, which make up our body. Such is the beautiful adventure of the universe, thanks to which each of us is the product of a 14 billion year history involving stars, galaxies, collisions and others star explosions.

Nature, Born from Chance and Necessity

Chance is at the origin of the diversity and variety of the universe. Democritus, a Greek philosopher from the 5th and 4th century BC, contended that everything happened by chance and necessity. This statement was long perceived as a paradox. It took 2000 years for quantum physics to prove it right. Indeed, whilst nature is largely ruled by structuring laws, that is to say by necessity, it also allows some room for creativity, and chance. Snow crystals, for example, structured according to an immutable law: six peaks and a hexagonal symmetry. Yet, each snow crystal is unique, shaped by wind and humidity. These crystals therefore blend laws and chance, a combination which results in their diversity.

A LESS BEAUTIFUL STORY: THE DETERIORATION OF EARTH BY MAN

In parallel to the story of the universe, spanning 14 billion years, we must also tell the less palatable and more recent tale of man's tightening hold over the planet. We are the only species to wage war against nature. The paradox resides in the fact that in the event of our victory, we will be lost.

The Role of Intelligence in Human Destiny

About 5 or 6 million years ago on Earth, an animal acquired a superior form of intelligence. Why man rather than dolphins or whales? No one can say. Man, a poor animal bereft of any convincing physical defenses, with no sharp fangs, powerful claws or shell, unequipped to fly or to escape, managed to survive in a hostile environment by the strength of his intelligence.

It is by drawing on this intelligence that he was able to invent weapons to defend himself: initially simple slings enabling him to hunt prey in the treetops, followed by bows, arrows, and eventually gunpowder and tanks. By dint of cunning and cleverness, the complexity of these weapons lead to the creation of the atomic bomb and its detonation over Hiroshima.

The products of our intelligence also make our existence eminently precarious. An illustration is provided by the events of September 1983, in the context the cold war, when Officer Stanislav Petrov, in charge of the Russian nuclear arsenal, was warned of the American launch of five nuclear warheads. With only a few minutes to analyze the situation, he decided to forgo retaliating and triggering an atomic war that would have proven fatal to humankind. As it turns out, it was a false alarm. Thus, the human intelligence that saved us in our beginnings might well now prove to be our downfall.

The Ravaging of the Planet by Human Beings

If nowadays the nuclear risk has grown distant, without however disappearing entirely, another threat looms on the horizon with the current ecological crisis and global warming, born from the fruits of our intelligence.

We are becoming increasingly aware that our planet is finite. This had long been established on a physical plane, since Eratosthene, a Greek scholar, measured the circumference of the earth in the 3rd century BC. But this finiteness is now taking on a new meaning. From this point forward, we face the possibility of natural resources running out, from oil to fish, in the not-so-distant future. The impact of mankind has become so powerful that its effects are felt on a global scale.

Our hold on the planet has become a threat. The image, seen from space, of the lights produced by human activity on earth is edifying. We can see the yellow beams of urban lights and motorways, as well as red clouds of burning methane in oil extraction sites. We can even distinguish, off the coast of Japan, the lights emitted by the thousands of small boats fishing for lamparo. Yet overfishing, a product of technical progress, causes fish populations to plummet in the oceans. We know that our fishing rate is twice that of their reproductive capacity. Take another example, half the oil stocks that took the planet a 100 million years to produce, were consumed in one century by man. Their combustion emits carbon dioxide, whose density in the atmosphere has been increasing exponentially since 1950, stepping up the greenhouse effect and heating up the planet, with well-known disastrous consequences: the melting of the polar ice caps and fields, probably contributing to a rise in sea level of two or three meters by the end of the 21st century.

Human beings also jeopardize biodiversity. Their activities destroy many plant and animal species, be it the insects pollinating plants or earthworms fertilizing the soil. Nearly half of them could disappear by the end of the 21st century.

Species extinction is certainly part of the natural course of the history of earth. We now dread a temperature rise of two or three degrees Celsius, but at the time of the dinosaurs, the whole planet had a tropical climate. In the same way, we are becoming alarmed by a rise in carbon dioxide of 30–40%, but its level was 15 times higher 250 million years ago. Our planet has undergone a number of massacres. During the third massive extinction, 250 million years ago, nearly 95% of species disappeared. Earth might have become barren. However, these extinction events have enabled other life forms that survived to proliferate and diversify in an unparalleled way.

The sixth extinction event, which we are currently living through, nevertheless displays one particular specificity compared to those which preceded it: it is unfolding at an accelerated rate due to human activity.

We do not know whether the planet's regenerative capacities, previously spread over millions of years, will be able to resist this.

Human beings have only existed for 7 million years and should take their cue from turtles, animals admittedly not renowned for their intelligence but known to have endured for 300million years. Turtles show us that the species which survive are those which adapt to new conditions and live in harmony with nature. If humanity cannot summon such capacities, it could be wiped from the face of the Earth.

Should Humanity be Saved?

Let's engage in an exercise of science-fiction, and imagine the disappearance of humanity. Some would judge this purely anecdotal. After all, have not millions of species declined? I maintain the opposite. Actually, humans brought to Earth three elements which no other species ever produced before, starting with art and culture. If humans disappeared, termites would not spare Stradivariuses, works of art, or books! Humanity's second specific contribution is science. We have been able to decipher the laws of nature, we have come to understand the mechanisms of life with DNA, reconstituted the history of cosmos... All of this knowledge would disappear if the human species were to go extinct. The third contribution of humanity is compassion. It has been observed in colonies of birds that parents prioritize the feeding of healthy fledglings, neglecting the frailer ones. Biologists explain this by the idea of "a logistical gene" leading to the favoring of the individuals most likely to ensure the reproduction of the species. No such gene exists in humans, who commit themselves to caring for their weak or sick fellow beings. Humans developed an ability throughout their evolution, like some other animal species, to suffer before the manifestation of others' pain and concomitantly, the desire to appease these manifestations. Thus were born the great organizations such as Amnesty International or the Red Cross. Here again, this feeling of compassion would run the risk of disappearing if humans disappeared from the surface of the earth.

Art, science and compassion: the three treasures in the name of which we must strive to save humanity and enable it to further develop its intelligence and creativity.

In the end, is intelligence a poisoned chalice? To avoid having to answer this question in the affirmative, it is imperative for us to review the role that intelligence plays in human destiny, by developing an expansive humanism capable of embracing nature on which we depend — far removed from Descartes' humanism which called to "become like masters and owners of nature." This new humanism is a vital necessity. We no longer have a choice.

THE YEARBOOK PROJECT

Nathalie Joffre
Artist

FROM ARCHEOLOGY TO ART-CHEOLOGIST

Objects from the past have always been central in my artistic practice. One of my very first pieces was titled 'The Dressing Gown'. It is a series of ten, black and white analog photos of my childhood dressing gown. It is in no way beautiful, and the story is that I kept this garment with me for years, even when it became too small. I did not know why, so I became obsessed by it, wondering where it came from. The only thing I could remember is that it was given to me as a present at one point during my childhood. I started taking photos of this dressing gown in different positions and locations in my parents' garden over a few months. It was very much an intuitive process for me. It offered me a way to look at this object, to observe it, to study it, and to stage it in my present, and it was also a way to remember my childhood. Objects from my past, garments, postcards, old photographs, pieces of wood, plates, hats, dresses, are still very important in my art today. I stage them, take photos of them, film them, and invent stories about them. I study them, but, in a way, I also archive them.

When I was 11, my idol was Howard Carter. He discovered Tutankhamun's tomb in 1922, and as such, is one of the most famous archeologists in history. For Christmas, my parents used to buy me books about archeology. I myself used to dig in my backyard. I had even planned to dig a tomb to leave it for future generations. One day I found bones, and needless to say, I was very disappointed when my parents told me it was the dog's bones. I grew up surrounded by archeology, old houses, caves, churches and mysterious woods. However, for various reasons, I did not become an archaeologist, at least in the traditional sense. As I grew older, I ended up far, far away from my woods and my caves, and ended up in Cergy Pointoise, studying at ESSEC. In all my time here, I was still very interested in art. I wrote poetry every day, and during my studies I made one of my most important discoveries, which has been an endless source of inspiration: the Surrealist movement. In my eyes, this movement represented pure creative freedom, and it gave me the courage to pursue my artistic vocation. I decided to study Surrealism in a more academic way, at the Sorbonne University.

After completing my MA thesis, I realized I did not feel very at ease using the vocabulary of the art historian, and this helped me realize that I had never acknowledged that my language was the language of the artist. So from that day on, I started experimenting, and practicing photography every day. I took black and white analog photographs of objects, particularly things from the past — rooms, old clothes, old walls in the street — and I experienced photography as a physical and empirical act of poetry toward the world. It was not about capturing that decisive moment, but rather wandering through familiar spaces to find traces and wounds of the past. Very rapidly, movement started to appear in my photography. In a way, work constantly evolves, transforms, even when you are not necessarily aware of it. A few months later, I realized I wanted to do videos, and so I started making films, and gradually, through film and video, I felt the need to explore what was happening to me as I was creating: the mistakes, the changes, the act of imagination, how temporalities collided into one another: present, past and future, how they are nonlinear and subjective, and unexpected dreams brought on by the exploration of the past.

In 2012, I understood that I was meant to be a professional artist, so I moved to London to study at the London College of Communication. During that period, I started looking at old photographs and photographic archives. I became more and more interested in early photography from the 19th Century, and especially in the link between photography and psychiatry. Through my research, I discovered a collection of old photographs conserved at the Bethlem Royal Hospital, one of the oldest psychiatric institutions in Europe. This collection of photographs is very interesting because they were taken just after the invention of photography. These photos feature mental patients and criminals, and photography was used, not as an artistic tool, but rather as a scientific tool. I started looking at these portraits, day after day, and the information related to them. I became more and more interested not only in the historical documents, but also in the relationship I was building with them. Instead of trying to look at these pictures as objective historical documents, I started looking at them as people, as stories, as physical objects, and I decided that all photographs and archives were not only dead documents, but also living documents. After the work I did at the hospital, I found this quote from Gaston Bachelor, "We are never real historians, but always near poets, and our emotion is perhaps nothing but an expression of a poetry that was lost." This symbolizes my vision of art, and how I feel as an artist: I am a poet archeologist. So, in a way, I did become an archeologist after all.

ARTISTIC DREAMS AND DATA LOSS

In 2014, my childhood dream came true: I was selected for a residency at the 104 Art Center in Paris on the theme of archeology. I had been invited by the University of Oxford as an artist in residence. I spent one year on excavation sites, talking to archeologists, reading their books, so, quite naturally, I was very happy. This research period was very unique, because, in a sense, I discovered the reality behind the myth of the archeologist, I saw the men hiding in the shadow of Indiana Jones, and I got more and more interested in the physical dimension of excavation. It is a very impressive task: people spending hours and hours digging up the ground, collecting, archiving small stones, bones, pieces of pottery, and they have very precise gesture and it is a repetitive process. So for my first piece at the 104 Art Center, I decided to work with mimes and actors to recreate the gesture of archeologists as if it were choreographed, in a piece titled *Apparitions*.

During my residency in Oxford, I took countless photos of the excavation site in Dorchester, a small town near Oxford. I was supposed to make a film about the excavation itself, but when I started taking pictures and shooting my film, I had a very bad feeling. I could not film what I had planned, I could not focus and I felt lost. It was as if when I was looking at the archeologists, I was lost in time. So instead of giving up on the project,

I decided to incorporate what was happening to me in the film and combine it with what the archeologists were doing. I decided to title it 'Data History Voyage'.

During the excavation, I lost half of my video files. This data loss was particularly painful. This event was initially very traumatic, but I came to realize that it was interesting in terms of my relationship with memory. I started asking myself how I could have lost the most important part of my film, how I could recover it, what my relationship to these files was, what my relationship to digital memory was, and most importantly, what kind of memory digital memory is and what future generations might excavate. Our hard drives? This traumatic event helped me re-think the entire project and my relationship to memory. So I decided that the part of the film I had lost should be a work in itself. I decided to create a memorial for this lost data in a piece which I titled 'X file'. I also did a map of the installation, to show where each file was positioned in the installation. The specificity of this installation is that it is infinite. Its scale can change and grow with the space it is in.

FROM OBJECTS OF AFFECTION TO THE YEARBOOK PROJECT

My fascination for objects of the past is a very important element in my work. Last week, I visited a very interesting exhibition at the New Museum in New York named "The Keeper." I found it very interesting because it was dedicated to the act of preserving objects, artwork and images. The centerpiece of the exhibition was "The Teddy Bear Project." This installation is made up of 3,000 family album photographs of people posing with teddy bears. For example, there is a photo of a soldier or aviator holding a teddy bear. If he wasn't holding a teddy bear, he would look very different and we would look at him very differently. This photo raises questions about his childhood, his identity, his personality and his individual history, which makes him more special in our eyes.

The installation featured another interesting photo: an image of a child posing with a teddy bear. This is the perfect example of a child's object of affection. All children have that special teddy bear, and children usually get it at the age when they are starting to be a bit more independent and build their personality, their identity. This project perfectly symbolizes how simple objects, like teddy bears, can be meaningful to us and are essential pieces of our identity from our childhood to our death. This is something which is backed by psychological studies. Between the age of four and 18 months, babies start developing an intermediate area of human experience between what they are on the inside and the outside world. This was described by psychoanalyst Winnicott in 1951 as the "transitional space." The best example of this is the adoption by children of an object to which they become very attached, known as transitional object. This can be a teddy bear, a blanket, a toy, etc. By cuddling such objects, children feel they are cuddling the mother and they feel comforted. This is their first bridge between their inner and outer world. In that sense, the invention of this object is perhaps our first true act of creation, because this is the first time we are able to use our imagination to create a new reality out of nothing.

The concept of transitional object was a very important element in my reflection about how I could tie this in with this week. As we just saw, objects can be central in the construction of our personal identity. Through them, we start our relationship with the outside world and we develop our creativity for the first time. Today if we look at the context and our experience, we live in a society where people are more and more interested in living experiences, rather than owning objects. However, people always feel the need to keep, to collect, to archive objects. By this I do not mean consumer goods or precious things, I am talking here about very special objects, the most personal and intimate that stay with us as a part of our identity and a part of our memory. Therefore, keeping, collecting such objects can be one of the most personal acts of creation of our life. Even if they are broken, cheap, ugly, small, uninteresting for most people, these objects mean the world to us.

This helped me define what we could accomplish together through this residency. I titled this project the 'Yearbook Project'. The goal of the project is to create an archive of your year by building an installation comprised solely of your personal objects, be it a teddy bear, a book, a photo, etc. In a way, this is a new type of yearbook, one which has with no faces, no names, just objects, while at the same time being quintessentially personal. I would like to thank you for your involvement in the project. I hope that getting involved in this project, thinking or talking about objects you hold dear enabled you remember or revisit places, memories or people from your past in a different way. In a way, you have excavated your own past, and your own story. Gaston Bachelard once said "we are never real historians, but always near poets, and our emotion is perhaps nothing but an expression of a poetry that was lost." I hope that this personal and yet collective artistic exploration of the past has enabled you to find your own expressions of poetry that were lost.

8

BIOLOGY, ETHICS AND COMPLEXITY

Prof. Henri Atlan

Biologist, Director of Studies at EHESS Paris

BIOLOGICAL REVOLUTIONS

In the history of biology, there have been two major revolutions: the revolution of molecular biology in the 60s, and the revolution of post-genomics, epigenetics and bio-complexity, which started in the 90s and still continues today.

The first bio-revolution uncovered things which had previously been completely unknown: firstly, the discovery of the physical substrate of genes, which in turn led scientists to discover that these genes contained special molecules, known as DNA. The second bio-revolution led to the understanding of the mechanisms of protein synthesis, which had been an absolute enigma until then. The revolutionizing discovery was the correspondence between the sequence of DNA and that of proteins, called the genetic code. It is through this correspondence that proteins are synthesized, expressing the DNA sequence.

At the time, most biologists who contributed to this discovery thought that everything there was to be known in biology had already been discovered. Jacques Monod even went so far as stating that nothing remained to be discovered in biology, arguing that biological structure could be compared to crystals, only more complex, implying that "more complex" was a sufficient explanation. However, at the same time, John von Neumann, the great physicist and inventor of computers, thought that, on the contrary, complexity does not explain, but rather should be the object of scientific enquiry.

The idea that with the discoveries of the first biological revolution everything was already within our understanding, was based on a number of assumptions accepted by almost all biologists, which would later prove to be false. Scientists assumed that the flow of information from genes was merely unidirectional, and that each gene coded for one given protein, which in turn was responsible for a given characteristic, be it structural or functional. The second assumption was that since the activity of proteins depended on their three-dimensional structure, then the way this chain folds in space was determined solely by the sequence, in other words, the unidirectional structure of the protein. The final assumption was that to think that these molecules, i.e. DNA and proteins, were information-carrying molecules. This was partially correct, because they do carry "information", however, information here was understood in its technical meaning, as used in information theory, leading to confusion between the genetic code and the genetic program. This was then used as a blanket explanation for everything, as if everything in a biological organism, be it its structure, its functions or its development, was determined by the structure of the DNA, in the manner of a computer program.

These assumptions were challenged by new, unexpected, discoveries and advances, such as animal cloning, the discovery of prions and viroids, and above all, the findings of the Human Genome Program. This program was launched as a research program aimed at sequencing and mapping the entire genome of several organisms, one of them being the human genome. Scientists had expected to provide a listing of characteristics, very much in the manner of a computer program. However, this was not the case, and triggered the second biological revolution, or paradigm shift if you will. For decades, scientists had thought that DNA held the answers to everything, but the findings of this program led to the emergence of the study of the complex interactions between genetics and epigenetics, i.e. what surrounds genes and controls them, a notion which had been abandoned for decades. The task ahead of biologists, then, was to study the interactions between proteins and DNA. This type of analysis is more adequately described as "modeling", a discipline which consists in building models of complex systems.

NEURAL NETWORKS

Modeling consists in making models of complex systems so as to be able to study them. The fundamental notion of this modeling is to consider each unit as a formal neuron. For that reason, this type of modeling network is more formally referred to as neural network computing, in which each unit can be in several states. For a simple analysis, this can be reduced to two states: each unit can be in a "rest" state, represented as 0, or in an "activated" state, represented as 1. Each individual unit connects to all the other units of the system in different ways. Units can receive stimulating, i.e. activating, connections, thereby switching to 1; or inhibiting, i.e. suppressing, connections, thereby switching to 0. At any given time, each unit computes its state by making the sum of the connections it has received from others, and the algebraic sum is compared to the threshold for this unit. If the sum is larger than the threshold then the unit switches to state 1, if it is smaller, then it switches to 0.

After a few steps of such a process, the network stabilizes, and the units no longer change their state. This "computed", stable state is compared to the complex system under study in order to attempt to understand reality. What this modeling process aims to establish is the connections between the units which make up the network. This, of course, leaves one significant problem, namely the under-determination of theories by facts, or rather, by observation. In layman's terms, this means that for one given system, several models may be able to explain it. Let us take the example of a network made up of five units. This network can only be in 32 possible states. However, we must then also take account of how the units relate to one another. Each connection structure is a potential model. In other words, it is one of the many ways the connections between units can be drawn. The connections can either be there, or not, which in turn leads to two possibilities for each individual "connection." This leads to a total of 25 possible connections, which in turn means the number of possible connection combinations is 2^{25}, i.e. 10 million. This means that even the simplest assumptions can lead to millions of possible models. Of course, among these 10 million possibilities, there will be tens, hundreds or maybe even thousands of possibilities which overlap, or predict the exact same states.

This means one should be very cautious in believing or not believing the relevance or accuracy of a model.

With such a level of under-determination, it would be impossible to achieve any findings. This can be reduced by increasing the number of possible states to be observed. In biology, scientists can build what is considered a "good" model, which explains the few observations we have, and can experiment with it in order to verify the predictions based on this model. However, when dealing with disciplines where there is no experimentation, such as economy, ecology, or the emerging climate sciences, even when very sophisticated computer programs have been used to build such models, scientists are faced with under-determination.

This type of model is what is called a bottom-up model: starting from real-life observations or measurements, scientists try to build a model which can describe and if possible predict the behavior of the system as a whole.

However, there is another type of model: generic models. In this case, one is not concerned with reality or how the real system is made. Generic models are abstract constructions, the purpose of which is to determine whether or not a given behavior or function is possible, and, based on these findings, to propose possible structures, which may or may not exist but are shown to be possible. One of the first generic models for self-organization was proposed by Heinz von Foerster, the architect of cybernetics. He carried out an experiment which consisted in analyzing cubes which were magnetized in such a way that three sides of the cube had a magnetic field in one given direction, either inward or outward, and the three other sides were magnetized in the other direction. As a result, some cubes would be attracted to one another, and others would be repelled by one another. These cubes were randomly placed in a box which was closed and shaken at arbitrary moments in time. From time to time, the box was opened again and from an initial state which was completely random, and he observed the gradual emergence of a structure. The cause of the emergence of this self-organization, was the magnetization, of course, but also the way and the random moments when the box had been shaken. In terms of information theory, this "randomness" is expressed as "noise." The fundamental principle this experiment proved was that noise can contribute to the emergence of structure, or what Von Foerster called the principle of "order from noise."

FROM FUNCTIONAL SELF-ORGANIZATION
TO SATISFACTION FUNCTION

In such a context, the role of generic neural networks is to provide a generic model of self-organization and emergence in a large neural network. Let us take, for example, the scene from the famous movie *Space Odyssey* in which we see great apes playing around with bones and learning to use these bones as tools and weapons. Making a model of this very complex system is very challenging. It is impossible to map a bottom-up model which would attempt to analyze every single detail of the actions of the apes, put it together and re-produce this behavior. However, this can be done by proposing a generic model, showing how such a behavior can emerge from a mechanical viewpoint.

The goal to be simulated here is the emergence of function, as seen in the scene from the movie. The apes invented a new goal: to use the bone as a tool. The apes start by playing with the bones with no intention whatsoever. By chance one of them happens to hit something or somebody else with a bone, then it understands it can repeat the same movement, but this time intentionally. How can this happen?

Such a question pertains to teleology, i.e. an action directed towards a goal. In general, when we look at causes and effects, the cause precedes the effect. But in fact, in a teleological action, there is a slight time inversion and the cause of the result actually takes place after the action has been carried out. In other words, when you want to do something, what you are doing is what seems to be the cause of your action but in fact it is the result of a process. In psychology, this type of time inversion is generally referred to as "a mental state." They are viewed as conscious mental states that are able to cause bodily movements whenever an intentional action is executed. The mental state, or the representation of the goal, precedes the action, and then this action becomes a mechanical, causal action. In other words, the cause is not the goal when it is achieved, but rather the mental intention. Psychologists use a basic syllogism to describe teleological movements: an individual "B" has the desire to be in state "S", "B" knows that "C" is a cause for "S", and therefore "B" produces "C." The problem with this syllogism is that it does not explain intentional action, it simply describes it, assuming intentionality: it explains the production of C as a means to produce S and implies the existence of intentional mental states which are defined as desires or knowledge.

In order to build a model which does not present this flaw, such a behavior should be explained by producing an internal origin of the goal, i.e. the self-organization of an emerging goal. This type of model is generally referred to as intentional self-organization. In order to achieve this, we can rely on a very interesting observation made by Elizabeth Anscombe, a philosopher who wrote a seminal book in 1957 entitled *Intention*. She observed that the practical syllogism mentioned above is different from the traditional demonstrative syllogism: "All men are mortal. Socrates is a man. Therefore Socrates is mortal." This particular syllogism is different because it is redundant, and could be reduced to only two propositions. Following this pattern, the practical syllogism above can be re-written as follows: B believes C is the cause for S therefore B produces C. The notion that B wants to induce S, is implicit in the idea that "B produces C." Based on this, the syllogism can be re-phrased in the form of a network. The network has learned, or memorized, a relationship between a state S and a state C, and when the network reaches this state S or is close to it, then this state S can behave like a goal, in the sense that when exposed to an input C, the network is driven to S again by the dynamics it has memorized. This is what happens in the scene from the movie. An ape is playing around with the bones, and by chance, it reaches the final state, i.e. it has hit somebody. The final state, then, is memorized together with the initial state. Another event may lead to the same final state, but since the final state has been memorized with its initial state, the whole process starts all over again, only this time it looks as if it has been triggered by the final state. This is what is referred to as an apparent "time inversion."

Not every final state produced by every input can be memorized in order to repeat the behavior or "state." There is a selection, or preference, between the final stages which are produced largely at random. Of course, such a satisfaction function cannot be programmed by the designer of the model, because such programming would be antithetical to the notion of self-organization. In fact, the same final state can be achieved simply by looking at what happens most frequently at random. This relative frequency is the "satisfaction function" which is not programmed, because it is the result of the structure of the network on the one hand, and on the other, of the history of the encounters the network has had with inputs from the environment, a history which may be largely random.

INTENTIONALITY: INTENTIONAL ACTIONS VS INTENTIONS

Following the ideas of Anscombe, action and goal are one and the same thing, and so the goal is not produced by what can be referred to as a "mental intention." This implies that intention and action are not dissociated from one another. On an *a priori* ground, every intention should be executed. But as scientists, we know that this is not the case. This then begs the question: why are some intentions executed and others are not? This may occur, for example, when an intention is not executed because it is inhibited.

The notion of intentional mental state is at odds with the traditional notion of free-will, and the causal relationship between intention and action. We all experience free will, have mental states, images, representations, conscious decisions and feel that these are the causes of our intentional or voluntary movements. However, in fact, this may not be the case.

Data provided by neuro-physiology on voluntary movement points to the fact that conscious will is not always the cause of voluntary, intentional actions. This data was obtained by neurophysiologist Benjamin Libet. A study using very precise timing of electrode activation in the brain of patients undergoing surgery demonstrated that when the patient consciously decided to make a movement, the initiation of the movement in the brain precedes the initiation of the actual movement. Interestingly enough, a parallel can be drawn between this neurophysiological premise and the philosophies of Spinoza and Descartes. Spinoza establishes a relationship between body and mind as being two aspects of one same thing; Descartes argues there is no causal relationship between mind and body. Not because they pertain to different substances, but precisely because they are one same thing expressed in two different ways.

The impact of such a view is twofold. On one hand, we lose our traditional understanding of free will and causation of actions by decisions. On the other hand, however, we gain an understanding of intentional actions without having to resort to hidden causal states of mental state. This leads to a statement which is difficult to admit for moral philosophers: the desire expressed in our practical syllogism is nothing more than unconscious drive accompanied by consciousness, in other words, the retrieved memory of the goal to which it is directed, with the knowledge that this consciousness is not the cause of action.

ETHICS AND RESPONSIBILITY IN THE FACE OF PROGRESS

In 1959, a famous conference, entitled "The Two Cultures", discussed the split into the titular two cultures: the sciences and the humanities. Sciences on the one hand, has become increasingly materialistic, looking for mechanisms which are as deterministic as possible; and humanities on the other, a field still dominated by philosophical tradition, both idealist and vitalistic, with important consequences on ethics in Kantian and post-Kantian philosophy.

For centuries, life and thought were considered to be specific to certain beings, which is what differentiated them from mere material bodies, and the soul was what made the difference. As opposed to inanimate bodies, an *anima*, the soul, made living bodies not only alive, but also able to feel, think and know. This non-material soul was endowed with sensitivity and intelligence, or at the very least, inception, behaviors which are supposed to culminate in what Kant refers to as the "human supra-sensitive domain of freedom", as opposed to material inanimate bodies. This view is still seen by most philosophers and theologians as the only possible view compatible with ethical thinking or moral philosophy. I, however, would argue this assumption is not correct. In all events, the gap is such that techno-science is often accused of dehumanization, of invading our lives and being a cause of both fascination and fear. In order to bridge the gap, there is a need for a new philosophy of nature which takes into account what we have learned from biological and cognitive sciences, always in a critical, non-reductionist manner, while at the same time avoiding idealist, essentialist definitions. This need is all the more pressing since we are constantly confronted with ethical problems raised by innovation in science and technology, and especially in biology, in a field which is referred to as bioethics.

Bioethics are defined as a set of problems created by biology and medicine which biology alone cannot solve. The term "bioethics" however, does not seem perfectly adequate, because it seems to imply that it is a sub-discipline of biology, as are biophysics or biochemistry. However, it is the opposite. These issues are complex because today, we are dealing with new scientific concepts, such as genes, embryonic differentiation and biological evolution to ancient ideas about life, reproduction, embryos, mankind and consciousness in ambiguous ways. Old definitions are no longer relevant, and new definitions are evolving over time based on new discoveries and technological achievements. New problems are arising, because what is being learned in biology seems to be at odds with what we have thought about life for centuries.

Today, a clear need for non-essentialist definitions has arisen. We need to give up trying to identify the essence of things (man, life, embryos, etc.) because we are dealing with evolving processes and, consequently, definitions also are evolving.

The technique discussed herein aims to study the individuality of non-coding DNA, i.e. DNA which does not code for any specific protein. It varies greatly from one individual to another. However, considering this is the source of individuality, or the essence of a being, would be as incongruous as considering a fingerprint, equally unique, as the essence of human beings.

9

THEORIES OF EVOLUTION AND THE MECHANISMS OF ADAPTATION

Pascal Picq

Paleontologist
Lecturer at the Collège de France

How can theories of evolution help the corporate world, and more specifically, its capability to innovate? These two worlds may seem very distant, yet they could learn from each other. Indeed, evolution theories shed light on natural patterns of innovation that can be applied to all species and groups. Besides, men develop different types of social behaviors and understandings of the world that make them more or less capable of adapting to these patterns, and therefore to innovate.

ITINERARY OF A PALEOANTHROPOLOGIST

Paleoanthropology — which comes from the Greek *paleo* (ancient), *anthropos* (man) and *logos* (knowledge) — covers a scope of fields that look into the origins of mankind and its evolution: genetics, archeology, prehistory and ethology. I came to this field after engineering studies — with no great conviction — after which I had turned towards theoretical physics. It was a woman who changed everything, a woman that I met in the 1970s. She was very old (3 million years old) and very small (barely a 3.7 feet), but very charming nonetheless. You might have guessed it, it was the australopithecus Lucy, with whom I sort of fell in love. I also met a great scholar,

Yves Coppens, who ultimately convinced me it was time to change paths, and I decided to dedicate myself to paleoanthropology.

The general public often only has a partial and caricatured vision of evolution, limited to dinosaurs, australopithecines or other Neanderthals. But that is only one small aspect of evolution, its historical component, which traces the story of life. Today, I would like to talk about another component: the mechanism of evolution. How can you spark evolution and innovation? How can you survive in the "world of the Red Queen?"

While working on a publication, I wrote 10 years ago on the theories of evolution and adaptation, I discovered that this subject interested people from the sphere of management and the business world. Which is not as surprising as it could seem. The corporate world and the defenders of theories of evolution already came together 200 years ago in the United Kingdom in the Lunar Society of Birmingham, a club of prominent and progressive personalities. For example, economist Adam Smith; poet, doctor and botanist Erasmus Darwin (Charles Darwin's grandfather); manufacturers Matthew Boulton and James Watt (Inventor of the steam machine); Josiah Wedgwood (founder of the famous ceramic factory that Queen Victoria was particularly fond of), and occasionally joined by the Americans Benjamin Franklin and Thomas Jefferson. Together, they laid the foundations of what would later become liberalism and free enterprise, strove for modern democracy and stood against slavery. They had understood a crucial idea: a society in which one group is exploited by another is not capable of innovating. They are at the origin of the theories of evolution.

They were true precursors. For example, as early as in 1797, Erasmus Darwin had published a treaty supporting the education of women and young girls. And we could say that Josiah Wedgwood invented marketing. He was from a modest family of potters, and suffered smallpox, leading to one of his legs being amputated. In order to still be able to operate the lathe, he asked his friends Matthew Boulton and James Watt to invent a mechanical system to make up for this disability. This was the first step of a flourishing manufacturing process. Wedgwood was the first to ever send out illustrated catalogs of his products, to use *sponsorship* by publicizing the fact that he supplied the King of England, to have offers like "buy one get one free", etc. For a person with such a frail physical condition, imagination was a matter of survival.

WHAT IS A THEORY OF EVOLUTION?

Forget everything you think you know about evolution: the fight between species, the survival of the fittest, etc. That is all nonsense. In fact, the theories of evolution look at changes in nature. Because for at least 3 billion years, life has been able to innovate, adapt and change — and without any managers, or R&D directors! When I work with companies, we study their ability to stimulate natural innovation models and to repress the cultural patterns and conceptions of the world that could hinder innovation.

Three Visions of the World

There are three main ways of perceiving the world, which in turn determine the understanding one has of evolution.

The first, and the most widespread, considers that the world in which we live was created as it is, without experiencing any form evolution, or that it follows a circular pattern which regularly brings it back to the starting point (for example, in the tradition of ancient Greece or India). This is a very ancient and universal conception.

The second vision appeared more recently in the history of mankind. It lies on the idea of progress. It estimates that mankind is capable of innovating, being creative, inventing technologies, cultures, artifacts, tools, societies, etc. It knows how to find solutions to live a better life, even if it implies fighting against nature.

The third conception of the world is evolution, as described by Darwin. It is often poorly understood, and even caricatured.

No Species is More Evolved than Others

How do the defenders of these three concepts face the truth that chimpanzees are the species that is closest to man? The first will say that man is made in the image and likeness of God, whereas Chimpanzees are in the image of the devil, and that this is immutable.

The second will say that men's ancestors are the great apes, which is perfectly erroneous. They consider that chimpanzees are less evolved than human beings.

The defenders of the third version, more correct with regards to modern science, argue that chimpanzees are our brothers in nature, and that we have common ancestors. Chimpanzees are therefore considered as evolved, just as much as human beings and other species.

Those who see chimpanzees as the ancestors of men consider that the latter is more evolved than the former, and therefore that men are superior. This is absolutely inaccurate: researchers know that today's chimpanzees are not the same as those from the past, no more than today's flies are similar to those of the past, or today's human beings the same as those of the past. The same can be said about all species, civilizations, cultures and countries. Darwin argued that no species can be considered as superior to others, that the most capable of surviving were not the most intelligent ones, but the most capable of adapting. To adapt is to understand the world and find ways to innovate accordingly.

But the second vision of the world, the one that claims the superiority of certain species, has not disappeared. Quite the contrary, it has had a high resonance in the western world and in Japan for more than a century, and it still has. As a result of its economic predominance during the 20th century, the western world seems unable to understand that every country and culture is equally capable of rising to the top. In that respect, we should not forget that for two millennia and until the end of the 19th century, China was the first economic and cultural power in the world. Very soon, it will be back on top. And the Muslim world laid the foundations of all European scientific knowledge!

If you have an erroneous conception of evolution, according to which some species, cultures or civilizations might be superior to others, you might end up last of the race without even seeing it coming. The world is changing! Africa, India and Brazil are gaining power and influence. Yet, in France, a recent report on competitiveness placed South Korea among the emerging countries. That is a sign of willful blindness.

Three Reactions to Change

The three conceptions of the world we have just described give rise to three very different attitudes from a geopolitical point of view.

Countries with a strong economy thanks to their natural resources are led by governments that are influenced by a fundamentalist view of the world. That is the case for example in Texas, prey to creationism; Canada, that withdrew from the Kyoto protocol to exploit bituminous shale under the influence of the Harper government; or Saudi Arabia and the Emirates, governed by conservative Islamic governments, or even Russia where Orthodox religion still has a strong hold. I would like to make an important clarification here. The question is not so much the religious presence *per se*, but rather a certain use that is made of religion, that considers for example, that natural resources are a gift from God to men for them to exploit them. It is easily understandable that these states may be reluctant to change.

In Europe, on the East coast of the US, in Japan and Korea, a certain idea of progress is predominant, with by corollary, a culture of manufacturing, transformation and innovation.

Finally, the countries that follow Darwin's evolution theory encourage entrepreneurship and creativity, as is the case in the Silicon Valley for example.

IT IS TIME TO CHANGE A WINNING TEAM!

As discussed previously, evolution theories focus on changes in nature. What causes them? Why does a change happen? The first reason is nature. Natural disasters such as earthquakes, volcanic eruptions and other meteor showers provoked drastic environmental and climatic changes. They demonstrate that evolution is not necessarily something that happens over a long period of time, but can also happen suddenly.

The second reason is tied to human activity, and more precisely, what I call the "Race of the Red Queen", a reference to Lewis Carroll's *Alice in wonderland*. On her journey, young Alice runs beside the Red Queen and is surprised to see that the landscape is following her. She is running, but she is not moving. The Queen then warns her: "*Now, here, you see, it takes all the running you can do, to keep in the same place.*" In other words, we must adapt to the consequences of our own activities, and at an unprecedented rate. If your company is successful, others will gear themselves up to catch up with you. And if they catch up with you, you in turn will have to change to stand out. Our ecosystem as a whole is in movement. Some might be tempted to stay out of the race, to avoid getting involved. And that is isolationism. But one thing we do know is that when a species or an ecosystem gets isolated, it is doomed to disappear.

Crises are a very normal event in the course of evolution. It can be caused by two main factors: an event unrelated to you (a volcanic eruption, the *subprimes* crisis, etc.) or success. The latter tends to convince you that no change is required, which will eventually lead you to your downfall. A good example of this is Kodak, a jewel of the world economy 20 years ago. Blinded by success, it did not prepare for the digital revolution that was coming. The company has nearly disappeared today. If you earn success but aren't ready for big changes, then you will disappear. Anticipate the fact that you will reach your limits. That is why it is important to change a winning team! Very old companies such as General Electric, Michelin or Saint-Gobain understood this well and continuously offer state-of-the-art innovations to ensure their survival.

INNOVATION BETWEEN LAMARCK AND DARWIN

The most common way to innovate in human societies and companies is the innovation identified by biologist Jean-Baptiste de Lamarck two centuries ago: active adaption, which is when innovation takes place to face evolutions in the environment and context. If the market changes, you have to offer new products, new ideas and be creative. This is typically the type of innovation offered by engineers. Continental Europe, Japan and Korea are very gifted in this field. This form of innovation is necessary, but it has a drawback: you stay within the limits of what is known. This is obvious when you look at the fact that the top 25 companies in continental Europe are all more than 40 years old, while in the States, a third of them (and soon half of them) are very young: Intel, Microsoft and Facebook.

Companies from Continental Europe have not yet been successful in making a place for themselves in new technologies and new fields of excellence, because culturally, this region is dominated by an engineers' vision of the world. They don't challenge themselves when everything is working fine, and innovate only when they are forced to. They stay within traditional, well-known sectors: aeronautics industry, construction, water management, etc. European universities teach students how to reinforce existing systems, whereas young American students are encouraged to create their own company as soon as possible. Continental Europe seems to be lacking a culture of entrepreneurship, risk-taking and failure. When we have good ideas (such as the MP3 system invented by a German laboratory), they are implemented in the UK or the U.S., where investors are ready to take the risk to support them. In other words, we know how to discover rather than innovate, which means introducing new applications onto the market.

But from a Darwinian perspective, innovation takes on a whole new meaning. Economist Joseph Schumpeter argued that the greatest book he had ever read was Charles Darwin's *On the Origin of Species*. He was the first to talk about economic evolution. Darwinian evolution goes through three phases: variation, selection and development.

Variation

Our genes can mutate, duplicate or create novel combinations. They are variation machines Darwin understood that variation was the fundamental basis for innovation. When you innovate, you must first multiply ideas in all directions, challenge certainties, change perspectives. That is how brainstorming works for example. It doesn't matter if the ideas formulated during it the brainstorming session are good or bad. The main objective is for them to provoke variations. Similarly, in a group, differences between individuals are a true potential for innovation.

Selection

The next step is to choose ideas from among all those that were suggested.

Development

In the final stage, the retained project must be taken to the end.

To imagine the sequel of the very successful animation film *Toy Story*, Pixar studios used a Darwinian innovation. All staff members were gathered in a large room, and were asked to contribute as many ideas as possible. At one point, somebody said "*I'm thinking of a house that floats in the air, pulled by balloons.*" The idea was written down, but wasn't retained for *Toy Story 2*. But it was used a couple of years later, and gave birth to the very beautiful *Up*.

I do not mean that there is a good and a bad way to innovate. You must be able to see when it will be more productive to follow Lamarck, and when you have to trust Darwin.

If you choose a Darwinian logic, it is primordial to respect the following principles in the management of the innovation.

- Everybody can offer good ideas. Research and Development is not a field reserved exclusively to R & D departments.
- You have to create circumstances in which people will feel comfortable and authorized to suggest ideas.
- An idea is not intrinsically good or bad.
- The leader of the innovation project does not necessarily have to be the person who holds the highest role in the company, but should be the person who has been recognized as capable of successfully driving the project. Chimpanzees for example, do not necessarily entrust a delicate hunting mission to the dominant male, but rather chose the male that is the most likely of being successful in catching preys. The dominant male accepts the leadership of the chimpanzee that was chosen. Once the prey has been captured, the booty is shared and every contribution to the effort is respected.
- Cooperation is paramount. Since 1985, when Gary Kasparov lost to Deep Blue, no single chess player could defeat a computer. But the hydra software was beaten twice during free-style chess competitions, where players joined forces with computers. Even if you are the best player in the world, the computer can understand your strategy and defeat you. But it cannot anticipate variations that could come from a diversified group. To have good ideas and be a leader in your field, you should surround yourself with people who can cooperate, rather than gamble on one leader and count on him/her to pull others with him/her.

IDENTIFYING CULTURAL AND SOCIAL OBSTACLES

Social hierarchy and group behavior can hinder innovation. Once more, monkeys can give us the proof of that! The island of Koshima in Japan is populated by macaques of which the local population is very fond, and they feed them sweet potatoes that they throw on the beach for them. In the 1950s, researchers noticed that a female macaque, called Imo, had had the idea of rinsing the sweet potatoes in sea water to get rid of the sand, giving them a salty taste that the macaques particularly appreciate. She had innovated. And it took 50 years for all the macaques of the island to do the same thing. Indeed, the hierarchy within this species is so rigid that it prevents a smooth transmission of practices and information, and therefore of innovation. Chimpanzees, on the other hand, have much faster transversal transmission abilities.

In the neoclassical *homo economicus* model, it is said that the rational behavior of an economic actor is to strive to obtain the best personal benefit from a transaction. Yet experiments inspired by gaming theories revealed that individuals do tend to share, even if it is not out of pure selflessness. Generally speaking, business deals generally concluded with a 55 % or 60 % for one of the parties, but seldom more. Because who knows what tomorrow might be made of? If I make a very unfavorable proposal to a third party, they might make me a bad one in the future when they have an advantage over me.

Experiments lead to similar results with monkeys. A large pharmaceutical laboratory was carrying out an experiment that involved two groups of macaques, one which received food and the other didn't. Surprisingly, this experiment failed. After research, it turned out that the macaques who were receiving food shared it with the ones who didn't. That way, if the situation were to change, they were guaranteed food. It was a matter of survival for the group, a form of interested altruism. As a manager, then, do not hesitate to count on cooperation!

A similar reaction was seen in monkeys from South America. They had to perform a task, and received cucumber, which they particularly like, as a reward. But when grapes, that they love even more, were given to some of them, they refused this "unjustified" privilege, and went "on strike." Monkeys, as humans, attach importance to how they are perceived and rewarded. So be very careful in how you choose to value and remunerate your innovators!

With these few examples, I hope I have proved to you that in terms of innovation, management and group management, change and adaptation, we have a lot to learn from anthropology and evolution.

10

SQUATTING AND "ARTIVISM"

Gaspard Delanoë

Artist and Activist
President of the 59, rue de Rivoli Association

LIVE ILLEGALLY OR DIE LEGALLY?

We live in a world where the 67 richest individuals have as much wealth as the 3.5 billion poorest. The squatting movement has often been presented as marginal. However, studies show that it has grown over the last 20 years. Today, globally, more than a billion people illegally occupy land, vacant buildings, forests and other abandoned places. They lodge, live and engage in activities there. This may include immigrants, single parents, young people from dysfunctional families, the homeless, students, the unemployed, artists, undocumented individuals, intermittent workers, welfare recipients, pensioners or retirees, former detainees, people from psychiatric institutions, etc. Although this movement is unstructured — it has no central unit, is executed through a variety of behaviors and, to different degrees — it affects a large population in the world.

Squatting, or the illegal occupation of a residence, has often been presented as the response of individuals driven to this end by the society in which they live and where having a job does not even offer the guarantee of being able to afford a roof over their heads. The terrible quote by Abbé Pierre is more relevant now than ever: he said that the poor, the humble and the disadvantaged have the choice between living illegally or dying legally. With squatting, people choose the former.

The accusation that we value illegality, based on our actions and our claims for squatters' rights, is correct. However, I stand by what I consider a constructive and positive illegality, which is distinguishable from other, extremely negative illegalities that I am the first to condemn. Sometimes laws produce so much injustice that they deserve to be questioned, even broken, in order to advance forward. This is similar to the processes that surrounded the laws against abortion, among others.

THE SQUATTING ARTISTS OF PARIS

Though marginal at first, the movement of squatting artists gradually gained ground over the last 30 years. The first of these squats was claimed in 1980 on rue d'Arcueil and was called Art-Cloche. The artists had settled in a place occupied by homeless people with whom they lived and tried to create a place of artistic production and exhibition. They were quickly expelled. For 20 years, the only government response to the illegal occupation was repression and expulsion, again and again. Over time, the practice of artistic squats has expanded to the point that the ability of the Prefecture to carry out evictions has been exceeded. At the same time, in 2001, when nobody believed in it anymore, Paris elected a left-wing mayor for the first time in 70 years. At that time, the parties supporting the squatting movement were also left.

For our part, we established our living quarters on rue de Rivoli, in a building owned by Crédit Lyonnais and which remained empty for 8 years. This national bank went bankrupt — perhaps in part due to the incompetence of some leaders — and its impaired assets were to be liquidated, including 200 vacant buildings in Paris. This became a godsend for us who were having to seek new shelter after each expulsion! After a first unsuccessful intrusion attempt (we had been reported by a neighbor), we were finally able to establish ourselves in this building on rue de Rivoli and the police lost interest in us.

Logically, we should have been expelled: ownership is constitutive of our laws, democracy and the Republic. Judges inevitably find in favor of the owners. However, during the trial, which was brought about by us, the State and counsel for the opposing party had explained that we were to be expelled urgently because this property had been sold. The judge was astonished at this sudden rush to sell since the place had been vacant for 8 years. This earned us a six-month period during which we were allowed to stay, which changed everything. The municipal campaign was in full swing and the left parties — environmentalists, communists and socialists — were ignited in our favor. Squatting movements flourished in the capital, which was scattered with empty Crédit Lyonnais buildings and those of real estate companies, which became the objects of speculation and guaranteed funds.

Aware that we were not causing a disturbance, that our being there served as an artistic production and taking into account that our doors were open to the public, the Prefecture preferred to wait for the results of municipal elections to react. We asked Bertrand Delanoë (with whom I have no relationship, Delanoë being a pseudonym) to write, in black and white, his promise to try to resolve our case if elected. No attempt to support our case had ever been publicly declared in the past. To our surprise and that of his entourage, Bertrand Delanoë kept his promise once elected. Therefore, the city of Paris committed €4.6 million to buy the building from the French government: specifically, the *Consortium de Réalisation*, which is a public company created by Edouard Balladur to liquidate the impaired assets of Crédit Lyonnais. What the Mayor did not know was that 4–5 years later, from the time that we had agreed on the objectives, the place would be closed for safety reasons, among others, and would require an additional 4 million for renovations. In total, the cost was 9.1 million. All that money just to help squatters!

We were asked to leave while the work was being completed, knowing that we would be relocated elsewhere. Then, if we were classified as an Association under the Law of 1901 (we were previously a class devoid of legal status), we would be allowed to take part in discussions for the signing of a precarious occupation agreement that would last for one or more years and would be renewable. We saw the process through to the end. Certainly, the city imposed a significant condition for its authorization: as it could not arrange for studio apartments in the building, because it would be too expensive, only open workshops were permitted, without the possibility of living there. In the movement, some refused to yield, others felt that it was worth the effort. By a vote, we opted for the compromise.

This movement has attracted the attention of media from around the world, from Japan to Brazil, South Africa and the United Arab Emirates. We received much greater support than we could have hoped for, mainly because we were proposing a different way of presenting art and creation. Usually in France, art is confined to institutional (museums) and merchant (galleries) locations. For our part, we invite the public to discover artists' work as it is being made. This guarantees easy access, and greater proximity and intimacy with the art.

As artists and residents of the squat, our way of life was largely based on gathering materials to create works of art, but that also involves food. In the photo, plastic bottles have been affixed to the left side of the facade and flattened tin cans to the right.

You can see that the slogan "Mr. Sarkozy, poverty is not a crime" is displayed on the front facade. This was because legislation regularly sought to toughen penalties for illegal occupation. For 30 years, 93% of squatting cases resulted in expulsion. However, more and more squats have been officially authorized over the past 15 years and some have been brought up to code and legalized. In addition to 59 rue de Rivoli, other places have been officially authorized, such as 111 rue Saint-Honoré or La Petite Rockette in the 11th district, which has become a place where objects can be exchanged and recovered and which now employs 10 people.

From 2005 to 2008, 59 rue de Rivoli and the movement of artists and squatters were supported by the left. After 7 years of occupation, to our surprise, this movement has the support of part of the UMP [French right-wing party]. This was unimaginable when we first began! Jean-François Lamour, President of the party, visited the squats. He acknowledged that Paris was suffering from a lack of affordable housing, forcing many to go into exile in the capital, and that it could be appropriate, if necessary, to discuss affordable housing solutions, in great detail and in a timely matter.

For years, our "Assistance group for buildings in danger" attracted the attention of Parisians to vacant buildings: why not invest in them? We thought it unacceptable that the buildings remain empty for years — 40 years in the case of Place des Vosges — while people were sleeping in the street.

We also make use of the street, as with our 27-second fashion shows that are completed in the amount of time one waits at a traffic light. Our outdoor performances cannot last for more than four or five minutes since rue de Rivoli is a thoroughfare and blocking it causes a phenomenal amount of disorder.

Here is a self-portrait of me.

How does this place function from an economic point of view? The Mayor of Paris set very low rental prices for us, but asked us to pay all additional costs (electricity, repairs, maintenance, water, insurance, etc.). For a building that spanned 1,400 square meters along 59 rue de Rivoli, this represented 70,000 euros per year. To cover these costs, each artist was asked to pay 130 euros per month for a 12-square-meter workshop. With thirty artists (a strong core of twenty people and dozens that came and went from the space), we raised 48,000 euros per year at best. However, that's only when artists manage to pay. But what should we do when they get too behind in their rent, expel them? The question is obviously difficult for a squat. Nevertheless, their lack of contribution challenges the equilibrium of the place as a whole. This is exactly what the city would need to expel us all.

For some squatters who cannot pay, we managed to establish partnerships with private companies. This primarily consists of Canson, which has donated drawing supplies to our grateful artists. Every year for 3 years, Canson has awarded a prize to an artist who is then allowed to display their art on the front façade of 59 rue de Rivoli for one month. They also select twenty artists who are then allowed to present their art on the ground and first floors. Canson's patronage brings in nearly 13,000 euros each year. Finally, visitors end up donating a little here and there. This is how we balance our budget.

59 rue de Rivoli sees nearly 70,000 visitors each year. It is open Tuesday through Sunday, from 1 p.m. to 8 p.m. Here, visitors can discover anything from art made of plastic to concerts on the weekends and, of course, admission is free. Everyone is welcome to come down and check us out!

CONVERSATIONS WITH A PUNK

11

Didier Wampas

Punk Rocker, Former RATP Electrician
"Punk Taught me that Future was Within Reach"

Xavier Pavie — Didier Wampas, you grew up near Paris, in Villeneuve-la-Garenne (in the île de France region); your father was a blue-collar worker, your mother a housewife, and they were both "humanist communists." Did this childhood make you who you are today?

Didier Wampas — To paraphrase a famous film, I was fortunate enough to have communist parents! They instilled deeply humanist values in me. Communists in post-war France truly believed that a big, beautiful world was possible. This strong ideology was the driving force of their lives, almost like a religion.

X. P. — To what extent do these values affect you in your life today?

D. W. — They are primarily reflected in my absolute refusal to play the great game of marketing. I am just not that kind of person, it's simply not in my genes. I'm not capable of selling myself, or promoting my achievements. I aspire to the exact opposite. My first encounter with Punk Rock at the age of 15 reinforced for me the idea that art is not a livelihood. Art is meant to disturb, shock people. An artist should not complain about not being able to live from his or her art.

As one of my songs says, I am a working class punk. When I was young, I worked in a factory for a year before joining the RATP, somewhat by chance: my father had sent my application to a number of organizations, and the RATP took me on. I worked there for 30 years. It gave me the chance to continue making the music I loved. What other choice does an artist have, knowing that his or her art is neither bankable nor mainstream? Does this mean that he or she should give up on the dream of making a living from art? I took responsibility for the choices I made, to make the music I loved while doing whatever else was needed to make ends meet. I was a "worker-punk" just as there were "worker-priests" in the 1960s: I worked round the clock so I was a bit out of things, a bit like a spectator. I loved the perspective that gave me on things. I enjoyed going to work for the human relationships and social interactions. When you work the night shift, you meet weird and wonderful characters, and experience situations that you could never find otherwise.

Being an artist is having something to say, something to share. Maintaining a "normal" life helped me keep my feet on the ground, and not live in a bubble. I know too many musicians who have nothing else left to say.

Above all, keeping my job was a way for me to make my music without needing to be a success. I could have lived from my music part-time as an *intermittent** but I always refused to do this. I'd much rather just be even a civil servant than be a servant of the music industry!

X. P. — How would you define punk?

D. W. — I was 15 in 1977, when punk music reached France. This new style offered me complete freedom of thought, of action, and a chance to live "in" difference. As a teenager, in my Parisian suburb, I felt quite inadequate: I didn't play football, I didn't like the Bee Gees, I wasn't invited to parties... I just didn't know what to do with my life. When punk music arrived, I realized I was not alone, and that there was a universe and an art form which matched my personality. This gave me hope: another world was possible. It is not the *no future* aspect of punk that resonated with me. Quite the contrary, punk music taught me that that a future was within my reach.

A student — Do you really dream of a punk world? Would it be livable?

D. W. — I often wonder. Having said that, we are not there yet! I worked at the RATP, without ever working too hard. I realized that there was not that big a difference between those who poured their heart and soul into their work and me, who stuck to the bare minimum ... If that's going to be the case, then why not be a punk!

---

* Editor's note: intermittent is the status for workers in casual employment in the culture industry.

To me, being a punk means doing what you want to, regardless of how others judge you. Unfortunately, punk has become a cliché in music, fashion and ideology — which is the exact opposite of the punk spirit.

A student — Is coming to ESSEC a punk provocation?

D. W. — On principle, I am open to anything — interviews for Punk fanzines, coming to talk at ESSEC, or going to a TV show. I do not go to these events to try and sell anything, but rather as an expression of my freedom and a sense of detachment. When I watched TV as a child, I thought it was boring, except when Coluche or Gainsbourg came on: they proved me that there was something else out there. Having said that, I think I would have been very embarrassed if anybody had asked me to appear on Star Academy, which embodies everything I hate.

A student — As a punk, what do you think of illegal downloading?

D. W. — I couldn't care less. My personal goal is to make music, not to sell albums. There will always be people who want to make music, those who simply want to listen to it, and others who want to make money by bringing the former and the latter together. A band earns approximately 10% of the gross price of a CD (excl. taxes), which is generally around €10. There are five of us in the band, so this represents approximately €0.20 each per album, and our last album sold 4,000 copies… At that rate, you may as well download it for free!

A student — If you had Manu Chao's bank account, would you go all the way to Congo, as you say in your song? Would becoming rich have changed your life?

D. W. — When you start out, deep down, you always want to show the world what you are worth. The older I get, the more I realize that I just don't care about being rich and famous, and the more I enjoy playing at small venues. I have come to realize that happiness does not lie in success.

X. P. — Did you actually become political, as the song *Chirac en prison* leads us to believe?

D. W. — I knew that the relative success of our song *Manu Chao* would give me media access. This does not mean that I wanted to go and sell my music on TV sets. If I was going to be in the limelight, then why not make it an opportunity to offer something different. I had seen a puppet show on censorship under Louis XIV with my children. The show ended with a question: and what are we doing with our so-called freedom of expression today? I took this quite literally, and wrote *Chirac en prison*, thinking I would see where it led.

X. P. — Does your political commitment go beyond your music?

D. W. — I think it is easy for a band to go on-stage and mouth slogans in front of an audience that is already won over. Moralizing seems a bit cowardly if you don't take responsibility for what you say. The mayor of a small town has to face up to how precarious life is for his or her constituents. It's not for me to tell anybody what to do. I express my political commitment through my actions, and in my life by the very fact of continuing to work while making music.

After the *Charlie Hebdo* terrorist attack, many stood up to say "I am Charlie", even fashion journalists for example, who are far from being "Charlie" in real life. I hope these attacks will lead to a real awareness, and goes beyond being simply a "slogan" that we posted on Facebook for all of a week.

X. P. — Where does creativity come from?

D. W. — It comes from the desire to contribute, each at our own level, to improving the world we live in. For me, this is through music because that is the only thing I know how to do. I am not so much concerned with creativity: I do not necessarily try to be original, I simply try to make honest and sincere music. Even apart from music, I try to live up to what I believe in, without desperately trying to sell CDs and getting on the radio. When I'm in the studio, I do not worry if people are going to like my music. Quite the contrary, I do everything possible to avoid falling into mainstream style.

X. P. — In your latest album, you talk about the difficulty of being an artist and of being honest. Is it that difficult to combine both?

D. W. — There is nothing easier than being honest. It's in human nature. Children are honest when they are young. Unfortunately, this is a quality we very soon lose. Society teaches us that you cannot succeed if you are sincere, honest and selfless. I am utterly convinced the opposite is true.

X. P. — At the end of one of your demonic concerts, I saw you holding the door for your audience as they were leaving and thanking them for coming. That surprised me: you put yourself on the same level as us.

D. W. — For a concert to be a good concert, everybody has to be involved: artists, the technical staff and the audience. Everybody matters. I try to convey to the audience everything music gave me. Rock music saved my life, and I hope to give back to others the same hope and happiness that music brought me. When I was young, I would have loved it if the bands I admired came to say "hi" to the audience! I have seen too many concerts where artists only did the bare minimum. Why bother? I want to give everything I have on stage. That is the least you can do when you are given the opportunity to express yourself in front of an audience.

A student — Is art necessarily corrupt when money is involved? Is it possible for an artist to preserve his/her integrity while trying to sell his/her art?

D. W. — I find it difficult to believe that is possible. Those who succeed nowadays, be they painters, filmmakers or musicians, really wanted success. There is so much competition that artists cannot attain success and wealth by chance. True, there are some examples which run counter to that, like Louise Attaque who sold 3 million albums without even trying. However, this is very rare. I am not a "hardcore" anarchist who is on a crusade against capitalism. I simply refuse to be a part of that system. I want to believe that it is possible to live on the outside, on the fringes.

A student — You say you compose your songs without worrying about whether your audience will like them. So, ultimately, who do you make music for? Is it for you, to prove to yourself that you are free?

D. W. — I think that even when I was 15, I composed for myself. Today, I do not try to "shock" the *bourgeois* because they don't listen to me! In the same line of thought, what purpose would it serve to condemn the Front National** when those who vote for them will never listen to my songs? I prefer to provoke those who are likely to listen to me.

** *The French extreme-right wing party.*

A student — Your message is that we can live a free and happy life, doing what we love. Is that right?

D. W. — Yes! And even working in business! Regardless of the position you have in life — HR Director, sales rep, police officer — you can do it honestly and sincerely. By giving in to the temptation of being a petty chief, we only end up making life impossible for those around us. I've witnessed this first hand at the RATP. Of course, when you are a sales rep and you MUST make money at any cost, then it must be very difficult to stay true to your principles. But the people I have been meeting today at ESSEC are changing the image I had of business schools!

SHAPING IMAGINATION

12

Marie-Paule Cani
Computer Science Professor at Institut Polytechnique de Grenoble

Imagine we could sculpt the fruits of our imagination in three dimensions, in a virtual environment, as easily as we would with Play Doh. Imagine you could even change, add detail or refine these virtual creations at will, by creative actions which would be as natural to us as drawing with a pencil and paper. This dream is the dream I pursue with my research team, named IMAGINE.

CREATING SHAPES IN MOTION

For time immemorial, humanity has always tried to create shapes. But how can we express them as directly as possible, especially if they are 3D and animated? How can we convey to others the idea we have of a moving object? Few tools exist for this. The same is not true of music, for example, where you can hum a tune as you are composing it in your mind.

In order to create shapes, we need a medium. It could be a sketch, a drawing or a painting. However, these remain nothing more than a planar projection of 3D objects. While sculpture can capture volumes, it is static and can only evoke movement by featuring situations of imbalance.

Beyond its creative or recreational character, an expression of which can be found in animation films or video games, the representation of shapes and movement nourishes a profound desire for knowledge and invention. Evidence of this can be found in the sketches through which Leonardo da Vinci dissected the organization of nature — the growth of branches, for example. This graphic stage helped him formalize his ideas and to better comprehend reality than through reflection alone. Similarly, he first put down on paper a 3D sketch of the flying machines he wanted to design. Generally, we need to see what we are in the process of creating. Research in cognitive psychology has in fact shown that interaction with a visual support enables creators to refine their idea, clarify it better than through a simple mental picture.

Digital media have invaded our lives, so much so that they have replaced standard pencil and paper. Why not use them to draw not in two dimensions but in three dimensions, or to sculpt shapes which are not static but in motion. These mediums offer multiple advantages: they free us from constraints of scale of traditional tools and mediums; they bring with them the possibility to do, undo, redo as many times as necessary; they save a great deal of time by duplicating elements in an instant.

Such is the ambition which I have assigned to my research team: to offer digital tools which can allow users, more so than traditional paper and pen, to communicate, specify and refine shapes in motion — in other terms, to shape the imaginary. In so doing, I embrace the ambitions of Colin Ware, who once said that "we should think about graphic design as a cognitive tools enhancing and extending our brains."[1]

DISCOVERING A PERSONAL PATH

What led me to this field of research about which I am passionate and brings to my life much more than a simple job ever could?

As a child, while I developed an interest for literature and history, I also found great pleasure in creative arts like drawing and sculpture. In the end, I studied science, which was then considered as the most prestigious academic path one could take. And that is how I joined the Paris *Ecole normale supérieure* to study math. I passed my *"aggregation"* in 1987, after which I decided to switch to a radically different field, and quite new at the time: IT. I was attracted to this field because, in addition to calling on mathematical reasoning, it involved structuring data, information and tasks, and what is more, solve problems. Since then, I have never stopped challenging myself.

---

[1] Colin Ware, *Visual Thinking for Design*, Morgan Kaufmann, 2008.

A Revolution in Computer Graphics

I then discovered computer graphics, a field I have never left since. This technique is sometimes confused with image processing, but it actually applies the reverse principle of the latter. While image processing works on an existing photo or drawing, computer graphics start with a strictly mathematical model representing objects, shapes and movements, which is then used to create a picture.

To produce an image like the one above requires three steps. It all starts by the geometric modelling. This consists in preparing the mathematical representation of a desired shape through equations. Then comes animation, which involves calculating object movement and deformation. The third step is the rendering, which consists in projecting 3D geometry onto the pixels which make up the image. At this stage, we simulate lighting and the physical properties of materials, namely the way in which they reflect light, to ensure the final virtual image has the right colors.

With current techniques we can obtain highly-realistic computer generated pictures, with each object made up of several million polygonal facets expressed in mathematical terms. But how is this wealth of data needed to design these images generated? Should this task be reserved exclusively to highly specialized professionals? That is question which interests us today.

At the end of the 1980s, the results we had achieved were not as sophisticated as today. Our research focused primarily on techniques for image rendering from the geometric representation of an object, with particular emphasis on how light is reflected on different surfaces. In the rendering of a virtual room which has one red and one green wall, for example, it is important to take into account issues of radiosity, by which these colors reflect onto the objects present in the room.

At the time, we also wanted to achieve smoother surfaces. In computer graphics, a surface is defined through a principle of meshes. For example, famous researcher Henri Gouraud drew a grid on his wife's face to reproduce it as a computerized image, the very first of its kind. The drawback of this technique is that if you only assemble each of the planar facets of the mesh, you obtain a surface which is not smooth.

I wanted to create and animate smooth organic shapes. In order to achieve this, I used a process which is very different from the one commonly used, by drawing inspiration on principles which were well known in the field of mathematics but never applied to computer graphics: implicit surfaces. The tool I developed enabled us to model flexible objects, which could lump together in clusters or flow in an irregular fashion, the way a drizzle of honey would trickle, for example. This approach was very innovative.

Unlike parametric models which define explicit coordinates of points, implicit surface formalism defines a surface as a set of points in space which satisfy a given equation. More specifically, I used "skeletons" surrounded by implicit fields, thereby creating thin shapes and layers of thickness. These shapes can come together in an invisible, "seamless" way, when these skeletons come close to one another. If they move further apart from one each other, the object stretches, deforms, until it breaks apart into two pieces.

That was my first great discovery in computer graphics. With this discovery, I designed a 3D movie which featured toys in a child's bedroom, and this was 10 years before *Toy Story*!

This research also taught me to work with artists; in this case I worked with students from the Paris *Ecole nationale des arts décoratifs*. Among many other things, they taught me how to design and follow a story board. During this project, I was also faced with an important issue which inspired the rest of my career: finding a way to skillfully combine visual realism, in all its fluidity, and the control which enables one to follow a precise script. This is a topic which I still explore today.

With hindsight, this experience gives me the opportunity, first of all, to give you a piece of advice: follow your heart! That is what matters most in a career. Find something personal, that you are passionate about, and don't be afraid to stray from the beaten path.

EMBRACING COMPLEXITY

After a couple of years, I got tired of simulating objects inside virtual rooms. It is important to understand that at the time, video games invariably evolved in a castle, leading you from room to room to collect objects. There were no outside scenes, simply because they were too complex to represent.

My team and I then undertook to model natural landscapes and natural phenomena. This was a very complex undertaking: complexity of shapes first, clouds for example; complexity of movement, be it the sea or hair; complexity linked to the profusion of elements present in the scene, for example, the multitude of small waves on the surface of the ocean. In order to overcome these difficulties, we initiated collaborations with scientists from a very wide range of fields, specializing in the natural elements we were trying to replicate. However, we could not apply their knowledge directly to the field of computer graphics, because we have specific needs. For example, meteorological models do not provide the keys for identifying the 3D shape of a cloud in the sky of a virtual world, no more than equations of the physics of fluids automatically give us the shape of a wave in a rough ocean. The scale we needed, perceptual, is not necessarily the same as that studied by other sciences. Another specificity of our activity is that in the field of animation, visual realism is more important than precision. Another determining factor in computer graphics is the speed of execution: an artiste who sculpts a virtual environment wants to observe what he has modeled directly, without having to wait for calculations to work.

These characteristics proved crucial in a tool for surgical simulation which we had developed. You can easily imagine that in this setting, speed, and the precision of control by the user are nothing short of vital.

Therefore, it is a matter of collaboration with other disciplines, where each of the parties brings specific skills and know-how, which enabled the emergence of solutions which none of us could have identified alone.

This research led to the emergence of a methodology thanks to which we overcame the complexity of the situations we wanted to process. It seemed to us that the best way to process a particularly complex problem was to decompose it into smaller, easier sub-problems. For each of the latter, we have looked for the best suited representation and obtained a number of sub-models, which we could then combine.

To illustrate this process, our modeling of a stream of lava can in fact be broken down into three sub-models. The first, based on particles, is used to determine the trajectory of a fluid running down a mountain. The second, based on implicit surfaces, is used to create a smooth surface around these particles, and the third gives an animated texture to the lava stream. The art lies in successfully combining all the elements of these sub-models, each of which solves a sub-phenomenon.

Let us now discuss a challenge given to us by *Infogrames*, a video game studio: they wanted their characters to leave footprints in the grass as they walked through the prairie featured in the game. What they wanted was for their players to be immersed in the virtual world, to the point that they could actually leave an imprint on it. This problem is particularly complex from a computer graphics viewpoint, because of the profusion of blades of grass in a prairie. Each individual blade of grass is easy to reproduce, but there are so many that simply combining them was more than any computer of the time could handle. In order to solve this problem, we used a trompe-l'oeil model. The blades in the foreground of the image were 3D and animated, whereas those midway were painted on sorts of animated windows. In the background, they were represented by simple textures. When the camera moved, the 2D blades became 3D. Players, however, had the impression that the entire prairie was moving. Computer graphics cannot replicate the world perfectly, but can simulate what is close to our eyes. In this example, we calculated a simple movement, i.e. how blades of grass react to a gust of wind. This motion was then applied to each individual blade, understanding that they did not interact with each other.

We applied the same strategy to create an animated anatomical model in which a set of tissues (bones, muscles, ligaments, etc.) can be combined in real time.

Within the framework of a collaboration with L'Oréal, we worked on simulating hair. This cosmetics company, which usually tested its hair products on real people, was looking for a more efficient way to model their effects. Here are some of the components of the problem: human hair can be compared to inflexible strands which interact with each other, and this interaction is defined by the shape of the hair at rest and in motion. In order to animate hair, we developed a multi-layered model: the principle was to replicate the overall dynamics by animating a limited number of "guide strands." This is how we developed the "super-helix" simulation model in collaboration with a Parisian physics laboratory which had developed a very relevant hair strand model. In this example, the strands are inflexible, the only degree of freedom they have is in their curving or torsion, which means no extremely complex equations are required.

We could then calculate the collisions between hair strands. When we displayed the image, we added a large number of geometric hairs, generated either by extrapolation around the guide strands, or by insertion, between two guide strands. For curly hair, even if the strands are inflexible in themselves, the curls can move with the movement of the character. We were thus able to simulate the dynamics of normal hair in movement in a very realistic way.

Once more, we overcame complexity by superposing different models for each sub-phenomenon.

The animation of clothes in real time raises a number of challenges in terms of simulations, because mathematical equations do not apply perfectly to these inflexible and incompressible materials. However, what we could do was simulate very soft springs in real time. We were inspired by this, and removed the constraint of the incompressibility of the clothes. The rule says that garments stay isometric to their 2D pattern. Therefore, on the pattern, we calculated the areas which would be compressed by draping, and added a series of folds geometrically. In order to calculate the size of the latter and connect them, we used implicit surfaces. All in all, we added layers of knowledge to the initial model to solve the problem.

These many examples encourage me to share a second piece of advice with you: embrace difficult problems and view them as an opportunity to grow. Feel free to break down a problem into multiple, simple sub-problems, which you can process, one by one. Gradually, you will understand how to solve situations presenting greater complexity.

UPCOMING CHALLENGES

Animation movies and video games bear considerable witness to the fact that today, we can produce virtual images based on mathematical data, which are as realistic as photos. It would be tempting, then, to think that there is nothing left to discover. Nonetheless, one question remains: who is most likely to be creating the vast masses of data to generate these images?

Until now, there have been two major approaches to automating the creation of content: reconstructing reality on the one hand, and automatic generation of data algorithmically on the other, which is referred to as procedural generation.

The first approach, seizing and reconstructing real movements or data, presents limits of scale. For example, it is simply impossible to capture the myriad elements which make up a landscape, with its trees, blades of grass, animals. Particularly when relying on existing objects, this technique stifles the actual creation of new elements, the pure fruits of imagination.

The second approach, procedural generation, is often used by scientists in particular, to express hypotheses. Thanks to planning laws, you can create a fishing village by the seaside, and laws pertaining to tree growth help us create virtual forests. However, can our imagination fully express itself through laws? Even if we found a law to perfectly express what we have imagined, how then could we find the initial conditions and the parameters of this law? This creation process would follow a trial and error process: if the image you got was not satisfying, you would have to modify the mathematical parameters and recompute the data. This is very far from the intuitiveness of creating with paper and pencil. What would be ideal would to be able to modify the virtual image directly by adding details or additional elements, without having to generate it all anew.

Therefore, both these automated methods for the creation of content come with limitations. For that reason, today, almost all virtual images are created by interactive modeling. Computer artists use extremely complex software based on the most advanced mathematical models to create all the contents by hand, blade of grass by blade of grass, hair by hair. This technique requires such mastery of the processing chain that it hinders the creative process and leaves no room for 'drafting'. In fact, computer artists often start by drawing a sketch using paper and pencil. Once they have finished it, they reproduce it via the software.

Rob Cook, the scientific director of the Pixar animation studio, states that the greatest challenge of computer graphics today is to make the tools as invisible to the artists as the special effects are made invisible to the public. When we watch a film like *Avatar*, we don't even think twice about what is virtual and what is real: we are happy to get caught up in the story. How can we give artists tools which can become an extension of their body, and let them get caught up in their creative impetus?

Towards Expressive Modeling

Making digital tools invisible, creating the conditions for expressive modeling, that is the challenge that the IMAGINE research group has set itself. We are trying to make virtual creation flow as easily as if you were sculpting or drawing in real life.

To this end, we developed a tool which projects a 2D sketch done by an artist in three dimensions. The artist can then see every side of the shape he or she is bringing to life, or zoom in on certain parts to refine them or add detail to them.

We have also designed the Hand Navigator. Similar to a computer mouse, it controls a virtual hand which sculpts virtual clay, in real time.

Does this mean we solved the issue of virtual creation? I'm afraid nothing is that simple. The tools I have just mentioned work for simple, homogeneous shapes, but cannot be used to sculpt complex shapes. For example, how can you enlarge a virtual mountain simply by drawing the silhouette of a higher mountain maintaining the same level of detail and precision?

Clothes illustrate this issue well. They are made up piece-wise developable surfaces, and consequently, of flat pieces which make up a pattern. They are difficult to create in the real world: you need extensive training to be able to draw a pattern. And in the virtual world, we need our characters to wear clothes.

How can you create virtual clothes from a sketch? How can we ensure they are animated realistically? How can we transfer garments and outfits to different body types?

In standard software, in order to create a garment, graphic artists draw patterns, and position them round a virtual 3D model. They then have to define the seams and enter the parameters of a physical simulation (elasticity, friction, etc.). The way the garment sits through the physical simulation generates a virtual garment. However, this physical simulation is very complex to implement, namely because clothes are incompressible, make folds. In addition to the constants of stiffness and friction, the delicacy of the meshing can have a considerable impact on the thickness of the folds calculated by the simulator. Therefore, it is a long, iterative and arduous process.

Fashion designers can draw sketches of clothes, why would it not be possible to go straight from a drawn silhouette of a 3D model of the garment in question? Then it would simply be a matter of cutting its surfaces to lay them flat to calculate its pattern which could even be used to produce this garment in real life.

Our first research focused on the design of clothes through sketches. For that, we applied very simple rules. And so, if a t-shirt is fitted when you see it from the front, then it will be the same all around the bust. It is therefore characterized by a constant distance from the body, information which we then include in the mathematical model. It then becomes possible to sculpt the shape of the garments in a distance field calculated around a 3D model.

However, garments designed that way often have somewhat of a plastic feel to them, as they lack the folds characteristic of developable surfaces. In order to address this, we initially imagined systems used to draw draping. But in order to achieve this, it is more interesting to integrate new data into the model. We know that a garment is developable. Therefore, from an initial surface we can approximate as close as possible through a developable surface in pieces. We can then calculate the pattern, and simulate the folds on this surface.

When you work on designing a garment or a shoe, the folds are an integral part of the design. How, then, can we draw them not only on a draped surface, as in the previous example, but also on a surface with folds? The great difficulty resides in the fact that, due to the drapery, the points which match the silhouette are no longer on the same plane — the silhouettes are no longer plane. The computer system uses certain properties of developable surfaces to optimize developability, by gradually identifying the points which are on the silhouettes thanks to a system of sliding constraints. Ultimately, this produces a real physical prototype of an imaginary object, like a boot for example.

How can we transfer garments automatically to characters with different body shapes? In this respect, we used a well-known computer process: copy-pasting. However, it is not simply a matter of loading the desired scale. You must distort the patterns of the initial garment. This leads to a very interesting question: how can two characters with dissimilar body types wear the same garments, when these patterns are different?

In mathematical terms, how can we preserve the design of a garment? By working on this question, we discovered that it was good to apply three principles: firstly, maintain proportions, and then preserve the fitting or non-fitting character of the garment, and, finally, in the parts which do not touch the body, preserve the positioning of surfaces with regards to the surroundings. All this was expressed in mathematical terms and converted into algorithms. That is how we can, for example, transpose the pattern of a "standard" dress to adapt it to a pregnant woman's body.

Following the same logic, 3D animation uses anatomy transfer. Films featuring a great level of precision and detail, as is the case of Avatar, require the representation of the muscles which we see moving under the character's skin, sometimes even organs (the lungs breathing, a heart beating, etc.) In the past, graphic artists dedicated tremendous amounts of time creating all these details for each new creature. That is why we designed a system to transfer a certain number of anatomic features automatically, from a human model to a virtual character. The principle is the same as for clothes, with the only difference that we work inside the body and not on the surface.

Let us imagine for example, that you want to transpose your anatomy to the character of Homer Simpson. He is quite chubby, which is not necessarily your case. You will have to crop the layer of fat surrounding the cartoon character's body, then transpose your own anatomical features. In order to do this, we ask our mathematical tool to respect a certain number of rules in its processing chain: the bones must remain straight, stay symmetrical in relation to the sagittal plane, muscle mass must be proportional to fat mass, etc.

The Dream of Virtual Sculpture

You now know how to create a 3D model from a 2D drawing. Let us now take this one step further, and attempt to sculpt directly in three dimensions in the virtual world.

This is where the virtual clay we developed comes into play, offering possibilities that go way beyond the sculpting possibilities with actual clay. With this tool, you can decorate a 3D shape with drawings or colors, but you can also preserve the layout of these elements of decoration if you change the shape of the object. This would not be possible in the workshop of a traditional sculptor.

In order to illustrate the sculpting tools of structured shapes, let us take the example of a three-dimension fortified medieval city.

As a first step, we identified the different elements (A, B, C, D, etc.) which made up the city (towers, fortifications, etc.). Then we applied a grammar specific to computer languages. In other terms, we made "words" in which the letters are combined based on precise rules. For example, you can remove B, or replace an A by a D without the buildings collapsing. These production rules indicate which elements you can modify in the model while ensuring it remains valid.

As interesting as this tool was, it was still a source of frustration. As it was, the tool enabled us to create an infinite number of fortified cities, but users did not have full control. In order to give control back to artists, we decided to adopt a different strategy. Rather than using elementary immutable components, we opted for a transformable material, similar to clay, to build buildings. This introduces rules of elasticity: if you curve a wall excessively, for example, it could jeopardize the overall structure. This wall will then automatically become a different, valid element, like a tower for example. If you stretch the wall on a linear plane, the constituent elements duplicate. As the creator sculpts, the tool modifies the objects as needed so they stay relevant.

A new challenge arises: applying our discoveries to animated content. The goal is to sculpt and draw movements naturally thanks to digital tools. For example, we animated the flight of a dragon by using a space–time curve. In a single movement, the user can draw a curve and factor in speed, trajectory and the mode of distortion of the original character. Once the movement has been generated, the user can refine the image (for example, modifying the direction of the creature's tail) without having to recalculate the image as a whole.

TOWARD SMART MODELS

A methodology has emerged from all the work I presented to you today. Thus, in order to make digital tools invisible to users and to viewers, two fundamental principles must be respected: enabling creation through simple movement, and integrating knowledge in the models.

Let us imagine, for example, that I want to model the conference room in which we are now. Once I have the result, I might want to expand my audience, i.e. make the room bigger. Would the mathematical model be able to expand the seats and audience, and risk distorting them? Would it not be better to expand the walls and flooring, and duplicate rows of seats for new audience members? In order to achieve this, you must have intelligent models, which can understand user intention when a user does something as intuitive as stretching an element of the screen. These models must therefore be built on knowledge.

In the future, I hope computer graphics will be able to offer "magical pens" which would become new creative mediums. A 2D drawing could then automatically transform into a 3D one, we could copy-paste elements which adapt automatically to their environment and which we can refine by sculpting in an intuitive way...

By way of conclusion, I would like to underline that all these discoveries were only made possible thanks to collaborations, often transdisciplinary. Which leads me to my last piece of advice: do not be afraid of people stealing your ideas, share them with others, who can, in turn, inspire you. Dig your furrow in a field about which you are passionate, be open to opportunities and develop your own, personal vision. Then, your work and your life will be aligned, so much so that you will not be able to distinguish one from the other.

What I love above all in my work is to invent new imaginary worlds, and novel mediums of expression. I also love the diversity and freedom doing research brings me, which has led me to teach, serve my community of peers (I am the vice president of the European Association for Computer Graphics), to explore very varied topics and to work with researchers from all fields, throughout the world, and has helped me build beautiful friendships.

To finish, I would like to challenge the prejudice that IT is a "man's world" Sadly, the rate of female students in this field is declining. Whether you are a man or a woman, I can only urge you to join the fascinating field of computer graphics, which has applications in countless fields and needs more diversity!

THE KNOWLEDGE ECONOMY: A SECOND *RENAISSANCE*

13

Idriss Aberkane

Researcher in Neurotechnologies and Biomimetics

Five hundred years after the turning point that the Renaissance represents for European societies, we are about to experience a second Renaissance, a deep-rooted transformation of the principles on which our lifestyles, our economy and our development are based. This second Renaissance is founded on three fundamental pillars: the Knowledge Economy, Biomimetics and the Blue Economy.

To fully grasp the magnitude of the transformations we are undergoing, let us look back at the first Renaissance, or better yet, project this first *Rennaissance* into our times, 500 years later. Three artistic geniuses would have been born a couple of decades ago: Leonard de Vinci in 1952, Michelangelo in 1975 and Raphael in 1983. Le Tintoret would be born 3 years from now, in 2018.

In art as in architecture, looking back to the past, going back to basics, is a common exercise. For example, the campanile of Berkeley University in California is inspired by the campanile of the Piazza San Marco in Venice, which was rebuilt in 1912. Stanford University decided to build one even closer to the original, and even higher than its Californian competitor.

Another example of how eras and times blend together might be the design of the Apple headquarters. Its design is a reference both to the most advanced technology — it looks like a UFO in the shape of a particle accelerator — and also to nature, with an interior forest of apricot trees, paying tribute to the nourishing land of California. At the same time,.it is also a reference to the ancestral myth of the Garden of Eden — beautiful gardens as they existed in Baghdad in the 9th century for example. Silicon Valley today, like many other technopoles, replicates the melting-pot that Baghdad was in ancient times, the city that was designed by a Jewish Zoroastrian architect, built by Christians and governed by Muslims.

When Apple calls its bank to know how much money it has, what do you think the answer is? Your liquidity is equivalent to the GDP of Vietnam! We are not talking about stock options, but of hard cash, to the tune of $160 billion. All this gathered by a company founded in a garage in 1976. This goes to show just how powerful the knowledge economy really is.

WHY KNOWLEDGE ECONOMY?

Imagine an economy in which each person is born with spending power; in which whatever I give you also remains mine; in which unemployed people have more spending power than workers. That is the knowledge economy.

Knowledge: The New Oil

One of the specific qualities of knowledge, just as of stupidity, is that it is infinite, whereas oil, gold or uranium, are finite. Striving for unlimited growth with an economy based on raw materials is illusory. However, it is possible with the unlimited material that knowledge represents.

This is the logic followed by American President Jimmy Carter as early as in 1977: if we base our growth on raw materials, by definition, this growth will be limited; but if we index it on knowledge, our growth will be infinite. However, his ambition to make the dollar the currency of knowledge did not succeed, because today the dollar is still the world's reserve currency. Whether you are buying oil, gold, uranium, wheat or frozen orange juice concentrate, the transaction will take place in dollars. This is very difficult for BRIC countries whose natural resources are ineluctably converted into dollars.

Nevertheless, Jimmy Carter's approach did have a considerable cultural impact. In 1984, when Apple was launching its first computer, Steve Jobs met French President François Mitterrand and explained that the reason France did not have a Silicon Valley of its own was because it was averse to failure. For him, France's culture was based on the idea that it was better to do nothing than to try and fail, which is the exact opposite of the Silicon Valley's philosophy: "fail early, fail often." Steve Jobs also asserted that software was the equivalent of the new barrel of oil. He could not have been more right. Today, the richest man in the world is not an oil magnate, but a software magnate. Today's most flourishing companies are based on knowledge.

We are already in the knowledge economy. One proof among many of this is that Barack Obama did not choose an oil magnate as his Energy Secretary but chose to appoint a Physics Nobel Prize winner, Steven Chu, thereby breaking with tradition. South Korea — which exports more than Russia despite having no raw materials, with a territory 171 times smaller than that of the Russian Federation and a population three times smaller — has already set up a Ministry of Knowledge Economy. When they want to develop a new scientific discipline, they do not develop new software or school textbooks, but they try to make it attractive and fun, via attraction parks filled with robots, called Robotlands, to persuade children from an early age (and their parents) that robotics is a promising activity.

The Economy of Knowledge: Prolific and Collegial

The total volume of knowledge doubles — in terms of quantity and not of quality — every 9 years, maybe even every 7 years. In other words, the number of problems raised and solved is multiplied by two every 7–9 years. Today, humanity produces more knowledge in this short period of time than it has during its entire history. This is the first property of the knowledge economy: it is prolific. Its second property is that it is collegial: everybody owns a share of it. This explains why Wikipedia is one of the five most visited websites in the world. Unfortunately, our ego pushes us to hold on to what little knowledge we have, and refuse to share it as if in doing so we could lose it. But quite the contrary! This is what the founder of Wikipedia, Jimmy Wales, understood when he abandoned his porn website business to create an on-line encyclopedia. For his first attempt, Newpedia, he paid Nobel Prize winners to write articles. At the same time, Microsoft had launched Encarta, a similar project equipped with unlimited resources, and could afford all the Nobel Prizes winners in the world. Jimmy Wales countered this competition by proving that money cannot buy inventiveness: he developed a new technology, the wiki, based on a collaborative dynamic of knowledge enrichment. Six months after the launch of Wikipedia, there were already 25,000 new pages. No need for Nobel Prize winners!

All the revolutions that have had an impact on our history — the emancipation of women, laptops, collaborative encyclopedias — all went through three phases of acceptance: the innovation was first seen as ridiculous, then dangerous, and finally accepted as being evident. After being mocked, it is considered as a risk before finally being accepted.

After he was fired from Apple, Steve Jobs founded NeXT and created the NeXT Cube computer, which was to define the design of the future Playstation II, 10 years later. This is the machine that Tim Berners-Lee, a "small" CERN engineer (the European organization for nuclear research) used to explore one of his obsessions: creating a network between the researchers working for the particle accelerator, who were from all over the world and from a variety of fields. He wrote a message on a post-it "This computer is a server, do not switch it off." He had invented the Internet. Taking the idea even further, he had the wonderful premonition that if the system worked for a community of researchers, it could be extended to the whole world: and so the WorldWideWeb came into being. I see this as a collective demonstration of knowledge. If we refuse collective learning, we will learn nothing in the 21st Century. I hope that when my children look up the definition of the word "expert" in the dictionary, the definition they read says that it is a group of people. Individual expertise has no value in the 21st Century.

The Three Rules of the Knowledge Economy

The knowledge economy radically changes the picture, just as quantum physics revolutionized traditional physics. However, it does obey a set of simple rules.

The first rule is that exchanges of knowledge are a positive-sum game. When I give you knowledge, I do not lose my own. The second rule is that knowledge is not instantaneous. We can operate billions of stock operations per second but we need time to assimilate knowledge. The third rule is that exchanges and combinations of knowledge are not linear. In a material and linear world, €20 + €20 = €40. But in the knowledge economy, 1 kg + 1 kg = 3 kg. When you combine two knowledges, you build a third one. Sharing material goods is a division, whereas sharing knowledge is a multiplication.

IA Spending Power that is Universal

The most beautiful dimension of the knowledge economy probably resides in the structure of the spending power it induces. When a lecturer shares his knowledge with an audience, for example, this audience also shares two priceless elements: time (the most precious resource of all) and attention. The flow of knowledge is proportional to the attention given multiplied by the time spent.

Time and attention can be seen as the spending power of the knowledge economy. This has significant social implications: whoever we may be, wherever we may be, we are all born with spending power. We all have time and attention. Unfortunately, we squander this spending power, all the more so considering that we can save neither. To date, humans have spent 7 million years in front of the video game *World of Warcraft*. By way of comparison, Lucy, the Australopithecus afarensis, is only 3 million years old, and people have spent less than a 50th of this amount of time since 1966 developing Apple. We could create a wealth equivalent to the GDP of Vietnam with only a 50th of the time we have spent in front of *World of Warcraft*! One day, might we be able to do the same by playing? Maybe you think this idea is ridiculous, and tomorrow you might find it dangerous, but maybe the day after it will become accepted as evident.

All this begs the question: to whom do we freely give our attention and time? To the people we love and to the things we are passionate about. In the knowledge economy, our spending power is maximized by love. Is that not a wonderful property? Even in a company, if you want to optimize knowledge exchanges, start by loving what you do!

RENAISSANCE THROUGH BIOMIMETICS

Imagine that, for generations, we have been living in a room filled with shelves full of things that burn easily. So much so that we use them as fuel in winter. But one day, we will discover that what we have been burning for generations to keep ourselves warm is books! Imagine pulling one of these books from the fire, opening it and discovering formulas, ideas, diagrams, etc. This library I am talking about is our planet, nature, whose technological refinement we are only starting to understand.

The science which covers the technology of nature is referred to Biomimetics. It helps us discover that if we compare microscopic phytoplankton made of silicone and a chip manufactured by Intel (also made of silicone), the more technologically advanced of the two may not be the one you think. To replicate what a water drop does, Intel had to spend a fortune (reducing the scale of an electronic circuit from 32 to 22 nanometers can cost up to $10 billion), use a spotless laboratory without the slightest piece of dust that could clog the machine, and meantime generates considerable pollution. Yet Intel Core i7 microprocessors have been floating in the sea for millions of years, produced by a perfectly designed industrial process which causes no pollution whatsoever!

By destroying nature and biodiversity, we are burning treasures of technological knowledge. Nobody would even imagine setting the Google X lab in Silicon Valley, which has been conducting research for 15 years, on fire. Nature has been working for 3.8 billion years: so why are we destroying it? Every molecule is the chapter of a wonderful book and is invaluable.

High-tech Nature

There are countless practical applications of Biomimetics.

Forests have long had their own form of Internet, in the shape of a small, yet extremely intelligent mushroom which connects trees by sharing the nutrients of one tree with another, without forgetting, of course, to collect a small commission every time. When an animal dies in the forest, this mushroom "pre-digests" its carcass and spreads its nutrients to plants. This intermediary can connect up to 10 million trees. For their part, humans have been struggling for more than half a century to solve the famous equation of the "salesman's journey" to try and find the shortest journey connecting a number of points (in our case, cities). This mushroom has already understood how to solve the very same equation connecting no less than 10 million points. A researcher from Oxford University conducted the following experiment: he opened a map of England and placed the mushroom on London, and placed an oat flake at the location of other cities to see how the mushroom would connect them. Two days later, he had a map of a railway network which was much more sensible than the one that currently exists.

Imagine that Air Liquide has to service 1,000 cities in the North of the United States. Take a map of the size of a lecture hall, place a mushroom on the starting point and an oat flake on each city you need to connect. Two weeks later, you will have the optimal route, and it could help you save $1 billion a year!

Let us look at the animal world. Shark-skin is made up of thousands of small teeth, and is the best anti-turbulence surface that we know of — much better than any material developed by nuclear sub-marines during the cold war. Airbus uses it for its A350 thereby reducing its fuel consumption by 5%. Speedo also used it as a model to design swimsuits for the Beijing Olympics, which were so efficient they were forbidden!

Abalone shell, composed of 10 million leaves, is the hardest known ceramic. It can even resist the blast of a bazooka. The green fluorescent protein of jellyfish inspired breathtaking innovations in the field of bio-technologies, leading some of their inventors to win a Nobel Prize. There are also bioluminescent bacteria which produce light only when they reach a certain quorum. This led Stanford University to imagine a bio-luminescent tree to illuminate the city. The ability of these bacteria to become dangerous only from a certain quorum is key to their survival: if they do this too soon, our immune system would find a way to fight them. By finding ways to counteract this quorum effect, we could create myriad antibiotics.

Samsung has been conducting research on a small squid whose skin has a higher definition than an 8K screen. It is also flexible, repairs itself and produces positive energy! Mercedes used boxfish jellyfish to solve a problem with which mathematicians were struggling: how to create a volume which was both aerodynamic and spacious. It paid due tribute to nature: the car was named the Boxfish Car.

A toxin produced by a small shell is worth €800 million per kilo (in comparison gold is worth only €30,000), and a specific toxin produced by bats can go as high as a billion dollars per kilo.

Each molecule, each organ, each set of organs is a chapter in the big book of our world, a chapter that could be worth millions.

I am enjoying this so much that I cannot resist sharing more examples with you.

Sandworms, which live in the sand, produce the best hemoglobin available: not only is it universal, it also has 50 times more oxygen than "normal" hemoglobin. It is perfect for organ transplants which require increased oxygenation to avoid necrosis and rejection. During the D-day in Normandy, the American army was in desperate need of blood substitutes: the answer was right under their feet!

The glue used by mussels to stick to a rock is the best glue in the world: it is efficient for weeks, in any temperature, in salty and non-salty environments, as well as being sun proof and biodegradable. It is used in hospitals to suture wounds.

Here is a final example: the Mantis shrimp is equipped with minute hammers that it can use at the speed of light to kill crabs, for example. It can shatter a bullet-proof aquarium! To protect itself from the lightning it generates due to this speed, its eyes have the best sun-filter known to date.

Our great-grand-children will probably wonder why, if we knew that oceans and forests held such unimaginable sources of wealth — ceramics, anti-turbulence coatings, glues, semiconductors, etc. — we continued drilling for oil. The ocean and forests are the oil platforms of the future. Some have already understood this, such as those involved in the Canopy Raft project, which analyzes the ecosystem of the canopy, or SeaOrbiter, a ship designed by Jacques Rougerie as an international ocean station.

Anything we can learn from nature is so much more valuable than oil. Most importantly, let us not destroy nature when we exploit it for the knowledge it can give us, just as we do not destroy a book by reading it. This opens up mind-boggling perspectives: we could generate infinite growth without destroying nature, by using it as a source of knowledge and not as a raw material.

THE BLUE ECONOMY

Blue Economy is based on the principle of applying Biomimetics to management. Imagine that there is no such thing as waste and that to explain what it is to your children, you have to take them to a museum. Ridiculous? But there is a place exempt of waste: nature.

Waste, by definition, is something that no-one wants. Nature knows no such thing. More precisely, the planet has had to deal with a "polluting waste" which caused the destruction of 99.99% of all life forms on earth, the most massive extinction you could ever imagine: oxygen. When oxygenation happened, 600 million years of evolution were swept away. At that time, no life form knew how to resist oxidation. However, it is this oxygen that makes the planet Blue. If life managed to transform the strongest pollutant it had ever came across into something so beautiful, could we not do the same with our own waste? This is the challenge of the Blue Economy. It is the natural step which follows after the Circular Economy (a term coined by sailor Ellen MacArthur) in which there is no more waste than in nature itself. We should force our industry to adopt the same production mode as nature, and not the other way around!

The American Civil War was between Northern abolitionist States and the Southern, anti-abolitionist states, the former being richer than the latter. Beyond the question of slavery, the economic disparity between the two parties made war unavoidable. How can we explain the apparent paradox that the North was more competitive than the South even though it had abolished slavery? When the North gave up on free labor, it quickly adopted the steam engine. Today, if we were to abolish pollution, this would bring us into a new era of industrial evolution, which would be incomparably profitable.

The inventor of the Blue Economy, Gunter Pauli, is the "Steve Jobs of Sustainable Development." When I discovered his work 6 years ago, I threw out the management classes I was giving at École Centrale. Gunter Pauli invented the management of the 21st Century.

The goal of the Blue Economy is to transform what nobody wants — CO_2 for instance — into a coveted commodity. For example, spirulina, an algae with strong nutritive properties, can capture CO_2. The waste generated when we produce edible spirulina is in fact an extremely expensive component sought after by the cosmetic industry and the biodiesel industry. In other terms, we could render production of edible spirulina profitable before selling it, while at the same time capturing CO_2.

When we drink an expresso, we only use 0.2% of the biomass that was used to produce it. But coffee grinds is a perfect compost for mushrooms, especially shitake mushrooms: they grow twice as fast than in soil. These mushrooms can be used to feed cattle — whereas caffeine would kill them. You can also use coffee grinds to give fabric the ability to absorb smells.

Another waste nobody wants, mineral dust, is very dangerous for lungs and could asphyxiate plants if it settles on their leaves. This is a big problem in China, the top producer of rare soil, because extracting it is very polluting and generates a lot of dust. A Chinese scientist found a way to transform this dust into paper, without using water or wood. Another benefit is that this type of paper is waterproof. Gunter Pauli got his book of children's stories on the Blue Economy published on this kind of paper, and it is told to young children in kindergartens throughout China.

In Colombia, a researcher invented a machine to plant trees that could reforest desert lands, to recreate biodiversity and make precious wood, replenish water tables and create bio-diesel from the turpentine from trees, and all this with a ROI of $17,000 for every dollar invested in the purchase of a hectare of arid land.

Nature is beautiful and intelligent, it has an MBA, a Masters in Brilliant Adaptation! Let us learn to live in harmony with our wonderful planet. We should learn to evolve, and jump right into our second Renaissance.

MOLAR

Patrick Roger
Chocolate Confectioner

15

HEARING COLORS: MY LIFE EXPERIENCE AS A CYBORG

Neil Harbisson

Musician, Artist, Co-Founder of the Cyborg Foundation

I was born with a rare visual condition called achromatopsia, which is characterized by total color blindness. Although I have never seen color, colors have always been a part of my life. They are omnipresent in our everyday life, and they have permeated language: yellow pages, Green Peace, the Red Cross, oranges, Bluetooth, Pink Panther, the Yellow Submarine, etc.

In a number of contexts, color is used as a code, to differentiate hot and cold water for example, or in maps. But when this color code becomes the only means of representation, as is the case for certain maps in Tokyo, it is very confusing for me. Some flags, for example those of France, Italy or Ireland, all look the same to me! If somebody were to ask me if I have seen a man with red hair, blue eyes and a pink jacket, the only information I would have is that they are looking for a man who has eyes, hair and that he is not walking around naked! Therefore, my desire to perceive colors did not arise from a desire to access their aesthetic beauty but rather from a genuine social need.

FROM A SOUND PALETTE TO A CHROMATIC PALETTE

I decided to study music, and more specifically piano, which I thought would not involve color. However, I quickly found out that many music theories linked sounds to colors. In fact, both colors and sounds are frequencies, one audible frequencies and the other light frequencies. Newton, for example, identified seven "simple" colors which he associated with notes of music.

So, during my studies, I decided to create a third eye which could enable me to hear the frequency of light: which note would be produced by red or blue? In 2003, this research culminated in a first prototype. It was a webcam connected to a software used to detect light frequencies and scale them down to audible notes. At first, I only had six notes, but 3 years later, the program had 360, matching the 360 degrees of the color wheel.

The scale of sounds transposed from light frequency is microtonal. Sliding from red to orange is the same as going from F to F sharp. There are 30 micro-tones in a semi-tone. Two notes separated by micro-tones are very similar but you can hear the difference. It took me 3 years to train my ear to differentiate the nuances. We tried to ensure the sounds were as pure as possible, i.e. that they represented a constant sine waveform. The early days were very challenging. For the first few months, I experienced terrible headaches as my brain adjusted to these electronic sounds and was taking in all this new information. After five months, hearing colors had become familiar, and this perception quickly turned into a feeling when I discovered my favorite colors through sound.

However, I was unable to feel color intensity, which is measured through saturation. In 2007, we managed to translate the level of saturation through different volume levels. Very bright colors emit a resounding sound, and as the colors get closer to gray, the volume decreases.

After acquiring this perception, I wanted to go even further and sense colors which go beyond human sight, such as infrared or ultraviolet light, which we achieved in 2008. This acuity allows me to detect if the alarm system of a bank or a shop is activated, for example, and most often, it is just a fake. My goal is to continuously extend my color perception beyond human perception to ultimately reach radio waves, x-rays and even gamma rays. Unlike the chromatic circle, the sono-chromatic scale could be represented as a straight line which extends indefinitely.

From the moment I was able to hear colors, I could "play" them. I started "painting" pianos instead of playing them by using the musical instrument as an artist would a canvas. A piano equipped with an antenna plays a C sharp when it is presented with blue, and F sharp for orange. In so doing, I transformed a musical instrument into a cybernetic organism, which I play through colors. Quite naturally, for my final composition for my degree, I prepared a chromatic book.

THE BIRTH OF A CYBORG

I then wanted to create a new bodily appendix which could enable me to feel color. I wanted an independent perception organ, which involved neither my eyes nor my ears, as would have been the case with glasses or headphones. First I contemplated getting a third eye implanted in the middle of my forehead, but finally chose an antenna which would not limit my perception to what was in front of me, but rather enabled me to access a spectrum of perception of 360°. The information is not transmitted by my ears but through bone conduction, by way of variations which are then transformed into sound data. The antenna implanted in my body produces different oscillations depending on the frequency of the color, and these become sounds in my inner ear.

Once we had designed the antenna, getting it implanted was a veritable obstacle course. A bio-ethical committee opposed my project, arguing a perception which went beyond human perception was unethical, and warned against the dangers of having a cybernetic device inside the body. They were also worried about the image that a person walking out of the hospital with an antenna would provoke. In the end, I found a surgeon who accepted to work anonymously. My skull was pierced in four different points. Two of them support the structure of the antenna. The third contains the chip which vibrates depending on the light frequency, and the fourth is an Internet connection which receives colors from all over the world and from satellites.

The operation was initially planned to last 45 minutes; in the end it lasted over three hours. It took two months for the antenna and the bone to merge. Now it is virtually impossible to remove it. It is covered by a thin layer of skin, which comes off should anybody pull on the antenna.

Thanks to the Internet connection, I can receive colors from the five continents. On each continent, there is a person authorized to streamline them to me. That way, I have an extended sense of colors, which transcends my immediate surroundings. Whenever I feel like it, I can watch a sunset in Australia.

The union between cybernetics and my organic self is so intimate that I progressively developed the feeling of being a cyborg. This is particularly true when I sleep, because then, my brain creates electronic sounds which are perfectly identical to those generated by my device, so much so that I cannot quite discern what is the fruit of my mind or the software.

In order to renew my passport, and for my antenna to be shown on it, British authorities requested me to provide medical evidence of my new cyborg identity and that my extension of my body and senses was more than a mere electrical device. Until then, I had not been able to travel; security controls at the airport were particularly problematic. Today, I can travel as I want, provided I renew my passport every time the appearance of my antenna evolves.

The New Life of a Being with Extended Perception

These new perceptions affected my brain in different ways and opened me up to many new perspectives. For example, I no longer dress to look good, but rather to "sound good." If I decide to dress in C major, I will wear the three corresponding colors. With minor chords, I will most probably be dressed for a funeral. Therefore, depending on the clothes I wear, I can wear a tune or even a song, simply by superimposing different colored stripes.

Thanks to this technique, I can design dress-songs, and I even designed a wedding-march dress, enabling the happy couple to save on a band! I painted my living room in C sharp by covering the floor with a shade of red, the lowest frequency, which generates a profound sound. The kitchen is purple, a high-pitched sound, and the ceilings are black and white, silent when I lie down. In my bedroom, there are three colors: B, E and D, thereby creating the word "bed." My front door is green, which is in the middle of the spectrum of colors, thereby becoming a tuning fork of sorts. Hearing green means I can "get in tune" before I leave, just as you would tune an instrument. Finally, my bathroom is covered with different songs.

My eating habits also have changed. Today making a meal is like composing music with food. I can eat my favorite song. I am currently working in partnership with restaurant *El Celler de Can Roca* in Gerona, ranked one of the best restaurants of the world, to offer the first sono-chromatic dish, and a *"food player"* thanks to which hosts will be able to listen to the sound

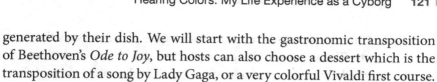

generated by their dish. We will start with the gastronomic transposition of Beethoven's *Ode to Joy*, but hosts can also choose a dessert which is the transposition of a song by Lady Gaga, or a very colorful Vivaldi first course.

Thanks to a microphone placed on my antenna, I can amplify the sounds I receive, and thus share compositions, concerts of colors with an audience. When I walk through a supermarket, especially in the household aisle with all the bright labels, I feel like I'm walking through a night-club!

In an art gallery or a museum, I can listen to a Picasso. Painters are my composers. The Scream by Munch is very microtonal, while Warhol generates a saturated sound which is so loud that I can hear it as soon as I step into the museum. Less saturated works, like those of Goya, Velasquez or Leonardo da Vinci, are more muted and you have to get closer to them.

However, the greatest change that I have felt is in how I sense people. I can now enjoy the sound of a face, whose eyes, lips, skin and hair produce specific sounds. In doing so, I can draw a sound portrait of a person and send it to them by MP3. The first sound portrait I ever did was of Prince Charles. He visited my university while I was studying, and although he was initially surprised by my request to listen to his face, he did accept to let me do my first sound portrait. I have done many more since then.

Everybody has their own little music. Judi Dench's hair, which is as white as snow, is perfectly silent. The sound of James Cameron's skin — and more specifically the shade of his nose — are very high-pitched. Al Gore's eyes, with their different shades of turquoise, produce two different notes. They are very melodic, as is the case for Steve Reich, whose eyes have a sort of pattern. The eyelids of Tim Berners Lee produce a very unusual sound. The sound portrait of Moby, who is completely bald, has one note less. Woody Allen's sound is very unsaturated, like an old painting. Philip Glass is microtonal, whereas Bono's glasses are very loud. Even the sound of identical twins always differs slightly.

I like doing what I call "face concerts." I start by playing the note coming from the eyes of one of the people from the audience, which I combine with a rhythm, then I play the sound of a second person, combined with a different rhythm, and so on and so forth until reaching a genuine concert from the colors coming from the audience. If the concert is bad, it is their fault entirely!

Finally, I never cease to be amazed every time a person says they are black or white. The way I see things, the former are a very dark shade of orange, and the latter a lighter shade of orange. It makes no sense to differentiate black and white: we are all orange, with slight variations.

Just as I transpose colors to sounds, I transpose sounds into colors. I have composed a painting which takes each note of the Queen of the Night Aria in Mozart's *Enchanted Flute*, and another for Justin Bieber's *Baby* — quite surprisingly, the entire song is pink. I also represented Vivaldi's *Four Seasons* and *4'33"* by John Cage, a silent piece.

Needless to say that when we speak, our speech is related to different colors, which I like to transpose in painting, syllable by syllable. Martin Luther King's famous "I have a dream" oscillates between C and E, whereas a diatribe by Adolf Hitler has no dominant color because the sound contrast between each word in his speeches is too big. Most often, however, there is a predominant shade which characterizes the voice of an individual. An accelerating car produces a rainbow, going through the entire spectrum of colors.

Within the framework of the city colors project, I am trying to determine the dominant colors of European cities, which inhabitants wrongly believe to be gray. Madrid is amber-terracota, Lisbon is yellow and turquoise, London is red and yellow. Thanks to a mobile app I have designed, people can point their smartphone toward public sculptures and can listen to their colors to hear their melody. Of course, at night, this melody is very different. For the food player, we have also created an app which will let users hear the dishes they make at home, thereby enabling them to make dishes which sound good.

All in all, my life has changed in many ways. My antenna has brought color to my life, quite literally, but it has also generated much curiosity, and has sparked unexpected interactions with others. People stop me in the street, and I am always amused at how their questions evolve over time. In 2004, passersby first thought I was wearing a light, then they imagined it was some sort of microphone for web chats, and around 2007, they thought it was a Bluetooth telephone. In 2009, people thought it was a GoPro camera, and in 2011 an accessory which was in some way related to the Google Glasses. Lately, a young boy asked me if it was a retractable selfie stick. But nobody, however, has ever imagined I am wearing an antenna which enables me to extend my senses. My hope is that in 2020, this idea will have become commonplace, and that there will be more people equipped with bodily extensions, new senses or enhanced or extended perceptions.

THE CYBORG FOUNDATION

In 2010, together with choreographer Moon Ribas, I founded the Cyborg Foundation, which aims at promoting the use of technology to extend our perception of reality. We share the strong belief that such amplifications are a means of engaging better with the Earth and with other animals, whose senses are much more developed than our own. We should make use of technology to enhance our perceptive abilities at least to the level of other species, maybe even further.

The word "cyborg" is the contraction of the notions of "cybernetics" and "organism." Such a union between these two notions can express itself in three different ways. First, the notion of "psychological cyborg" refers to individuals who feel they are psychologically connected to cybernetics. This is the case for most of us. This can be seen in how today we no longer say "my phone is running out of battery" as 15 or 20 years ago, but rather "I am running out of battery." The next stage is a biological union by implanting this technology into our biological bodies. This is followed by a phase of neurological integration, i.e. how our brain is modified by cybernetics.

Among the extensions created with Moon Ribas, there is an internal radar, which comes in the form of a chip attached to the ear lobe, which vibrates whenever an object or body moves in front of you. Infrared chips on both ears emit vibrations whenever they detect movements, from left to right for example, and they can calculate their speed. This way, a pair of earrings offers the possibility of retrovision, letting you know if somebody is behind you for example.

If we all had such tools, this would change the way we behave. Among many other things, pedestrian traffic would be much more fluid. New sports and dances would be created, based on a 360° perception.

The Cyborg Foundation has also worked on the Fingerborg, a project involving a young man who has a bit of a finger missing. Our first step was to ask him what digital appendix he wanted to get implanted. In the light of his hesitation, we explored different possibilities: a lighter — but he didn't smoke, scales to know the exact weight of objects. In the end, we decided to implant a mini-camera. It could easily be used as a sensor to emit vibrations to provide information on whatever he wants, color for example. But for now, he uses it to take photos. To recharge the camera, all he needs to do is lift the little hood at the end of his finger and plug it in.

Another sensor which will be available this year is the internal compass. Implanted in the lower section of the leg, it vibrates whenever you face north. Its sensitivity can be configured either to point to the true north (North Pole), or the magnetic north. This will create a veritable sense of orientation.

We are also developing cybernetic eyes for blind people, which will detect not only colors but also distances and shapes. The visually-impaired learn colors very quickly. A young boy was able to differentiate the frequencies of three colors in just a few seconds. A person who was not blind from birth can even associate the sound of a color with the mental representation he or she has kept of it.

As for the Earborg project, the reversed equivalent of my antenna, it is for people who are totally deaf. It detects the dominant frequency of a sound and transposes it 40 octaves higher in order to transform it into a color which is displayed on a little screen. This device will enable people to identify the tone of a discourse, information which can then enrich lip reading.

Just as some animals have bioluminescence abilities, I, too, got a dental implant equipped with a lamp which switched on by snapping my teeth together. This was not cybernetics *per se*, and this could have been very useful, if only the lamp hadn't switched on at awkward moments while eating.

One last example, a museum in Barcelona features a cyborg sculpture which represents the shape of my head and antenna. Visitors can show it colors, which are then sent to me. This is one of the ways I have found to interact with the public. Based on the same principle, the left arm of Moon Ribas, and its replica in the museum, are equipped with a chip which is connected to seismographs around the world, and vibrate whenever there is an earthquake greater than 1 on the Richter scale, which happens approximatively every 8–10 minutes. Her other arm is connected to moonquakes.

CONQUERING SPACE

I now aspire to a permanent connection with space. Since 2014, thanks to the Internet, I can already connect intermittently to NASA's international space station. My goal is to be connected to it all the time, but it is a very overwhelming activity. Until now, I have not been able to stand it for more than two hours at a time. By 2017, and with practice, I hope to be able to be connected to the colors of both Earth and space permanently. The Internet thus would no longer be a simple tool, but would become a sensorial extension, or even a sensory organ in its own right, operating beyond the limits of our environment.

Space is opening up a new and bewildering universe. My first two attempts at a public concert of space colors were not a great success. The first time, the profusion of ultraviolet lights, which are characterized by a very high-pitched and loud sound, gave me such a headache that I had to stop. Most of the audience had run away anyway! Ten minutes after the beginning of the second concert, somebody in the audience had a seizure, and we had to call an ambulance. The third concert ran smoothly.

There are two ways of exploring space: going there physically, or extending our senses so as to feel it from where we are. Given the rapid progress of 3D printing, we will soon be able to send a printed version of ourselves to Mars for example, and use the Internet as an extension of our senses, to feel our bodies out there, from right here.

Some believe it is unnatural to be a cyborg, some are even afraid because they think it is "dehumanizing." They consider that a cyborg is closer to machines than humans, which I contest: on the contrary, being a cyborg brings us closer to other animal species, nature, and ultimately, to reality. I personally feel much closer to insects, because, like them, I have an antenna, and to dolphins, because, like them, I hear through bone conduction. I also feel connected to nature, through the ultraviolet and infrared lights I can perceive. Moon Ribas shares a very intimate connection with Earth because she feels it in her bones, and she feels closer to animals because she can anticipate earthquakes. All in all, cyborgs are closer to animals than they are to robots. Why should we not extend our senses, at least to the level of other animal species?

16

CREATING IS ABOUT BEING GENEROUS

Christine Ferber

Pastry Chef, Chocolate Maker, Confectioner and Jam Maker

ALWAYS AIM FOR PERFECTION WITH HUMILITY

Every day, when I am making my pastry, chocolates, confectionery and jams, I work with something which is alive, versatile, and any day, it can play tricks on me if I get overly confident. Working with such beautiful, perfect raw material is something very humbling, and I feel it is my duty to bring all my professional qualities to the work of transforming it into a product which is equally remarkable.

An article published in *La Tribune de Genève* said that I made "*the best jam in the world, and the best chocolates in the world, in such a simple place.*" I was very touched by this. Not so much because I think I make the best products in the world, but rather because this simplicity is exactly what I want to preserve. I want my little local shop that my parents bought many years ago in tiny little Niedermorschwihr to stay a simple place, which is accessible to all.

THE ARTISTIC APPRENTICESHIP OF PASTRY

Ever since we were children, my sister and I helped our father, who was a baker, and pastry chef: my sister was in the front shop, because she was always such a pleasant person, and I was behind the scenes, because I was the grumpy one. When I turned 15, I felt I had gone as far as I could in pastry making: I now wanted to discover the world! My father did not share that dream. He convinced me that I should take the time to finish my training properly, so that I would be able do this job anywhere in the world, to travel, or maybe even to teach. In 1976, he took me to a wonderful exhibition, *Sucre d'Art* [sugar artistry] where many pastry chefs expressed their creativity by working sugar into every form and shape: pulled, spun, cast, etc. There was a specific piece that particularly struck me: a piece by Pascal Niau from Dalloyau, which required nearly 400 hours of work. It helped me understand that this profession is artistic, and so I was ready to embrace it.

At the time, nobody in France would have accepted a woman as an apprentice, so I decided to move to Brussels for a three-year course. When I got back in 1978, my father had plans to expand his shop, and wanted me to work with him. However, I still had dreams of seeing the world. In the end, we found a compromise: since boys had to go away for a year for their military service, I, too, would be allowed to travel for a year. I knew that no laboratory in Paris would ever accept a woman, so I decided to enter an artistic baking competition — which I won. After this, Monsieur Peltier, who had the best store in Paris, in the rue de Sèvres, invited me to join him for a year. He gave me a very thorough and precise training in baking and confectionery, and shared with me his avant-garde spirit.

Back in our Niedermorschwihr shop, I started baking and making pastry on a daily basis. Until then, my father had kept that only for weekends and celebrations. He was very pleased to accept this help because it gave him more time for his own passion, which he only shared with me quite late in life: to be a cook. As a baker, he had always worked like a cook, by experimenting, testing, tasting and correcting. Today, I take a similar approach with my jams. When you are creative, you cannot simply follow recipes. It is important to do what you like to do, the way you like to do it.

However, I started feeling lonely in this tiny 360-inhabitant village which was too remote to attract anybody. I discussed the idea of opening a store in town with my father, on a busy street, where my cakes could be seen, and attract passers-by. His answer to this was that if this were the condition for success, then how could I explain the success of Marc Haeberlin and his Auberge de l'Ill being awarded three Michelin stars in the tiny Illhaeusern in Alsace? He assured me I could follow in Marc Haeberlin steps if I respected some fundamental principles. He told me to be patient, to play the long game, to do what I love and most importantly, to do something others don't do: to give, be generous, even if that meant working at a loss. Deep down, I knew he was right, and decided to stay and fully embrace pastry making at Niedermorschwihr. In fact, I found that the flow of seasons in the Alsatian countryside, its regular traditional celebrations with their culinary specialties, the rhythm of flavors — chocolate from September to April, confectionery and ice creams in summer, and bread and pastry making all year long — suited my creative and artistic nature. My village is lulled by a gentle rhythm, bathed in light. I find its colors and the colors I use in my products invigorating. I would never have been as creative as I am today in a city. It is important to live in a place that makes you feel good to be able to create and produce beautiful things.

WITH MY FINGERS IN THE JAM JAR

One day, jam came into my life. Well, to be more accurate, it was a customer who brought me a basket full of Montmorency cherries. Rather than using them to garnish a black forest cake, as I usually would have done, I decided to make jam with them. This upset my mother, who was the exclusive jam-maker of the family for our pastries and donuts. I was to return to my cakes. All she would accept was that I make a couple of jars to decorate the shop window. She even refused to sell them to the first five customers who wanted to buy them! When the sixth customer asked for jam, she reconsidered. Selling jam, why not, but at what price? Since a Bonne-Maman jam of jar cost 7.25 francs in supermarkets, and since I had pitted the cherries myself, I decided to sell my jars for 7.80 francs each. I had failed to factor in that I needed a full hour to pit two and half kilos of cherries. Anyhow, at that stage, I had no plans of renewing the experience. Our customers, however, kept asking for more. By popular demand, I started with raspberries and blueberries, to the extent that it even ended up taking up a big part of my free time. When the famous pastry chef Pierre Hermé, a family friend, came to visit us, my father shared his concerns with him: all these jars, just sitting in the basement and an investment acquired at considerable cost (buying the jars, the fruit, etc.) were not very lucrative. Pierre Hermé encouraged me to persevere if that is where my heart was.

Since then, I have dreamed up nearly 1,200 different sorts of jams, chutneys, and sweet and sourn jams. Each year, I work on 250 to 300 different products, and regularly offer new flavors. I don't really promote them in any particular way, my customers do that for me. I never have enough jars to satisfy wholesaler or importer demand. I feel my greatest achievement is that I succeeded in convincing my customers to taste real, seasonal flavors, even if that meant being disappointed not to find their traditional strawberry jam. They learned to be open to the unknown, and to let themselves be surprised.

TIME AND GENEROSITY

Steadily, our store grew, whether for cakes, confectionery or jams. I dedicate my afternoons to making jam, and mornings to making cakes with my pastry chefs and confectioners. We make everything in the same workshop, and I would not give up my copper pots and pans for anything in the world, even if they can only hold four kilos of fruit at a time. We are currently having new premises built in the village to house two workshops, one for confectionery, and the other for chocolate. It will also include a kitchen, because over the last 50 years, my family has been developing specialty pâtés, condiments and foie gras. That is my brother's area of expertise. I will be in charge of the bakery, pastry and ice-cream workshop which is attached to the shop, and hope to set up an adjoining sampling salon and small cookery school.

My dearest wish is to continue creating in a way which reflects the seasons, with generosity and without having to count the hours. That, I believe, is the key: you have to give yourself enough time to let your imagination mature, to create, to transform matter while respecting it, and without spoiling it. Of course, I could save a lot of time by using a centrifuge, to separate the pulp of a peach from its skin and pit. But this technique damages the fruit, and the pulp oxidizes immediately. This affects the final product, whether it is an ice cream or a jam. The result is completely different if you choose beautiful pieces of fruit that you poach, skin and pip by hand, and then cut and cook in small batches. The first secret of a good product is to give it the necessary time to reach perfection, without seeking to make profit from it. I strive to respect this principle every time I create a new product. It is only later, during the second phase, that I look at new ways to organize my work and be more efficient.

SEDUCED BY EDITORS

If someone had told me 30 years ago that I would end up writing books, I would never have believed them. This is definitely not something to which I aspired. Yet, today, a number of my books have been published. I owe this to the people I met — particularly my co-authors Philippe Model and Bernard Winkelmann — and also to choosing generosity over profitability. When commissioning editors from Payot publishing house first contacted me to hear my thoughts on their next project *Six siècles de confitures* [Six Centuries of Jams] my friend, Pierre Hermé, immediately warned me: I was about to give away 20 years of my knowledge, to people who were only interested in making a profit! In fact, I had agreed to provide them with my help free of charge, because, in exchange, I got the opportunity to benefit from all the fascinating discoveries they were making in the archives of the Bibliothèque Nationale. Not without some hesitation, I followed my instinct and decided to go ahead with the project. The authors spent three weeks in Alsace, testing and re-writing recipes. The final result was so successful that the director of Payot decided to offer me a percentage of the sales of this book, and said he would also be happy to publish my books in the future. He was even ready to let the contract be submitted for endorsement to the suspicious Pierre Hermé!

That was a good life lesson: if I had not been generous and curious, if I had given up for financial reasons, I would not have had the opportunity to embark on a journey into the wonderful world of books! Creating is first and foremost about being generous.

FROM THE VOSGES FORESTS TO STARRED DREAMS

Jacques Genin
Chocolate Confectionner

Let me tell you the story about a young boy filled with dreams, and about a man for whom passion, pleasure and work are one and the same thing.

As a child, I wanted to become an actor or a dancer. My father made me face up to reality: I would not be able to make a living like that. Here was I thinking that to "earn a living" meant being happy in your chosen career. So I decided I would do research. But when I was 12 I started an apprenticeship in an abattoir in the East of France. Such is life! This activity was certainly anything but delightful, but it was a way of surviving, and keeping alive the hope of doing "something" with my life. And yet, I was still haunted by my dreams.

FIRST STEPS IN PARIS

When I was 19, on a whim, I decided to leave my home region, the Vosges, and I hit the road. There I was walking along the highway, with no destination in mind. A trucker stopped, and asked me where I was going, and so I decided that wherever he was headed would be my destination. And that is how I landed in Paris. But what to do next? I did not want to go back to the butcher trade, because it just did not make me happy. I got a job at the Café Dreher, place du Châtelet. When the owner saw how few skills I had, he put me behind the bar. It was a source of particular pride for me: I liked the idea of making cocktails. At long last, my life was about to change! In fact, all I did was wipe glasses all day long.

There was a night club in the basement of the café which intrigued me. It was a jazz club, and I could hear this music that was new to me, without even knowing who was playing it. The boss finally gave in to my repeated requests to work in that "den" to which I was so drawn, on one condition: I was to not speak to anybody and reveal my accent. The first time I entered the room which was bathed in darkness, I could make out trumpets, saxophones, and musicians, who, to my surprise, were all black. It was a new world. One night, when we were closing, one of the musicians talked to me in a language I did not understand. Someone finally told me he wanted a whisky, and for me to go and sit with him. He picked up his trumpet and played a tune for me. I learnt, some years later, that it was Miles Davis. It still makes me shiver when I think about it.

A STARRED NOVICE

Such was my arrival in Paris: filled with emotion and dreams. I could feel the magic of the city, that it was a place where I was free to make my dreams come true. But with the succession of all sorts of jobs, I was becoming disillusioned: I worked for one bad boss after another. One day, I finally realized that I had a problem with authority. And so, at age 21, I decided to open my first restaurant. Until then, I had never touched a pot in my life. I couldn't even make a simple vinaigrette. This absurd idea to venture into the world of cuisine came to me one night after a party. My girlfriend and I walked passed a restaurant which was for sale, 5 rue de Tournon, and she dared me to take it over. A fortnight later, I showed her the keys, and told her the good news: we were the happy owners of the place. I had just signed a pile of papers making me its owner. Of course, I had not understood the explanations given to me on "assets" and "liabilities." It did not matter, I would find a way to make it work! It did not take me long, however, to understand what "liabilities" were all about. It was a rocky start, but one year and a half later, I got my first Michelin star.

My life has often been guided by a feeling for a place. One day, I went for a walk at St.-Jean-de-Beauregard in the Essonne region and I discovered a beautiful spot, with an old building and a wash house. It was made for me! That became my second restaurant, the Auberge de Beauregard. Three years later, Patrick Dubois and I got our second Michelin star. I eventually passed on the lease of my restaurant rue de Tournon to the Aquarelle group, who had their heart set on it, at any price. So be it! I gave them a random, exorbitantly high amount — seven times what I had paid for it. And the deal was sealed. Once again, I had followed my gut instinct, true to my way of life.

I have never been interested in material possessions. And so, I sold the Auberge de Beauregard and took a four-year sabbatical. My daughter had just been born, and I decided to spend all the money I had just earned on a trip around the world with her. I had never had a childhood as such, I wanted to give her one, and most importantly, I wanted it to be filled with dreams. If I was ever to enjoy it, it was now or never. When I came back, I was penniless, and had no other choice but to go back to work. I was then 23, I had proved myself as a chef, and aspired to new challenges.

DIVING INTO CHOCOLATE

What new adventure would I take on? Once more, inspiration came from my daughter: I wanted her to have the best birthday cakes ever. So I decided I would take on chocolate confectioning. It is very difficult to make your way into this world without the right diplomas. But there was no discouraging me, and I knocked on the door of Robert Linxe, the founder of the famous *Maison du Chocolat*. He explained that he did not need an assistant, but that he would entrust me with a new line of pâtisserie. I accepted on the condition that after 4 years, I too would be able to create chocolate. In the meantime, I developed recipes for him, such as chocolate cream, a caramel éclair, a galette, all of which you can still find at the *Maison du Chocolat* today. After 4 years, I had held up my end of the bargain, it was Robert Linxe's turn to do the same. "Only a fool would let you go…. as a pâtisserie chef!" he said. It was time for me to move on.

I left the *Maison du Chocolat* right then and there, to open a laboratory in the 15th district of Paris. My ambition was clear: I would serve only the greatest chefs in the world. Five years later, I was the provider for no less than 200 Michelin-star restaurants in France and throughout the world. Business was going well, but after 8 years, weariness took over. It was not about success: with only two employees and a 23-square meter facility — which had required minimum investment — I was generating a turnover of 2 million Euros. And yet, I was bored.

That is when I fell in love with a magical place, an 18th century Parisian house located rue de Turenne, an old rose garden. I contacted the owner, and signed a cheque All that was left was to find the money.

That is the way I work, I follow my instinct, like an animal, without thinking. Of course, it is important to have experience and knowledge. But not everything can be rationalized. In the professional world, if all you do is to think, you become a mercenary. On the contrary, work should be a source of satisfaction, and fulfillment, just like love.

The chocolate shop and workshop on the rue de Turenne — like the later one in the rue du Bac — required an 8 million Euro investment. Today, it has 55 employees. It took 2 years' work before we could even think about the opening. It was an arduous start: the work was finished in October 2008, just as the financial crisis erupted, and banks were starting to fail. I was unable to get the remaining loans, so started with a deficit of 700,000 Euros. The first 2 years were extremely difficult. We had to produce continuously. When the bailiffs came knocking, I swore to myself that nobody would take this business from me. Fortunately, I had a lot of support. In 2014, I had paid back my loans, the chocolate shop in rue de Turenne belonged to me. It was performing well, through good years and bad, so I took out another loan and decided to set up in rue du Bac. On top of the creative process itself, I enjoy challenges. When it comes down to it, I never fully grasp the risks I am taking. Maybe because I never went to school or did a real apprenticeship, I improvise with the resources I have, with my gut.

ENTREPRENEURSHIP: ALL ABOUT FEELING AND SHARING

To work and to create, is all about sharing and instinct. To give you a taste of this alchemy, I would like to talk about some of my creations.

Instinct as My Guide — Fruit Caramel Bonbons

Let us start by the story of a caramel. The chef who officiated at the Georges V, Philippe Legendre, a client of my laboratory, once asked me if

I could make caramels. How could I confess the truth to such a great name, three Michelin stars that in fact I hate caramel, for no other reason than that it sticks to your teeth. He placed an order for the end of that week, promising that if my caramels were to his liking, I would become his sole supplier. There was nothing else for it than to get cooking, in search of a recipe. I did not want them to be sticky, and most importantly, they had to be a bit special. This led me to exploring caramel with fruit. Needless to say that this week of searching was stressful I don't know how to explain how I did it: without thinking, I used that precious animal instinct which has always followed me. Before creating a product, I already know what taste I want it to have. All that remains, then, is to find the ingredients which will bring it to life. That is how these caramels were created, and their fame continues to grow.

Chance Encounters — Capers and Hazelnut

A chocolate can also be born from a chance encounter. Two years ago, I was feeling down one night and decided to go out for a bit, to drown my sorrow in alcohol. I walked into a bar, and as soon as I sat down, I started talking to my two neighbors. We ended up spending the entire evening drinking together. Sometime later, a friend, Richard came to visit. He wanted me to taste some capers, which were divine. I had to have some! Richard promised to introduce me to their producer. Months went by and I still had no news. One day, Richard told me that a Gabrio Bini was going to come by the lab. An Italian man turned up on the doorstep of the lab with two boxes of wine and capers. It turned out that he was one of my drinking companions from that night out. After 40 years as an architect, he gave it up to set up in Pantelleria, an island off the coast of Sicily, where he cultivated vines and capers. At that point, I knew I wanted to create a chocolate bonbon around these capers. I combined them with a praline of hazelnuts from Piedmont, butter, covered in chocolate from Madagascar, 71% cocoa. Today I am unable to explain how the recipe came to me, but what I do know is that it works. Products are filled with human stories and stories of encounters, stories of passion and guts. That is what I love above all else in this job. I am proud of this subtle marriage of flavors offering immediate notes of hazelnut, followed by the more latent plant taste, while revealing a beautiful acidity which is reminiscent of the lands of Madagascar. With a good white wine, it is simply magnificent.

What I love as an entrepreneur are all these encounters which nourish me. Life may have driven me away from the professions I aspired to as a child — acting, dancing and research — but I never gave up on my dreams. I will follow them till the end. The main drive of a life is to want to do something, to be inspired and to dream. It does not matter what you end up doing. As far as I am concerned "to live to work and work to live", are two statements that cannot be separated. I could not live without working because I would lose what is most precious to me: contact, interaction, others. I would not want to live in a world which operated like a gas station, a disembodied world, where you fill your tank alone, in front of a machine, before continuing your journey, alone. We spend most of our life working, we may as well make it an opportunity to give and to exchange. What particularly motivated me throughout my ventures, was to know that what I was creating provided a livelihood for families, that I was giving myself the means to help others.

Highly Technical Treats — Sophie's Rocher

Let us now talk about a veritable treat, a chocolate bonbon which my partner, Sophie, created. When she presented it to me, I loved it straight away. She had the beautiful audacity to combine macadamia, caramel, with a covering of milk and grilled, caramelized almonds to make a *rocher*. This is very technical because the actual bonbon has a liquid base. That was added proof that I had managed to pass on to Sophie my taste, but also technique.

Sophie has been by my side for 12 years. She accepted sacrifices when we had to cut back, and was nothing but supportive. Soon, she will be the first French female chocolate chef! I will hand over the reins of my company to her and my daughter, who graduated from HEC and has passed the bar. It is important to leave something behind for those who are a part of your life. When you are at the head of a business, you cannot think only about yourself. You also have to share. That is part and parcel of the job. You cannot ask people to follow you if you do not give something in return. I want to create a society fueled by sharing, exchanging, and by passion. That is the very essence of what I do.

In the lab, only four of our 50 employees are male. Long before politicians became concerned with parity, I had already implemented it.

For matters like this, as in any other, I only follow one principle: everybody deserves a chance. There are more and more women joining our businesses, thereby bringing greater elegance and sensuality to our trade.

The Dedication of an Entire Team

I am where I am today thanks to the support of my team, which believes in me and stands by me, in good times and in bad, and who become involved in my projects despite my immense demands. Over the years, I have got to know the people who accompany and support me. I love each and every one of them, and these bonds are what sustain me. Alone, we are nothing. Being an entrepreneur means showing consideration to those who walk with you, who get invested for you.

During my first years as a chef, I was a very harsh boss. I was intimidated by no one. I wanted my employees to become more like me, maybe even to become me. However, I gradually came to understand that in order to get results, I had to ask them to be themselves, while at the same time conveying my vision to them. I had to invite them to let their instinct talk. This way of seeing things radically changed my relationship to others, and brought a magical dimension to my laboratory. Today, I have an amazing relationship with my employees, because it is they who have raised me all the way to the top. But I have never lost my soul in the process, because one of the things they like about me is who I am. I leave room for them to express their energies, because they will run my company tomorrow. Soon I will only be there to guide them, because other adventures await!

I once had a young intern, Mathieu. His teacher had actually advised me against taking him on: he was disruptive, he came from the ill-famed neighborhood known as the "*cité des Tarterêts.*" I decided to give him a chance. At the beginning, it was difficult, I could hardly understand anything he said. He had to become acculturated to the workshop's common language. The funniest thing is that today, Mathieu expresses himself perfectly correctly when he is in the lab, and as soon as he walks out the door of the lab he switches back to slang and *verlan!*[1] I took the time to listen to him and to get to know this young man, who has now become one of

---

[1] Coded French slang that inverts syllables.

my deputies. He has such a wonderful heart. The very one whose teachers considered doomed to failure simply needed someone to prove to him that he existed and that he was useful. I have several boys like him in my team. I must confess that my recruitment strategy is based solely on impressions. Not only do I not understand three quarters of a resume, but more importantly, I hire somebody for the fire I can see in their eye, for their aspirations. I have no selection criteria. What matters to me is what the person is looking for: is it pleasure or salary? When your life is reduced to pursuit of a salary, you end up going to work as if you were heading down the mine. The worst thing is that we are all going to spend at least 40 years working! To work, for me, is to get up in the morning, motivated by the desire to give and to exchange with others, and not wish my weeks away, hoping it was Friday on a Monday morning. To be a boss, you must be a leader, but you must also respect your employees so that they too, are motivated by the desire to come to work. Never forget that an employee works a full month before getting their reward. Such a commitment must work both ways.

I think it is a shame that we are limited to a 35 hour work week in France. We should all be able to dedicate the time we want to our chosen profession. And those who limit themselves to 35 hours a week should not complain about not feeling fulfilled! Of course, I do not spend a lot of time with my loved ones. But how could I create anything without giving myself entirely, body and soul, to my activity? On average, I work 18 hours a day, every day of the week and rest assured, it is never by obligation. Yes, I live to work, but thanks to that, I have achieved so many beautiful things! I have become exactly who I wanted to be, and nothing can stop me, and I never felt I was missing out on the world, or on having a social life. I share so much at the lab, and I meet so many people! Soon I will be 60, and I have no intention of stopping now.

ENDLESS DREAMS

Life has worked out well for me. It brought me what I had not had the opportunity to do, i.e. dance, acting, research, but transposed to another setting, in a kitchen, through cooking, gastronomy, elegance and sharing. Today, when I create, I conduct research; my culinary demonstrations are a form of acting. This profession has given me the opportunity to stay at the most beautiful and luxurious hotels, to taste the most wonderful dishes and the greatest wines. And yet there is still so much for me to discover! Some years ago, I tasted the Romanée-Conti, the best wine of Bourgogne. I am still stunned by this experience. When you are given the chance to access to such subtle flavors, you can only be the happiest man on earth.

Over the last 3 years, I have been working on a new project. I often travel to Japan to teach. I have chosen a place to set up. I did not want just another shop, on a busy street, lost in the crowd. I have purchased a 140 year-old house on the island of Hokkaido. I have decided to set up a laboratory there, and to open the first Japanese Jacques Genin chocolate house, with a workshop, a retail space, and a tea house. Since it is a listed building, I have maintained its entire structure. It will be the treasure chest in which I will design my products for Japan. It is scheduled to open in September 2016. This challenge is exhilarating, but not without apprehension. It has required an investment of 8 million euros. Once more, I am lucky to have no notion of figures, and to not be able to fully assess the risks I take. I do not quantify my goal in terms of financial gain but rather in terms of effort. I know it will require effort, blood, sweat and tears, but most importantly, it requires happiness. After opening, I will only spend one week a month in Japan. My real challenge will be to pass on my knowledge to a local team and to bring the French and Japanese cultures together in a harmonious encounter. All in all, that is my only concern. Financial issues are secondary. I have often visited this country, but I do not know it. I am very fond of its traditions, but I cannot claim to know it. I still do not know how my proposal will be received.

My dream for tomorrow would be to have a vineyard. In life, a man can leave a mark in a number of ways: through progeny which carries the same name, through musical or literary works ... and why not wine? If I could leave a mark like that of the Romanée-Conti, with a product whose name would survive centuries, I would be the happiest man in the world. Then, I will be able to retire.

18

MY IMAGINATION GIVES ME WINGS

Kathrine Larsen

Sommelier

My imagination gives me wings
It allows me to explore my ideas and thoughts before them being reality
It adds all the colors of the rainbow to a rainy day
It is really such a wonderful thing

I use my imagination all of the time
I use it when getting dressed in the morning
I use it when thinking of the day that lies ahead
And when baking a cake

I use it when planning future travels
I use it when buying a dress
I use it when choosing a restaurant
And when reading the menu

My imagination permits me to look in the past
It lets me explore cherished memories anew
My imagination permits me to look in the future
And paint a picture of tomorrow

I use my imagination to marry food and wine
I can imagine aromas, flavors and textures and how they will combine
With my experience I can imagine classic duos
And with my creativity I can conceive brand new ones

My imagination allows me to travel to vineyards and countries not
    yet explored
All I have studied and been taught will give my imagination wings
Within mere moments, entire landscapes
And row after row of vines appear in my mind

I can imagine the characteristics of a new vintage before it has yet
    been bottled
I can imagine what the sun and the rain gave
What the soil and rivers endowed
And what the hands of the vigneron granted

My imagination will allow me to envisage goals of mine yet to be achieved
It will serve as a driving force
Constantly carrying me forward
While revealing new possibilities before me on the way

My imagination gives me wings
It empowers all my thoughts and ideas
It adds all the colors of the rainbow even to a sunny day
It is really such a wonderful thing

CHOCOLATE

19

Pierre Marcolini

Chocolate Confectioner

THE MAN BEHIND THE BRAND

I founded the company in 1996. I bought a small boutique in the Brussels region, which was to serve as both the store and workshop. When I started out in this business, I had one concern: finding a way to innovate in an already-saturated market. "Belgian chocolate" is such a renowned institution worldwide that it seemed impossible to bring something new to the table, and I did not want to be just another Belgian chocolatier. At school, we were always taught that in order to build a successful career, we had to define a strategy, have a five-year plan, with clear milestones. My intent was not so much to succeed from a business viewpoint, but rather to find a way to innovate, to surprise. I therefore opted for a more empirical approach, and started out in my small workshop-boutique with one leitmotif: I wanted to make a chocolate that was a reflection of who I am. I did not analyze consumer expectations or prepare market studies; my business plan was to explore how I could leave my own mark, share a bit of myself with people. This, I believe, is the first difference between craftsmanship and profit-driven ventures. Large corporations rely on extensive and well-researched analyses to define both what they do and what they offer; artisans on the other hand, explore ways of expressing who they are, and how they can bring their creativity to life. Today, some of my creations, such as the "Saveurs du Monde", "Macarons", "Carré2 Chocolat" or "Les Cœurs", have become iconic. However, I did not create them with this intention. This came over time, through my relationship to my trade and to my customers. And this is the driving force behind craftsmanship: it is about finding ways of sharing emotions and conveying pleasure, and in that sense, it is an art form. Artistic expression is the DNA of my business, in quite a literal way. As a chocolatier, this desire to express who I am and share emotions takes on many forms, because chocolate is not only about tasting. Aesthetics play an important role in the whole experience, and therefore in my work, because we all eat with our eyes first. I also find inspiration in other art forms, such as cuisine, fashion or winemaking. They continuously find new ways of expression in fields where everything has already been said and done, and I find this very inspiring. This encouraged me to establish partnerships with Olympia Le Tan, Kistuné, Tom Dixon, Peter Pilotto, and AMI, to create signature "collections." I have been very fortunate, over time, this venture of self-expression grew into a successful international brand.

FROM PRECIOUS RAW MATERIAL TO UNIVERSAL CONSUMER GOOD: THE PRODUCT

Now, let us use our imagination to travel back in time. Five centuries ago, a boat manned by Conquistador Hernán Cortés landed on the shores of Mexico, and was welcomed by Aztec Emperor Montezuma. He handed Cortés the local trade currency: cocoa beans. Montezuma introduced Cortés to his favorite drink 'chocolatl,' served in a golden goblet. Five centuries later, the very same product has become a consumer product which has undergone centuries of transformation and is now drastically different from this first encounter with it.

After Cortés returned to Spain, and for nearly two centuries, people struggled to see how they could use cocoa. The Aztecs crushed the beans and added spices and plants to make a drink which they called "Drink of the Gods." For ritual and religious purposes, the Aztecs added annatto to turn the chocolate into a blood-red liquid. The addition of hot and spicy additives was not palatable to the Spanish consumer and two centuries later, they were substituted with sweet additions, such as cane sugar, cinnamon and honey, to make it into a sweet drink. Contrary to the Aztec tradition, where cocoa was a democratic product, chocolate became a luxury only the wealthiest and most well-connected Spanish nobility could afford. Over the centuries, this product has undergone many transformations and has now become a pleasure, a treat and a commodity. It has achieved what very few products have: it has become truly universal. Whether in Japan, in Shanghai, or in

Europe, chocolate always sparks a sense of wonder, enchantment, and pleasure. Still today, after all these years, I wonder what in nature makes chocolate so appealing to all. It transcends cultures and tastes, and offers a "point of convergence." Just as classical music, wine or gourmet cuisine, chocolate has succeeded in transcending borders and cultures; chocolate has become universal, something which people love and crave.

FROM TRAVEL AND INSPIRATION TO STUNNING RECIPES: THE ACT OF CREATION

In the past, an artisan chocolatier was someone who transformed, worked and produced their own chocolate. Today, however, this definition has evolved. After World War II, the purchasing power of the middle class rose significantly. During the post-war boom, known as the *Trente Glorieuses* in France, consumers could afford more, and indulge in treats much more than they could in the past. Instead of buying chocolate once a month, people went once a week, and therefore demanded a greater variety of products. Clients expected chocolate confectioners to become more creative, more inventive. People wanted to treat themselves, and in a far more luxurious way than in years before, and most importantly, much more frequently. The rise of labor costs and this growing demand led to the emergence of couverture producers, who offered semi-finished products: blocks of ready-made chocolate that confectioners could then use to make their creations. This left confectioners more time to focus on their imagination and inspiration. In turn, this led to a burst of creativity, particularly in the 1960s and 1970s. The downside of this trend, however, was that flavor became very linear, as all confectioners used the same "base", Valrhona for example, and their creativity was expressed primarily through the "packaging." In so doing, the industry seems to have lost sight of its origins, and got somewhat lost along the way. I feel this somewhat denatures the very essence of chocolate in general, and most importantly, of our trade.

In recent years, consumption trends have evolved, and a "revolution" took place. There has been a growing demand for purity in products. This was the case with olive oil and water, for example. The same took place with chocolate, and people started focusing on the percentage of cocoa in chocolate bars, seeking up to 100% purity. But in the case of chocolate, the quality of chocolate is not measured through the percentage of cocoa.

As is the case with wine, cocoa beans are, in fact, a terroir product. Just as there are different varieties of grapes, Merlot, Cabernet or Syrah, for example, which give the wine its distinctive aromatic characteristics, the same applies to cocoa beans. Some of the most renowned varieties of cocoa beans include Carenero, Puerto Cabelo, Nacional Equateur, Sur Del Lago, Occumare, Chuan, Porcelana or Amenolado. Just as two identical varieties produced in different soils, with a different exposure to sunlight, will produce different wines, the types of soil, the PH, the exposure to sunlight will all contribute to the flavor of the chocolate. Some varieties offer a floral, spicy or even a fruity note.

In response to these two trends, some confectioners have chosen to look back to the past, and go back to the origins of the trade. This gave rise to the "bean to bar" movement, a movement by which chocolate confectioners choose to make their own chocolate, directly from the bean. This path led me to Venezuela. I met a local producer, and asked for the criollo variety, because it is considered the "queen" of all beans. This rare bean represents only 2% of the worldwide production, and is renowned to be exceptional. The producer looked at me, smiling, probably amused by my obvious lack of experience, and simply presented me with different varieties. At that moment, I felt I had opened up a door to a whole new universe, to a trade which I knew and yet that I was discovering anew. Today, I focus on bringing these flavors to people.

Of course, couverture manufacturers were not enthused by the idea of me making my own chocolate from the bean! They offered to help me select the beans and transform them for me, but I was determined to do this on my own. They felt I was robbing the added value they had to offer. By focusing on the beans, I was able to take my craftsmanship to a whole new level. By deciding which beans I work with, how I want to roast the beans, I can give the chocolate more soul, it becomes the reflection and expression of who I am, and that is what makes it signature chocolate.

FROM ONE MAN AND HIS DREAM TO A STRUCTURED ORGANIZATION

As a self-taught artisan, I struggled to get the equipment I needed. There simply are no machines for making your own chocolate. People dissuaded me from trying, saying it was too expensive, that I did not have enough room. The initial quote I received to adapt my workshop was as thick as a phonebook and estimated at EUR 4 million, and I was told my workshop was too small, and that it would be virtually impossible. I purchased second-hand equipment, found a coffee roaster in Portugal, a bean crusher in Brazil, etc. This period of my life was a time of considerable despondency, suffering and doubts, but at the same time, it was very exciting and invigorating. It was absolutely exhilarating, and when we produced our very first chocolate, the whole workshop was bubbling with excitement.

Our clients noticed this shift, and some even came to us and said they no longer liked my chocolate. I then had to explain that previously, it had been somebody else's chocolate, and that the chocolate I was making now was my own. While this was difficult for me, I had to stay true to this new-found calling.

The bean to bar movement promotes the shift to direct and more transparent relationships with growers, while improving trade relationships and the lives of communities through a more equitable sharing of profits. Going to plantations raises one's awareness about a range of societal issues, from lower than normal wages, to child labor. As an artisan, when I find a plantation which offers beans I want to work with, my goal is to sustain that cocoa plantation, which in turn enables me to practice my art form. As such, it is my duty, and social responsibility, to ensure our trade is ethical. While globalization has many downsides, the positive aspect of it is that we can reach plantations anywhere in the world. This has enabled us to access extraordinary beans. On average, a ton of beans is paid between USD 2,500 and 3,000. However, in order to make a decent living, the grower needs a minimum of EUR 3,500, but they only receive half of the market value of their produce. Through the bean to bar movement, a ton of beans is worth between USD 3,000 and 10,000, and sometimes even up to 14,000 for exceptional beans.

The traditional representation of the chocolate confectioner is a man in his workshop, surrounded by chocolate, working day and night, alone. Today we strive to show a more positive and modern aspect of artisanship, slightly more "connected." By traveling, I was able to take a step back from the operational aspects of the job, which helped me re-connect with the produce, the trade, others, and therefore with my creativity. The primary driving force behind acts of creation is human connection, learning to give oneself to others, but also to trust others. When you launch a business, you do a bit of everything, but this can distract you from what made you set up the business in the first place. One of the first things I did was to create a team. I surrounded myself with artisans and professionals from different branches, all of which perform their duties with much more talent than I ever could. This enabled me to focus exclusively on my creations. My team enables me to be the chocolatier I want to be. Creativity comes from a place of serenity and peace, and moments when you are disconnected from everything in order to reconnect with your creativity.

FROM A LOCAL NAME TO AN INTERNATIONAL BRAND

Transformation has been the leitmotiv of this journey. There was the transformation of the man, of the product, of my approach and focus, but let us not forget the transformation of the company. We started off as a 30 meter square boutique, and through intuitive marketing, we started to grow. As the company grew, we were able to attract talented individuals, and experts from around the world expressed an interest in collaborating with us. They contributed to our becoming international and to our growth from a "Maison" to a brand.

From the outset, I decided to work for pleasure. One year early on, we had had a great Christmas and made 25% of the yearly turnover. I was the creative mind of the business, I did not manage the financials, nor was I interested in that aspect of my business. My banker called me in, and I thought it was to know how I wanted to manage all this money. And to my great surprise, they told me that if we continued on the same path, I would be facing a cash drain in six months' time. I, naively, asked him whether that was a good or a bad thing. This was a terrible wake up call for me. I had poured my heart and soul into this business, but I realized that while making good chocolate was satisfying, it was not good enough from society's viewpoint. I realized that I wasn't adequately equipped to achieve my ambitions. And so, I joined a business school to learn how things should be done, and simply understand the universe I was to survive in. I came to understand that the added-value I could bring was very specific. As the company grew, we were able to attract talented individuals, which

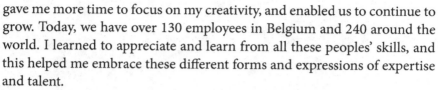

gave me more time to focus on my creativity, and enabled us to continue to grow. Today, we have over 130 employees in Belgium and 240 around the world. I learned to appreciate and learn from all these peoples' skills, and this helped me embrace these different forms and expressions of expertise and talent.

When your business starts growing to the point where you have 30 stores, and you are at the head of an eponymous brand, you must be aware of your responsibilities as a leader. Over time, I realized that all the people surrounding me and sharing in this adventure all wish me well and are genuinely concerned for me. They regularly ask me how I am, if my health is on track. When you are the founder, the one breathing creativity and life into the project, your responsibility is to ensure the sustainability of your business, and you must make every possible effort to ensure that your company, and the people who work with you, can continue to thrive. Gaston Lenôtre understood this well. His name was renowned worldwide, and yet he managed to detach his creativity and pass it on to ensure that his vision and philosophy of patisserie survived. He has been dead for 49 years, and his soul is still here. He founded a school, and successfully shared his knowledge, and passed on his spirit. Following in his footsteps, I strive to model my creativity, so that it can serve as a source of inspiration. I try to ensure this creativity is repetitive, so that it can be reproduced, with or without me, and that this creativity, which is part of my own DNA, becomes the DNA of the company.

ART AND IDENTITY

20

Alan Chong

Museum Director
Asian Civilizations Museum

The theme of this series of lectures and sessions is "work to live and live to work." The museum industry often struggles with what a museum is. Is it part of society? Is it a tourist attraction? Is it a cultural enhancement? An 'extra' as opposed to an essential element of the social fabric? Until fairly recently, this was the case in Singapore. Culture and museums were viewed as neither being essential to the economic development nor as a potential financial drive that could develop the economies of South East Asia. It was only the enlightened approach of a few cabinet ministers, former servicemen in fact, who saw the role culture could play in enhancing society, not only in developing a notion of nation building and patriotism, but also as spurring creativity in society as a whole. These recent developments, both in Singapore and other South East Asian countries, have sparked a genuine questioning on the role of culture, the nature of creativity, and on what art can tell us about how we approach ideas of governance, innovation, science and business. I personally believe that all museums are political institutions. We all need to play a role in society as a whole. The role we are trying to accomplish at the Asian Civilizations Museum is to trigger a reflection on the artistic heritage of the Asian regions in order to foster an understanding of the diverse cultural heritages of Singapore, their connections with the world and their interconnections.

The museum is located in the colonial hub of Singapore in the historic Empress Place Building. This building dates back to the 1860s and was used for over 100 years to house colonial and later Singapore government offices. The location of the venue is both important and symbolic. It sits on the port of Singapore which we used as the starting point of our reflection on what we wanted to offer our visitors. In the very structure of the museum and our geographic location, we have tried to explore the history of Singapore. Positioned on the waterfront, we constructed a new building looking on to the river, thereby shifting the traditional alignment of the museum, facing the city, back to facing the river, the heart of Singapore's history. At night, it becomes a lively area where people can re-engage with the river, with bars, cafés, etc. It is a reminder that this particular part of Singapore is where commerce took place, where money was made, but also where people and ideas came in contact with one another.

The Asian Civilizations Museum is designed as a museum of heritage and cultures. It is meant to reflect the immigrant cultures of Singaporeans as a whole: Chinese, Indian and South East Asian. What is striking is that colonial Europeans were left out of this narrative. In many nations, the role of Europe in Asia was written out, except in the most negative ways, as an antagonist, a colonial force, as an imperialist power or a bringer of war. This is very problematic because Europeans have been in Asia ever since the 15th century. One of the key issues we try to explore in the museum is what exactly 'identity' is: a nation, an ethnicity, a religion, a language, or maybe even a combination of all these things?

We have tried to replicate this multiplicity in the museum, and tell these complex, contradictory or conflicted stories. In order to do so, we have looked at the heritage of being a port city. The British settlement in 1819 was built on what already existed in Jakarta. Stanford Raffles led a successful military invasion against the Dutch colony on the island of Java during the Napoleonic Wars. He spent 5 years in Jakarta, then known as Batavia, a port city set up by the Dutch, which instantly attracted immigrants from all over South East Asia, India and especially China. This influx of migrants created a dynamic economic community. Raffles wanted to replicate this in Singapore: he established a free port, made sure people were welcome and ensured they were not simply brought in as indentured labor. He encouraged free immigration, especially from China, to encouraged people to come and live and work in the city of Singapore.

We now know that Singapore's history as a port city started long before that. Archaeological evidence shows that during the 13th century, Indonesian and Thai kingdoms had set up port cities in what is now Singapore, and this history stretches all the way back to the Yuan dynasty; the British merely 'resettled' Singapore. Early Portuguese maps from the 16th century already show the name Singapore at the location of today's Singapore, even though at the time this probably only represented a population of no more than a few hundred people. Of course, trade brought people and made money, but what interests us, is that it brought people in contact with one another, which led to the exchange of ideas, and the emergence of new forms of creativity, new kinds of art which blended different cultures. It also led to people converting from one religion to another, and most importantly perhaps in our area, to intermarriage, thereby leading to the emergence of a multi-ethnic, or what I like to refer to as a hybrid, community.

We recently took charge of a very large shipwreck from Indonesia dating from the 9th century (Tang dynasty). This is the earliest major shipwreck ever found in Asia. It contained a colossal cargo of nearly 70,000 Chinese objects that were bound for South East Asia and the Persian Gulf. We thought this was an important starting point for the history of trade, because already in the 9th century, thousands and thousands of objects were being mass produced in China and shipped to the Near East and to South East Asia. This small, 16-meter, Arab ship sailed from the Near East to China, packed to the gills with some unknown cargo which it probably delivered somewhere in China, and then stocked up with Chinese objects before it sank on its way back. One cannot help but marvel at the fact that, already 1000 years ago, trade, mass production, and a currency of exchange were already at play.

China produced high-quality ceramics and porcelain for the world. It had access to technology and to clay which could not be equaled anywhere in the world. And so, it produced objects for the Near East and South East Asia and then later for Europe and the Americas. The cargo from this shipwreck is rather extraordinary. It contains some of the earliest blue and white porcelain ever made. For example, the cargo contained two porcelain dishes created in China in the 830s based on Iranian examples. The glaze, shade of the colors and design are typical Iranian features, which were copied in China to be sent back to Iran. This is a very interesting early example of the adaptation of one culture to the needs of another, the making of a product based on the specific, artistic needs of another culture in response to a given demand. One of the things we are trying to do is to emphasize how art informs commerce and trade. In order to produce a product, you need creativity on the one hand and to be responsive to the creative needs of another culture, your consumer, on the other. These items are particularly exceptional, and to date we have found no other specimens, and so they are very significant examples of the early trade between the Near East and South East Asia. This is all the more important to us in that we are trying, through our work, to delicately highlight the extent to which China has depended on the Islamic world for more than 1000 years for its prosperity and its well-being. In so doing, we are endeavoring to highlight the idea that that civilizations are opposed to each other because of religion or ethnic tensions is false. This is one of the important messages we must deliver especially in this particular moment in history.

Trade is not only about money; it is about art, ideas and cultural contact. Our galleries have been set up following this theme of identifying cultural contacts. Luckily, the government has given us the means to enter the art market to build a new collection, be it through gift, donation or the purchase objects which reflect this idea. For example, one of the other things of which we need to remind our visitors is that Buddhism has its roots not only in India, but also in the Near East. The idea of representing the Buddha or Bodhisattvas, enlightened individuals, actually comes not from Asia but the Near East, from Gandhara which represents Pakistan and present day Afghanistan. In fact, the representations of Buddha arise almost simultaneously in the Kushan Empire which ruled central India and Pakistan in the 1st and 2nd centuries. One example is the very large head of a Bodhisattva which shows not only the subject matter of being a Buddhist deity, but is heavily influenced by the classical world in the Mediterranean. Greco-Roman art played a very large part in the Near East, the Roman and Hellenistic Empires made their way to the Indian border and played a very important role in Ghandara, which is a major civilization from the 1st century BC to the 3rd century AD. This particular item is a prime example of this influence: the Bodhisattva continues to wear typical Indian jewelry, but the idea of a naturalistic sculpted face created in three dimensions in a highly realistic manner, is very much influenced by classical, i.e. the world of Greece and Rome. More representative of the Roman influence, we also have a cup which was probably made near Jerusalem in the first few decades of the Common Era. It presents a semi-erotic theme, as could be found in cups for drinking wine. It was made in the Eastern

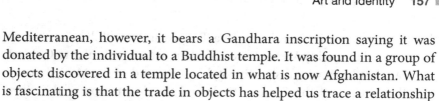

Mediterranean, however, it bears a Gandhara inscription saying it was donated by the individual to a Buddhist temple. It was found in a group of objects discovered in a temple located in what is now Afghanistan. What is fascinating is that the trade in objects has helped us trace a relationship between cultures and religions.

Our collection includes a beautiful pitcher representing a dancing woman. For decades, this kind of object was associated with Japan. There are many old Japanese collections which have similar examples. Very recently we discovered that the Mughal Emperor Jahangir, who ruled during in the 1600s over Northern India and Pakistan had an almost identical object. It is drawn in one of his manuscripts next to a passage from the Quran. What is fascinating is that this tells us that something which was always assumed to be native Asian was actually being collected by the Islamic ruler of India. This shows that, not only there was a sort of universality of demand, but also that people were interested in other cultures. They did not need things made specifically for them, in the image of what was traditional or known. Sometimes, they were delighted by an unusual form or pattern.

More familiar is the fact that certain Chinese courts and reigns were particularly open to outside influences. This is especially true in the Ming dynasty with Emperor Zhengde. He was particularly interested in Arabic and Muslim culture and in Islam in general. One of the great explorers of the Ming dynasty, Zheng He, was in fact Muslim himself; so, we have found objects which express this interest for both cultures. For example, we have a typically Chinese blue and white porcelain paintbrush rest shaped as a mountain, which has an inscription in Arabic. The integration of Islamic forms and inscriptions as a trend grew throughout South East Asia. It is found especially in South East Asia, as the great sultanates were Islamized from the 14th century onwards, if not even earlier.

The ups and downs of trade over time are immediately traceable through art, as one producing nation declines and removes itself from the market or experiences political crises. As they fail to produce objects, the market picks up in other areas. China, as an art producer and exporter, had competition from other parts of the world, namely India and Vietnam. During the early Ming dynasty, when Chinese porcelain was not exported as a result of a political crisis, the kilns in Vietnam began to produce high-quality stoneware for export around the world. We have found shipwrecks and excavation sites in Java, Borneo and the Philippines, which show very high-quality Vietnamese porcelain, which is similar to Chinese porcelain but has a very distinctive style. At the end of the Ming dynasty, with the collapse of the Chinese trade and the destruction of the kilns, areas of Japan instantly started to produce porcelain to meet the demand coming from the European market. In showing this, our gallery tries to hint at the fact that the cycle of trade, innovation and competition as we know it today is nothing new, and that these global forces are in no way unique to our age.

The second major thrust in the hybridity of the region is religion. It played an important role in shaping the region, and Singapore in particular. Most famously, Buddhism spread from India to China, Japan, and South East Asia, south to Sri Lanka and west to what is now Pakistan. Buddhism moved forward and contracted. It migrated into the Himalayas and Tibet; in Pakistan it was replaced by Islam and in India by Hinduism. In addition to these religions, we must also talk about Confucianism, Taoism, and the spread of Christianity and Islam. We must re-embrace important factors. Christianity plays a major role in Asia, not only in Manila and Korea, but also here in Singapore.

The story of Christianity is something we have focused on recently and have begun to highlight, because it offers great opportunities to display things which are unfamiliar to the public, to show how Christian objects were created in China, Ceylon and India, in exquisite and very interesting ways. For example, our exhibition features an ivory sculpture of a Madonna and child made in Ceylon in the early 16th century, possibly for the Portuguese market. In keeping with the traditional nativity imagery, she is standing on a crescent moon. However, her robes are particularly detailed and drape in the way a Buddhist monk's robe would be represented. Very interestingly, she has three folds on the side of her neck, which in Buddhist symbolism represents the sign of holiness. It is very interesting to see how the carver has used such Buddhist elements to characterize a Christian Madonna.

One of the most extravagant and beautiful forms we have in the museum is a shrine which is a composite of different elements, combining different aesthetic traditions. The basic form is a writing desk, the top section has been turned into a Christian shrine with Christ on the cross, surrounded by two wood-carved saints, all decorated in Chinese lacquer. The panels of the shrine are decorated in typical Chinese lacquer. It is a wonderful mixture of cultures: its traditional British form is complemented by Chinese decorations, probably made in Macau or Canton in the 18th century. The figure of the Christ was carved in ivory, probably from Goa in Western India. It was brought from Goa to Macau through Portuguese trade lines. This object is representative of the wonderful combination of cultures that could be seen at the time. People put elements from different traditions together to create an interesting and aesthetically pleasing whole.

Finally, the mixed community of Singapore and related towns like Malacca and Penang created their own forms of porcelain and decorative arts. The Peranakan generally indicate a Chinese-Malay hybrid community, who maintain connections in dress, food, language and religion with both communities, even though they identify very strongly with the overseas Chinese community. This led to the emergence of unique forms of porcelain, or batik produced for Chinese religious practices. We have fascinating examples of Indian or native Malay batik makers making Chinese religious objects for local Peranakan communities and their altars.

Later in the 20th century, we have strongly cross-cultural individuals who point the way to the modern world. In the museum, we reflect this reality through the portrait of a particular individual, Oei Hui-lan, who married the famous Chinese diplomat Wellington Koo. She spent most of her life swanning around the world in different cultural centers, Paris, Milan, London, and at the end of her life, in New York and Singapore. We analyzed her life, the languages she spoke and the identity she had, and it was very interesting. She grew up as a mixed Malay-Chinese girl in Sumatra. She spoke Malay at home with her family, she claims to have spoken Cantonese to her Chinese staff and servants. She went to school in the Dutch Indies in Sumatra, where she learnt Dutch which was the language of commerce and business, and learned her own native language, Teochew, from her father. So she had different identities as a child. She married a Chinese diplomat while he was Ambassador to France. She later moved to Beijing, but was ridiculed by local society because she could not speak Chinese correctly, so she spoke English or French to put them in their place. Later in life, she moved back to Singapore and took up Singaporean citizenship again, and at the end of her life she settled in New York, and became an American citizen.

In a sense, she is a typical modern person, who has so many identities, languages and roots that her identity cannot really be defined in any clear or tangible way, and I think this is part of what it is to be modern, to be part of a port city, of a community where you come in contact with and are influenced by people and ideas from all over the world. In the end, although we are a Singaporean museum and we try to tell the history of Asia in various ways, what we are trying to express is that Asia's identity is a fluctuating one, and that Asia exists only because of its relationship with the rest of the world. Islam has played a role for thousands of years, not only through the Islamic identity, but also through the wealth of East Asia, and today, still continues to play a role in the wealth of Singapore. It is these shifting patterns of religion and trade that we are trying to embrace and highlight in the new museum.

TO LEAD ONE'S LIFE, AN ACT OF CREATION

21

Eric Michel

Light Artist

Eric Michel was born in Aix-en-Provence in 1962. He studied art and music from an early age following the Martenot method. Initially trained in classical music, he then moved on to rock and underground music, and came back to painting and sculpture towards the end of the 1980s. After completing scientific studies, he first turned to the world of finance, while maintaining his artistic activities.

Eric gave a significant Eric Michel number of exhibitions in Japan, where he lived until 2002 while working as head of an American bank. In December 2003, his work was presented at the Kawasaki International Biennale Contemporary Art Exhibition. When back in France, he was selected to exhibit his work at the Salon de Montrouge in 2004 and in 2005. In 2006, his work was exhibited in London, New York, Miami, and he took part in the Nuit Blanche in Paris with a multimedia installation called "Nuit Fluo" [fluorescent night]. In 2007, his video "Swimming Fluo" was presented at the Shanghai Museum of Contemporary Art, and subsequently in most of the modern art museums in China for the "Sport in Art" exhibition, sponsored by the Beijing Olympic Committee in 2008. In 2009, at the invitation of Daniel Moquay, Eric took over the Yves Klein Archives for a multimedia installation entitled: "Lumière et Immatériel" [light and the immaterial] along with a performance around a sound-piece by Yves Klein. The same year, his installation "Passages de Lumière" [Light route] was showcased at the Nice Museum of Contemporary Art (MAMAC). His monumental light installation "Les Moulins de Lumière" [Light Mills] for the Grands Moulin de Pantin (near Paris) was inaugurated in March 2011.

In 2013, his exhibition "Passeur de Lumière" [Light Boatman] offered a dialog between the architecture of Le Corbusier and Xenakis at the La Tourette convent.

Eric currently lives in Paris. His work on light, especially in his paintings which are saturated with pure pigments, his videos and fluorescent installations, follows the traditions of the quest for the immaterial, following the lead of Yves Klein, James Turrell and Dan Flavin.

Many determining events in my life, events which shaped the path I was to take, happened when I was your age, when I was a student. It is not just for the sake of reminiscing that I will talk about certain elements of my experience, but rather to share with you some moments that might enlighten the decisions you make, today and in the future.

A CHILDHOOD OF ART

I received artistic training from a very young age. When I was nine, I was enrolled in a school which followed the Martenot method, offering an education based on art and music. As a teenager, I had to choose one of these fields, and when I was 14, I chose music. From that point on, I felt that art was an integral part of my life. However, because I was a good student, I followed a traditional curriculum, and did a Scientific Baccalauréat in 1980. I won the *Prix de l'Education*, awarded to the best pupil of the entire *académie*, and was awarded a 3,000 francs scholarship, which gave me the opportunity to travel to the United States. I discovered the Museum of Modern Art in New York as well as the great names of contemporary art — what a shock! The three pillars that were to be the foundations of my life became clear to me: maths, art and international outreach. I wanted to open myself to the world, in the broadest sense possible: I wanted to become an astronaut. I was forced to give up on this dream because my eyesight was not sharp enough, so I turned to the earthly world instead, and chose to spend my time traveling to explore the widest possible playing field.

When I started the scientific *classe préparatoire* in Paris, at Louis le Grand, I had the opportunity to meet students from khâgne and hypokhâgne and to forge friendships with philosophers. This opened me up to social sciences and gave a certain depth to my reflections.

Without a specific goal in mind at that time, I became aware of what a project, a destiny, a life could be. I sensed that the simple fact of living a certain lifestyle could be an act of creation, unceasingly renewed creation. I felt I could have an effect on the circumstances of my life, but also that exogenous events (accidents, opportunities, threats) would affect this trajectory every 4–5 years. I also needed to define what I wanted from life, and to be flexible enough to absorb shocks, and maybe even to turn threats into opportunities.

I followed both a scientific education (by entering the École nationale de la Statistique et de l'Administration Économique, [ENSAE]) and an artistic one (by doing music), all in an international environment. At ENSAE, I founded a photo club, got the school to rent a piano for students, and created a rock band which won ESSEC's Tremplin rock competition (one of the band was a student here). This led to a recording deal with the studio where Indochine had made all their albums. This convinced me that art was my life. I thought I was probably destined to become a musician, although I was also very interested in video. Through my studies at ENSAE, I did an internship in Chicago. This is where I first discovered the world of finance, options in particular, in which I specialized. I also had the opportunity to travel to Japan for a study trip, where I worked with the Ministry of Finance on the economy of Japanese households. Since then, I have never severed my ties with Japan.

Military service, mandatory at that time, was a pivotal and decisive moment. I decided to perform my service under a cooperation agreement with a French company in Japan. I had to leave a couple of weeks before our band was scheduled to perform at one of the capital's big venues: La Locomotive. Our drummer was in a similar situation, and so the band had to be dissolved. In Tokyo, I turned back to visual arts. The initial shock, namely the death of my rock band, in fact allowed me to discover new horizons.

GETTING READY FOR THE BIG LEAP

Back in France, I joined State Street, the pension funds management leader. Progressively, I became one of the world experts in overall asset allocation. In parallel, I continued my work as an artist. In 1998, I went back to Japan, as President of the Group's subsidiary.

A new intuition about my life started growing in me: earning my living by working offered me a form of freedom, and would ultimately give me the opportunity to take the great leap and live as an artist.

I suffered another blow: my son was diagnosed with cancer at the age of eight, and practically at the same time, the twin towers collapsed. These were catalysts: my term as President was coming to an end, my son was getting treated in France, so in 2003 I decided to leave the world of finance and to pursue art. It was at this same moment that I was invited to the Kawasaki modern art biannual, which I interpreted as a sign. This was because in 2000, I had won a competition to present my work in a collective exhibition at the Big Dome in Tokyo, with the possibility of being selected for another two-week exhibition in the Japanese gallery. This was the first time that I had ever exhibited my work to the public.

The only time I deviated from this new-found career, I worked as a consultant for 5 years with Axa to guide it in its development in Japan. So I did not fully turn my back on the corporate world, and this experience helped me grow as an artist.

When I entered the world of modern art, I wanted to understand it, and do a "market analysis" of it. I had a body of multimedia creations, but they were rather disparate. It was difficult to understand its guiding thread. I studied the landscape of galleries, possible partners, and established ties with galleries in the United States, England and in France. Orders started flowing in: a video for the Beijing Olympics, a piece for the *Nuit Blanche* in 2006. From 2007 to 2009, I lived in Rome, because my wife's professional career took us there. This stay helped me take a step back and understand the core of my work.

CULTIVATING AN ABILITY FOR DUALITY

I am sometimes asked how I came to work with light. It was not a sudden decision, but the result of a sequence of events that marked my life, of which I was not always fully aware at the time. In Tokyo for example, I covered the pale neon light that lit my first room with a piece of colored paper — my first subconscious light installation. In the Tokyo Big Dome exhibition, I presented fluorescent plaques with black light, which became one of my trademarks — in fact, I even patented it. So, light was already part of my work. In Rome, I had time to put things into perspective and wrote the following text, describing my relationship with this medium.

"The ferryman"

"I love light. It is the privileged vehicle of my sensitivity, of my work. It flows through the rivers of our lives. It irradiates our universe. It opens doors. Light is unique in that it is simultaneously corpuscular and undulatory, material and immaterial. I believe an artist needs to be a ferryman, between the material and the immaterial, from the real to the imaginary, towards pure sensitivity. What more natural then for such a commitment than choosing light as a vector of one's proposals? Light as a medium, but why not an end in itself? Did I really chose light? Did it not impose itself on me? Light speaks. I hear it. Sometimes."

When asked about what constitutes the act of creation, Francis Bacon explained that it was an ability for duality. Artists act, work, paint, and at the same time, are capable of observing their work to judge whether the end result is acceptable. Artists know when their work is finished.

Similarly, in life, one must combine the ability to drive our short-term, daily lives, while also stepping back to judge whether we are going in the right direction — but in order to do this, we must have decided on a direction in the first place.

Understanding this and formulating it was a genuine liberation for me. I started working on a larger scale; here are some examples.

Vivre la lumière
Intervenant: Eric Michel, artiste lumière

The light installation *"Les Moulins de Lumière"* [light mills] for the Pantin Mills (near Paris) was inaugurated in March 2011.

 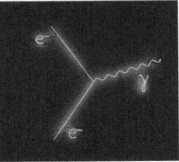

The installation *La lumière parle* [light speaks] was presented at La Maison Rouge in Paris, and was what gave the first *Néon* exhibition show-room its name. Above and beyond the light-language, this affirmation has a performative character: at the same time that you read the sentence "light speaks", light actually speaks to you. The scientific version of this sentence, a Feynman diagram, represents an electron emitting a gamma photon in space and time. This is precisely what happens with neon light: because of the high-energy excitation, plasma reaches a certain threshold and emits light. These are two layers of interpretation of light and its perception.

This monochrome of light is made up of a fluorescent paint activated by black light.

Biblioteca fluo, a work in tribute to Umberto Eco. It was created for the 50th anniversary of the Treaty of Rome.

This installation was presented in Rome. It was surprising to see that adults stayed outside the trapezium of light that was drawn on the ground, whereas children stepped right into it and played with the projected images. We should always strive to preserve this ability that children have to wonder, their ability to step right into things, without any pre-conceived limitations.

Lumière et immatériel [Light and the Immaterial] was exhibited in the Yves Klein archives.

   This installation was exhibited at the Nice Museum of Modern Art as part of the *La couleur en avant* exhibition in which artists were invited to retrace the history of the use of color from Matisse, the after-war period, to nowadays. This piece is first and foremost a neon perspective, but this luminous vanishing point becomes a horizon as you go further into the exhibition room. As in life, your perception of a given reality changes as you distance yourself from it. I would like to encourage you to live in the moment, while also being able to maintain critical distance, to see the bigger picture.

This installation was presented in the context of an exhibition titled *Quid sit lumen*. It offers a reflection on our relationship to light. On the floor, fluorescent tubes embody the soul of the watchmen. They are connected to old switches, the remnants of an old dormitory. Natural light, with a pink filter, comes to meet the inner light of these souls. This is a reminder of the light in which we are constantly bathed although we do not always see it.

This exhibit in the Couvent de la Tourette engaged in dialog with the architecture of Le Corbusier. There were two light installations in the atrium which interacted and generated interaction on the oratory which was just opposite.

This work was commissioned by the *Archives Klein* and the Luxembourg Philharmonic to stage and light Yves Klein's *Monotone Symphony*. This musical performance consists of two long moments of silence which frame a single chord held by choir and orchestra. The building was bathed in Yves Klein's favorite blue, and in the concert hall, variations of the blue monochrome coincided with the choir's lip movements. Light was the link between sound and silence, between full and empty, with this constant duality characterizing the artistic approach on which much of my work is constructed.

Vivre la lumière

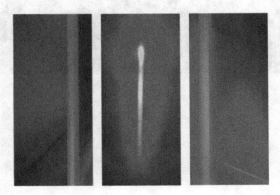

This triptych was installed on the ESSEC campus at the beginning of 2015. It is made up of light moments, i.e. "raw" fragments of photos I have taken at different points in life. People find it difficult to believe that I have not edited them, but I have not! This experiment is an invitation to re-learn how to see, and more specifically, how to see light.

I can think of no better way to end than with a quote from Yves Klein, who, answering the question "what is art?" answered: "Art is life!"

DISCUSSION

How do you Constantly Renew Yourself, Continue to Live and Bring Life to Your Work?

The key question here is freedom. You must always ensure you are in the greatest state of liberty. I invite you to remember Malevitch's essay, *Laziness: The Real Truth of Mankind*, in which the artist invites us to free ourselves from work and to win the freedom of doing only what you want to do, in this case, the act of creation to which each of us aspires. During the earlier part of my life, I acquired "shares of idleness" that later enabled me to experience true freedom. The true challenge is knowing what to do with this freedom. The day I reached a state of being free to do exactly as I wanted, I did not feel the anguish of writer's block. Quite the contrary: I filled 10 pages with what I wanted to do! Of course, time brings with it its own share of doubts and questions. To keep your source of creativity alive, it is essential to preserve your freedom. If you fall into the trap of seeking recognition, of doing what people expect from you, renewal is impossible. I know that external shocks might cross my path, and I may not be able to continue doing what I am doing today for the rest of my life. With advancing years, I want to share more and more, and give more and more conferences and master classes. This is the reason I wanted to become an artist as early in life as possible: after doing a job that let me put enough money aside, I was still young enough and had a lot to say. The day I no longer find freedom in my artistic endeavors, I will probably start something new.

CONVERSATION WITH AN INSPIRED, COMMITTED AND FREE MAN

Michael Lonsdale

Actor

THE COMING INTO BEING OF A COMEDIAN

Xavier Pavie (X.P.)

This year, iMagination Week focuses on the topics of imagination and transdisciplinarity. In your line of work, imagination is a determining factor. For those who do have imagination, do you think this is linked to a particular talent? Is it something one can work on?

Michael Lonsdale (M.L.)

No, it is not something that can be worked on. A child who starts playing the piano or the violin, or has a beautiful voice at a very early age, is talented. It is a privilege. For others, talent can manifest itself later in life. I regard it is a gift — I might even say a gift from God.

X.P.

Do you think that, as an actor, you received a gift from God?

M.L.

I felt the need to become an actor, in a very compelling way, probably because my life has been a strange story. I came into the world illegally in the eyes of society, because I was born out of wedlock and my parents never reported my birth. So, I was hidden away for the first years of my life, especially given that my grandfather was also an illegitimate child. In my family, this was the pattern across five generations! My mother did not want to show me to her father. However, children notice and pick up on everything that unfolds around them. I feel that, subconsciously, because they all wanted to hide me away, I wanted to prove to the world that I existed. I felt the need to be recognized and accepted. Today, I am happy to be my illegitimate self. I got over it, I no longer carry the weight they laid on my shoulders when I was nothing but a baby.

X.P.

Does this mean that each of the parts you have played was a rebirth of sorts?

M.L.

Yes. I felt an overriding need to perform. As a child, playing was the only thing I was good at. I did very badly at school.

In 1939, we moved to Morocco, where my father, who was English, had found a job. Initially it was only going to be for six months, but we got trapped by the war and ended up staying 10 years. It was a very turbulent period. I went from school to school, my grades in mathematics were terrible. If a teacher asked me *"how much is two plus two"*, I would think long and hard about it, and answer *"22."* I was much better at telling stories or writing essays. But there were so many spelling mistakes in them, that my teacher invariably wrote "what a shame" in the margin. I was just not made for school. One day, reciting *"rosa,* rose", that was it. Latin was the last straw.

Being the son of an Englishman in Morocco during the war put me in a bit of an awkward position. Children from Vichy-sympathizing families tried to bully me. Fortunately, I found "body guards" my own age, because I despise fighting and violence.

I felt the desire to perform after the first time I went to the cinema. It was in London, where I lived until the age of ten. Someone took me to the museum of scientific inventions, where they were showing Charlie Chaplin films. That was the first time I saw images projected onto a screen.

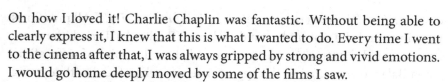

Oh how I loved it! Charlie Chaplin was fantastic. Without being able to clearly express it, I knew that this is what I wanted to do. Every time I went to the cinema after that, I was always gripped by strong and vivid emotions. I would go home deeply moved by some of the films I saw.

This need gently made its way in my mind, until one day in 1944 when, in Morocco, a rabbi invited me to take part in a TV show for children which required singing and acting. My very first part was Sneezy in *Snow White and the Seven Dwarfs* — so my career started with a sneeze! After that, it was Andersen's *Little Mermaid*. Every time, playing a part gave me so much pleasure — it was work that was play. This need for performing grew within me, becoming increasingly prominent over time. However, there was no arts school in Morocco, and no drama classes at all for that matter. I had to wait until I came back to France, in 1949, to get a chance to learn the profession.

At the beginning, I was so shy and self-conscious that I could not muster up the courage to enroll in an acting class. I could not summon up the courage to go to a workshop even though I had taken up painting. I developed a great passion for color and the great masters: Rembrandt, Matisse, and above all Chagall.

One day, an article caught my attention: *"Are you made for acting?."* I took the bait. After a two- or three-day trial, I was told that, indeed, I did have it in me, but that it was going to take a lot of hard work: I was too withdrawn and had to find a way to express my feelings. In any event, that first course turned out to be a farce.

"I IS ANOTHER"

At the same time, my conversion to Christianity was developing. Following the advice of the chaplain to artists, I enrolled in the class of Madame Balachova, emeritus professor and *grande dame* of theatre. With her I took a great leap forward. Her class was wonderful! I got to work with Delphine Seyrig, Laurent Terzieff, Jean-Louis Trintignant: all pupils who would later become leading figures in acting. One day, Tania Balachova told me that she wanted to see me get angry, and to perform something other than characters from Feydeau or Tchekhov. So, there I was, preparing the first scene of Moliere's *The Misanthrope*, in which Alceste is fuming with rage after Célimène has turned him down. I was doing my best to interpret irritation and aggravation, but the result was not convincing. Tania Balachova kept on telling me *"He is angrier than that, he is infuriated. Try!."* All my efforts were in vain: I did not understand violence. The harder I tried, the more I sweated and the stronger my heart pounded, to the point of suffocation. Tania Balachova reacted in the appropriate way when faced with a young man like myself. She told me: *"If you cannot prove to me that you know how to be violent, I will not be able to keep you, there is no point"*, in front of the entire class. You can imagine my embarrassment. In my final attempt, I yelled, waved a chair around, and ultimately finished by throwing it to the ground. It ended up in pieces. *See how good you can be when you put your mind to it! But you owe me a chair.* She had understood that the only way to get through to me was to threaten me. She was not going to get anything out of me through kindness. Yet, I despised violence. I hope you, too, can find professors who, every now and again, push you hard. Some people need to be challenged before they can reach their full potential.

Tania Balachova' teaching was extraordinary. When she opened an improv class, I could literally feel my wings spreading, I started to fly. I had the good fortune to get auditions and was hired by a great stage director. At first, I had terrible stage fright. My heart was pounding, my knees were shaking, I was in a state of panic. This faded over time, and gradually gave way to the immense privilege of becoming "another." This was certainly something I needed. Rimbaud wrote *"I is another"*… I went from project to project with wonderful artists, each more fascinating than the next, from Orson Welles to Steven Spielberg, Fred Zinnemann or in all of the plays of Laurent Terzieff. I have had the privilege of working continuously for nearly 70 years.

X.P.

You have performed in hundreds of movies and plays. How do you explain this compulsive need to always be "another"?

M.L.

It is a liberation. I was baptized when I was 22, by a wonderful Dominican who was my spiritual father until the day he died. One day he told me that I would *confide in my audience much more than I ever would anybody else,* and he was right. In Marguerite Duras' *Indiana Song* which I recorded for the radio, I had to shout and cry my love for a woman, Annamaria Guardi, for two full hours. In the work of Marguerite Duras, love is madness. She was mad about love, and nothing else mattered to her other than writing. This role liberated me. I got to let go of something which had been troubling me for a long time, a lost love. I freed myself from it, and it was very cathartic.

A Student

Are there any personality traits which you particularly admired among the characters you have played?

M.L.

I took great pleasure in performing in *L'Échange* by Paul Claudel. I played a magnificent character, an elderly American man who falls in love with a young French woman. It is one of the plays which I enjoyed most. I also had the privilege of working with a wonderful partner, Madeleine Renaud, in *L'Amante anglaise* by Marguerite Duras. She had an instinct for theater, and an unerring talent for always conveying the right intention thanks to which she always performed very passionately. We produced it in 1968, and played it for several years, until she died. It was magical. That is what happiness feels like!

A Student

You worked with Steven Spielberg. Was that experience different from working with other directors?

M.L.

I have worked with a number of great American directors, starting with Orson Welles in *The Trial*. He had a genius for the grandiose — and he was a precocious genius: when he was only 5 years old, he put on Shakespeare plays for his puppets! He was only 25 when he filmed his masterpiece *Citizen Kane*. Later, I worked with the great Fred Zinnemann for *The Day of the Jackal*. Then came Steven Spielberg — working with him was pure pleasure — later, there was Joseph Losey. These artists had such an intelligence for cinema, their interpretations were so accurate and they encouraged you to give your best.

A Student

Was it always self-evident to you that you were made for acting? Did you ever have to put this passion aside to follow a more rational, comfortable path?

M.L.

It was clear to me that I would never find anything that satisfied me more. I did consider joining a religious order for a while, but that would not have been possible materially: I had a family I had to take care of. I could not live my life and abandon my loved ones when they had nothing. Moreover, this vocation was not pressing enough for me to dedicate my life to it. But my life was and still is filled with wonderful relationships with ecclesiastics, whom I admire and are role models for me, such as Guy Gilbert or Jean Vanier.

INVENTING PARADISES

A Student

Six years ago, your paintings were featured in an exhibition in Paris alongside the work of Jean Revol. Is painting a refuge for your own, personal creativity? Does painting fuel your acting and vice versa?

M.L.

I have always been very sensitive to color. I was absolutely fascinated when I visited museums in London or in Paris: Bonnard, Monet. It was magical to me. I felt an irrepressible urge to do the same thing. I started to draw a little, without ever daring to go to a class. One of my aunts, who was an artist, explained to me how to paint. I painted, painted and painted, tirelessly, for 30 or 40 years, always driven by a desire to create an imaginary paradise populated with countless flowers. In the 1950s, when I lived in the south of France, I went snorkeling to explore the seabed and what

I saw left a deep imprint on me. There was such an abundance of algae and plants. I needed all of this because for me, matter is sacred. When I see a Rembrandt, a Titian or a Caravaggio, I always admire the care with which they dealt with matter, and how in their paintings, they managed to bring a small, inert piece of matter to life. These paintings emerged from caresses filled with love, precision, delicacy, and sometimes violence also, as is the case in some of the works of Caravaggio. It is both terrible and magnificent.

Over the past years, I have been too busy with my acting to paint, but painting is the breath of fresh air in which I can invent paradises, be they lost or imaginary.

PUTTING INSPIRATION IN THE LIMELIGHT

X.P.

You mentioned your religious conversion. Do you see a parallel between this conversion and the conversion entailed by each new character you play?

M.L.

Yes. The need to believe came on very early, quietly, discreetly and gradually. When I was 8 or 9 years old, before I even knew how to speak French, somebody gave a book called *The Life of Jesus*. As I read this book, I felt touched by this man, and got a first glimpse of the intense pleasure and sympathy I could feel for and through him. When I moved to France in 1949, I tried to look for somebody who could explain to me what Christ was. I met several Dominican priests and a wonderful godmother, who fell from the sky. I was baptized in an atmosphere of intense and incredible joy. It felt like a dream. I felt illuminated by what the Christ was offering: love, love above all else, and nothing but love. I did not feel this was incompatible with my acting. As the Dominican priest told me, *in life, you will have to play many roles, so you may as well be outstanding at it.* If I was going to perform, I was going to excel. This love that was shown to me was to be a source of fulfilment and openness, rather than a haunting complaint or longing which haunted me and pulls you down.

A Student

Have you ever turned down a role because of your religious beliefs?

M.L.

Yes, of course. I turned down uninteresting, negative, pitiful roles depicting monstrous characters. I did not want to play a part in that. However, I have played unlikeable characters, because it is important to be able to play the entire range of human emotions.

A Student

Is drama a vehicle for expressing your faith?

M.L.

I have produced some plays based on religious texts. The first was *The Way of a Pilgrim*, the story of a peasant who had lost everything, and who, one day, walks into a church and hears that he must "pray without ceasing." He searches at great length to understand the meaning of these words, until a monk explains the meaning of continuous prayer (*Lord Jesus Christ, have mercy on me*) which is recited uninterruptedly. I also produced a play on Saint Francis of Assisi, an inspirational man who fully embraced the way of poverty and surrendered to what is most beautiful in Christ. After that it was Thérèse of Lisieux, with whom I have always felt a very strong spiritual bond. What could this young girl, who died at the very young age of 24, have known about life? Everything! She was gifted, gifted with grace, full of grace. I directed another show on Madeleine Delbrel, a woman who deserves to be better known. I wanted to shine a light on these people and tell everybody what they had understood and achieved.

I also think of Sœur Emmanuelle, whom I knew personally. This woman is a wonderful life model. When she was 62, she collected millions to save this horrible slum in Cairo, where children ate among filth. She nearly fainted the first time she went there, and then decided to take action. She built a hospital and schools, taught women to work and saved the lives of millions of people. She was transported by fearlessness and freedom to act.

Let me tell you an anecdote which perfectly illustrates this. One day, Robert Hossein invited her to a very nice restaurant on the Champs-Élysées. She stood up, and went from table to table, introduced herself and said, "I am here to ask you for money" — because she never minced her words! She left with 2,000 euros. She could do anything. She was truly inspired! Not to mention Mother Teresa, an example of complete dedication to Christ. There is no greater love than giving one's life for those you love.

BE GENEROUS!

X.P.

These examples illustrate people who gave themselves to society. One of the topics of our week is the role each of us can play in society. What is your role, as an actor?

M.L.

My role is to bear witness to the beauty of texts. It is a beautiful experience to read in places where people need it most, and rejoice in our being there: hospitals, retirement homes, etc. There is a long journey one must undertake in order to help the poor or those who are struggling, and offer some kind of relief.

X.P.

What would be your message to the students who are gathered here today to help them develop their imagination, and imagine the policies and politics of society? Would your message be one of optimism? Or would it be pessimistic? What would your message to our youth be, the youth who will build the society of tomorrow?

M.L.

I think that we are currently at the beginning of the end of civilization. The African world could oust us, even if only in terms of their population. I feel the messages we hear today lack clarity and are particularly unsettling. In politics, for example, I cannot seem to understand the language used by those in power.

X.P.

We can assume that those who are in power today are not those who will build the society of the future. What would your message be for those who will build the future?

M.L.

To those of you who have a heart — and I dare think you each have one — I would like to remind you that each and every human being is a unique treasure which must be cherished. Never forget this. We are all the children of God. If you have any interest in others or feel called to a spiritual journey, you must try to live according to the precepts of Christ: the way, the truth and the life. His life program is the most beautiful I have ever known. I studied Buddhism, I studied Islam, but I am resolutely Catholic and Christian. I was born on Pentecost, my little gift from life! Follow the Holy Spirit, pray to the Spirit constantly. Hope. Think only of doing what is good. Many young people and future workers aspire to being rich, to do as they please, and to manipulate. This is not the right path. Give the money you earn to those who need it. Be generous.

23

GIVING ONE'S LIFE A MEANING AND BECOMING ONE'S SELF

Nicolas Huchet

Founder of Bionicohand

CHAPTER 1: WHAT?

The first chapter of the book of my life would be titled "What?": what should I do with my life?

When I was a kid, I really did not know what I wanted to be; and when I was a teenager, I didn't even want to think about it. When somebody asked what I wanted to do, what I really wanted to say was "be a musician!" But why bother, since I knew what they were going to say: "music isn't a real job..." So at the end of secondary school, I was given a choice between following a general education by going to high school, or a technical education.

And so, I opted for a technological school, and it was a disaster! I was surrounded by people like myself: young people who did not know what to do with their life and only wanted to have a good time ... After graduating, I joined *Les compagnons du devoir*, a large community of nomad craftsmen and artisans, the hobos of our times, in a way! Joining this community is an opportunity for young people to learn a trade while experiencing community life. As an apprentice, you get the opportunity to practice your trade while learning different techniques from highly-skilled and competent people first from all around France, through the *Tour de France,* and then from around Europe through the *Tour de l'Europe*. It was a truly wonderful experience for me.

One day, I had an accident at work, and I lost my left hand. It was the end of my world for me. I was 18, full of dreams, and what was supposed to be the best time of my life became the worst. My hand was amputated, and so were my dreams.

CHAPTER 2: WHY?

And so began the second chapter of my life, which I would title: "Why?" Why did this happen to me? What had I ever done to deserve this?

My self-esteem was so low I wanted to die. I wanted to jump out the window of my hospital room, but when I realized my room was on the first floor, I had to come up with a new plan! So I took a notepad, and made a list of my dreams. Of course, one of them was to play music, another was to travel around the world. At that point, I decided that since I was going to stay on earth, then I had to do something with my life. A "normal" life, a 9-to-5 job, driving to work every day, was clearly not for me! If that was the only option then I would rather have gone up to the fourth floor to jump from there!

I decided to study mechanical engineering. After graduating, I returned to the *Compagnons du devoir* for 2 years. At that point, I was 22. I took all my savings and moved to Ireland to study English. I picked up odd jobs, but couldn't really hold anything down because my English was far from perfect. During my time in Ireland, I did not only discover Ireland, I discovered Europe. I was studying with people from all over Europe; and we all had one thing in common: we all wanted to discover other cultures, but most importantly, we all wanted to move forward. I felt I was witnessing Europe in the making. This helped me understand that the point of life is to be together and come together around our differences.

I was looking for yet another job, and one day I came across a recording studio, where I saw a mixing desk. It occurred to me that since I could never be a musician, maybe I could do that instead! I worked there for a year, and eventually became a sound engineer. The more you focus on something, the more likely you are to actually achieve it. Good things happen through positive thinking. If you think it is not going to work, the chances are that it is not going to work. Never lose sight of what you want and what it takes to achieve it. Even if you do not know exactly what you want to do — which is more than normal at your age — do not lose sight of your purpose, of what you want from life.

Three years after my accident, I still had not worked out the point of my being on earth. I decided to travel around the world to find myself, to get lost, to be on my own and to meet people, and most importantly, to take time to think. My adventures led me to the realization that happiness can be found neither in material things, nor in freedom, or at least not in these things alone. We all search for happiness, but what does that actually mean? Having a car, a job, stability? If you look for happiness in material things, you will constantly be filling one void after another. Often, people believe happiness is being free. But the problem with freedom is that it is overwhelming. As human beings, we are so used to doing what we are told — go to school, do this, do that, be careful what people think about us — that we are at a loss when we are given freedom. I came to the realization that happiness, in fact, is finding a certain state of peace of mind.

CHAPTER 3: FINDING MY WAY

After my travels, I came back to France. I had money, I had time, but I had still not found happiness. I had been looking for answers, and while I had found some, I still had not found the answer to "why." I am from the so-called "Y generation", and spent a lot of time wondering "why this", "why that", etc. You, however, are the "why not generation": everything is possible. If you want to do a job that does not exist, then create it! The job I am currently doing does not "exist." Every day the world is different from what it was the day before.

2012 was dubbed the "year of change." The Mayan calendar predicted 2012 would be the end of the world. In France, it was the year of the French presidential elections, with the famous slogan *"le changement c'est maintenant"* [change is now]. Change, however, is not something that happens once at any given moment. The truth is, change is the only constant in life. However, as humans, we feel the need for security, stability, so we define answers to certain questions, even though by the next day they may no longer be valid. You are young! You have the choice to embrace change, to adapt, and to find yourself. And this is precisely what makes it both beautiful and challenging.

On a more personal level, 2012 marked the tenth anniversary of my accident and so, too, of my prosthetic hand. When I was first given my prosthetic hand, I could not help but wonder what it might be like in 10 years' time. I have used my hand a lot, it has been my loyal life companion since 2002. I was given a myoelectric hand. It is made of muscle sensors with electrodes, which converts muscle activity into electricity, the same way a car transforms thermal energy into mechanical energy, or your ear transforms acoustic energy into electric energy. When I move my muscles, the energy is converted into energy thanks to amplifiers, which, in turn, control the motor in the hand. There is one sensor on the top and one on the bottom, to control the open and close movements of the hand. In order to control this prosthetic hand, I had to learn to imagine moving the hand I no longer had. With a lot of effort, and the help of the people close to me, I finally managed. This success was the result of a lot of personal hard work, of course, but it was only made possible by the people who surrounded me and supported me. So remember, do not simply choose what you want to do, choose who you want to do it with. The people you surround yourself with are the people who will help you grow.

The hand itself cost €6,000, and the socket, which holds the sensors and the battery, costs approximately €4,000. In 2012, I discovered the new generation of prosthetic hands. There had been a clear shift: prosthetics were no longer seen as a mechanical response to a disability. Now they were offering something more, something better. New prosthetics are polydigital, they have several degrees of freedom which means prosthetic users can move all five fingers, as opposed to only being able to open and close their hand. The only problem with these hands is the cost: they cost approximately €27,000 and are not covered by social security.

I approached my Doctor to discuss these new solutions, and he strongly discouraged me from looking into this because he considered it would not be a suitable solution for me. My immediate reaction was "How would he know?!" Do not let other people tell you they understand your needs better than you do. For 10 years, people had been telling me what I should do, how I should lead my life. But they do not always know what they are talking about. Of course, it is important to listen to the people around you and to take their input into consideration, but it is also important to remember they are not always right, and they do not always know better. I trusted him,

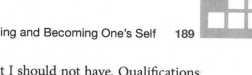

or rather, I trusted his qualifications, but I should not have. Qualifications do not give legitimacy to one person more than another. Experience, however, is key. So travel, learn, meet new people. That is what will shape you as well as shaping what you can achieve.

Around the same time, in October 2012, I stumbled upon a group of people who were using a 3D printer. I asked them if this type of machine could print a hand, they answered, "Yes, maybe." When I discussed my idea with them, they were all very enthusiastic and fascinated. They invited me to the FabLab, a public fabrication laboratory, where people from different backgrounds and with different skillsets come together to work on collective projects. It is not reserved exclusively for experts. It is a place where people like you and I can work on projects. At that point, I was 30, had no job, and working on a project was exactly what I needed. Being involved in this project opened me up to a world of machines, computers, and most importantly, it opened me up to the open-source movement.

The open-source community is motivated by the idea of sharing files or software freely, without licenses. Anybody can participate and propose improvements. We downloaded the InMoov hand: an open-source project available to everybody. This is what triggered my inner-change: I discovered a whole new world. I contacted the man behind the project to ask if it was feasible to use it to make a prosthetic hand. Our idea was that if the hand could be controlled by a keyboard, as was shown in the demo of the project, then it could probably be controlled by the sensors of the prosthetic hand I already had. Two days later he replied, saying "Probably not, but give it a try!" Where there is a will there is a way.

Luck had it that he was based in Paris, and that one of my colleagues from the FabLab knew him. So we started to work together. We made the parts of the fingers with the 3D printer, and used an Arduino electronic board, which is an open-source electronic platform.

We used two fishing lines for each finger: when you pull one line, the finger closes; when you pull the other; the finger opens, much in the manner of a puppet. The plastic parts printed by the 3D printer simply need to be assembled with acetone. After the hippie, punk and hipster movements, "Makers" have initiated a new movement! The "maker" community make what they need instead of buying it, re-use things instead of throwing them away. In our case, we combined the maker movement with technology and with a little effort from all of us, we were able to make a hand for a grand total of €200.

This taught me the importance of working together and the value of collective projects. Alone I would never have achieved this. We are a team in every sense of the word. There are ten of us, and what we hope to achieve is to combine disability, art, technology, education, humanitarian actions, and open source. For that purpose, we have set up an association which we have called MyHumanKit (https://twitter.com/hashtag/myhumankit). We hope my story will be multiplied for all the disabled people in France and throughout the world, to transform disability and to encourage people to embrace their disability through creativity.

How has this changed my perception of disability? I used to be ashamed of it, hide it by covering up my arm with long sleeves. Now I am just enjoying it and spreading the message.

24

MEDITATION: FOCUSING ON THE NOW

Fabrice Midal

Philosopher, Writer, Founder of the Western School of Meditation

BREAKING DOWN PREJUDICES ON MEDITATION

In Western societies, meditation is still subject to many prejudices: it is a tool for relaxing, for becoming more "zen", a magical recipe which is abundantly featured in magazines. Meditation, however, is something different entirely.

Meditation is Useless

The primary characteristic of meditation is that it is strictly useless, a disconcerting property in today's world, obsessed with performance. The frantic rhythm to which we are subject hinders us from engaging in an intimate relationship with our inner self, our intuition and our creativity so that we can engage with our feelings. That is why it is critically important for our well-being to find some time for ourselves during the day for doing nothing, which serves no purpose.

Human life would lose all its meaning if it were to be entrapped in usefulness. What, then, would be the point of falling in love? What would be the point of beauty and freedom? What matters most to us transcends notions of pure profitability. Meditation can free us from the simplistic question of "why", "what is it all for", "what purpose does it serve?"

Accepting that meditation is useless is also accepting and giving oneself the freedom to practice this exercise with no conditions, without setting specific goals or expectations which, if not met, place a veil of frustration between the now and ourselves.

Accept Doing Nothing

Paradoxically, meditation is an exercise which requires doing nothing. For example, it is not a matter of trying to concentrate. This is completely at odds with today's culture of constant occupation, and yet, we must embrace/accept the idea that doing nothing opens up a space of radical transformation. Hypnosis or psychotherapy have understood this. Artists also express the idea that it is through such a process that the emergence of creativity can take place. Doing nothing is a means of rediscovering how much our sensorial perceptions open us up to and connect us with the world, to life and to what surround us.

Meditation: An Exercise in Attentiveness

The recent emergence of meditation in our society could be compared to the discovery of sport in the 20th century. Our great grandparents, rural dwellers, had no need to do sport in order to be healthy. Their lifestyle meant they were constantly active, which kept them fit. Urbanization has generated a detrimental level of sedentariness, compensated for by doing sport. Today, meditation addresses the issues brought on by our new lifestyles: dispersion, divided attention, absorbed by incessant flow of information, digital media, advertising, etc. On average, an American teenager sends 100 SMS every hour! As for employees, while most say they check their emails every hour, observations have shown that in fact they check them every six minutes. The massive incursion of mediation in American companies is trying to addresses this phenomenon, and aims, more globally, to heighten employees' emotional intelligence and to prevent employee burnout. In France, the movement is only in its infancy, even if meditation is gaining increasing popularity, especially for children suffering from attention deficit. Sooner or later, meditation will become a routine activity, which people will carry out as a means to ensure their well-being, and become part of what is considered a healthy lifestyle, as naturally as we brush our teeth.

How, then, can we preserve our ability to concentrate in the face of constant demands? How can we maintain our ability to think and make our own decisions if advertising constantly insinuates itself into our minds? The massive communication budgets for the American electoral campaigns even lead us to question the risks for democracy of capturing people's attention. In this respect, meditation can help safeguard our freedom.

Cultivating Mindfulness

Meditation springs from oriental traditions, impregnated with spirituality. When the western world adopted it, it secularized and rationalized it. Science looked into how it affects our brain mechanisms and can affect us in a positive way. Those who do not aspire to such a spiritual dimension can thus explore meditation in its simplest expression, which consists in connecting with what is happening, and exactly how it is happening.

Throughout our lifetime, we are constantly exposed to new skills and new techniques which help us face up to situations we come up against, yet we often lack mindfulness. .And yet, mindfulness, being in the moment, is precisely what can save us in a job interview or an exam! Meditation is an invitation to cultivate this, to be in sync within ourselves and what is happening, so that we can be truly present in the moment.

Meditation, however, is not an internal exercise. By decluttering our relationship to the world, by sharpening our awareness, it opens us up to the world and to others rather than helping us focus on ourselves.

Another preconceived idea is that meditation requires you "clear your mind." In fact, it is the exact opposite because meditation refines our perception of the world and makes us connect with it in all its wealth.

Meditation: A Source of Care

When I survey participants of my meditation workshops on the lasting effects they have drawn from it a couple of months later, most state that they feel more caring. Many studies, namely those conducted by the Max Planck Institute in Berlin and the University of Stanford, confirm the wonderful virtues of meditation in this respect. However, driven by the constant obsession with success, we often have a deep lack of care towards ourselves and others. Despondency and denigration often take precedence.

While economic growth was expected to generate wealth and greater well-being, and as the living standards of western societies continued to grow, the incidence of depression increased markedly, as did suicide rates among the young. In the face of such intense manifestations of stress and burnout, mediation could constitute a salutary solution, particularly through the practice of care. By focusing our attention on the present, meditation offers a source of confidence. Not blind self-confidence, but rather confidence in what we have to do or say, in what our calling is, in life.

Finally, it would be a mistake to believe that meditation is merely a pleasant experience. If you want to relax, quell your anger or to get relief for your back pain, you would be better to have a hot bath or a massage. Through meditation, you will engage in an open and inquisitive relationship within yourself and your torments, but you will not eradicate them.

Let us now indulge in a simple meditation exercise.

Start by sitting without leaning on the back of your seat. Your feet must touch the ground, your hands lie on your thighs, your head is directly in line with your body. You can look down (but without lowering your head) to limit your field your vision and sources of distraction, or close your eyes. Do absolutely nothing else. And yet, your sensorial perceptions are expanded: you hear sounds, feel the contact of your hands on your legs, your feet on the ground, your clothes on your skin. Through the pores of your skin, you can feel the temperature of the air. Do not modify the natural rhythm of your breathing, simply be aware that you are breathing. By breathing naturally, you will maintain all your vital functions, embrace the life flowing through you. You might experience physical discomfort and want to move. Feel these feelings. You might be flooded by thoughts or emotions. Do not judge them, do not analyze them, and do not reject them, simply experience them in the now. Connect with what you think and feel, without trying to change anything.

Westerners are often confused by the physical dimension of mediation. And yet, how we sit has a bearing on how our mind works. Mindfulness is inextricably linked to corporal presence.

25

THE WORLD BELOW EVEREST

Yip Yew Chong
Artist

ACCOUNTANT BY TRAINING, CREATIVE BY CALLING

If I were to describe myself in just two words, I would say I am a "creative accountant." Not because I engage in creative accounting or cook the books, but because I am an accountant by trade, and I also let my imagination fuel my creativity. According to the theory of left-brain or right-brain dominance, left-brained people are very logical, analytical, and see things in a very systematic manner. I must confess that as an accountant, I fall into this stereotype! Right-brained people, on the other hand, are known to be creative, emotional and intuitive. I connected with that part of my brain rather late in life, but today, I am happy to be able to exercise both parts of my brain to the fullest, and to have the opportunity to present to everyone how I see the world.

When I was in the national service, I enrolled in engineering. Once there, my commanders recommended I go into finance because it was more versatile. At that stage, we did not have as much choice as people do today. Looking back, I could have chosen art, but at the time, these decisions had to be very practical and logical. I knew that it was hard to be an artist, so I chose the path of least resistance, on which I stayed for 22 years. I hold a full-time job in a leading financial services company, I manage a team of 70 people across various parts of the world, from Australia, to Egypt, China and Japan. However, I constantly felt drawn to the creative arts. I always did a lot of sketches in my free time, but it was nothing more than a hobby, until I came across the work of Ernest Zacharevic, a Lithuanian-born artist renowned for his murals in Penang. One of his pieces caught my attention, and it suddenly became clear to me that after over 20 years of being "stuck" in accounting, I could do something else, for Singapore and for myself. At that point, I decided to let my creativity express the collection of experiences which touched my heart and imagination, and pour this into my art.

In 2015, I took an eight-month sabbatical to focus on myself and my creative aspirations. I approached a property owner with a sketch, and asked if I could do the painting on the building facade. While in principle he was not opposed to the idea, he was Peranakan, and so asked me to do something which reflected his culture. I did not have that experience, and I did not feel this was something I could connect with. Nonetheless, I managed to propose an image, which the agent approved. I applied through the appropriate authorities for approval, and so began my first mural.

I was pleasantly surprised by the public's reception of this piece. People appreciated my work, and this encouraged me to continue. The more murals I paint, the more I appreciate the interactive aspect of my work. I personally believe that each of my pieces is meant to live. People interact with my creative work with their own imagination, and through this virtuous circle of imagination, my art becomes alive.

MY SOURCES OF INSPIRATION

I was born and raised in Singapore's Chinatown. I grew up among coffins and funeral parlors. Every night and every day we saw wakes and funerals, and all these images got etched in my mind. I have very fond memories of these streets, the markets, the neighborhood. As the country developed and progressed, houses started sprouting up from the ground, and the city's skyline became more and more clearly defined. I loved climbing to high places to contemplate the view. These heights intrigued me. As Singapore developed, the old houses were demolished and replaced by skyscrapers or tall residential buildings. In 1983, at age 14, we moved in to public housing flats, from the second floor of a small, traditional shop-house to the 25th floor of a tall, modern building. It was so beautiful, I could see the entire skyline, and literally saw Singapore grow from the ground.

Having a bird's eye view lets you appreciate the big picture, and I felt I could imagine the world beneath me. When you look down, you can see everything, and at the same time, you have to rely on your imagination to fill in the gaps. Oddly enough, I apply the same principles to accounting: I always strive to step up, look at the bigger picture and to not let myself get buried in numbers.

I have many sources of inspiration for my art. My art is filled with the things I have seen, the places I have been, the people I have met, all etched together and put into my creations at the service of my imagination. Both in my professional life as a finance executive, and in my personal life, I have had the opportunity to travel around the world. This enabled me to absorb the world, its differences, its colors, and meet wonderful people; and has fueled my imagination in many ways. I also draw a lot on nature. I am a nature lover; I cannot but marvel at what the world has to offer, and I genuinely believe that we live in a beautiful world. My imagination lets me see things in nature I want to share with others. I enjoy walking and running. Due to a health condition, I am no longer allowed to run, but nobody said anything about walking the marathon! So, in 2014, I walked the full distance in eight hours. When I am walking or running, I enter state of contemplation and meditation, which awakens my creativity. I constantly imagine things, and at the same time, I reflect, I observe, I contemplate all the experiences I have gone through. All these interests and experiences nurture my creativity.

ART AS A WAY OF CONNECTING

Through art, I found a way to give back to the community, and to share. It enables me to pay tribute, to embellish, and to make a place for stories or identities, and to leave a positive imprint on the city. I remember one day I did a walking tour of my murals with a group of families with autistic children. It was wonderful to see children who struggle so much to fit in, and who are ostracized, interact in and through public spaces. I felt very honored to see these children who are normally hidden away interacting with my work and having their photos taken in a positive way. My work was contributing to making a difference, and including them through interaction.

My style is very simple. This is by choice: there is no hidden message, no deeper meaning to my work other than what you can see. I am an accountant, after all! I am very factual, therefore my art too, is factual, as antithetical as that may sound! My work offers "slices of life." Most of my pieces blend with the environment, and they are always on a human scale, because I believe that sometimes you just need to get down to earth, to soak up the experience, to make it more real.

While my murals all tell a story, the stories in them are not mine *per se*. They are built through the way people interact with them. For example, with *The World Below Everest*, the piece I did for Imagination Week, you can make your own story, you can climb Mount Everest, you can tilt towers, you can jump, it is all up to you!

THE CHALLENGES AND ASPIRATIONS OF A CREATIVE ACCOUNTANT

My greatest enemy is time! I always fight to find time for my creative endeavors. I am an accountant by day, this means I have a nine-to-five job, five days a week. I have a senior, high-responsibility position, which means that I often have to put in extra hours, take part in teleconferences at night, etc. I also have a family, I want to spend time with. This also means that I struggle, or fail, to find not only a work-life balance, but also a work-life-art balance.

Another, less philosophical challenge, is bureaucracy, the paperwork. Some of the authorities are a bit bureaucratic and that can slow down my progress, or hinder a project.

After my sabbatical, I was offered a position in finance, which I accepted for a number of reasons. I have reached a level of expertise and recognition in my field, and I did not want to turn down what I felt was a good opportunity. On a more pragmatic level, I also feel that I have not yet gained financial independence. I want to make sure that my children have everything they need and have finished their studies before taking such a risk. Once I am assured they are all sorted, then I will be able to take my leap of faith and do what I like forever.

I feel I lack training. I do not consider myself self-taught, but rather a "learning" artist. I am not trained in any forms of art, I just did what I did because I felt compelled to. I also feel that I lack a depth in understanding the literature and the history of art. I hope one day to become a great artist, by learning more about the philosophy and the history of art, the culture surrounding art, and by acquiring more techniques.

One of my dreams is to, one day, paint in Chinatown. It is my place of birth, and so it would mean a great deal to me to leave an imprint on a place which has left such a big imprint on me. After completing all my current commitments, I would like to start exploring new styles and new forms of expression other than murals. I do not want to limit myself to one form of expression, I want to try new things in life! However, before I totally move on from murals, I want to produce a book to memorialize them before they fade away. Many years ago, during my first sabbatical, I studied film-making. One day, I may very well take the plunge!

At the end of the day, what my story shows is that it is never too late to try new things and explore yourself! Whether you use your left or your right brain, ultimately, you do not have to choose. You can be both! Embrace the multiple aspects of yourself and you will probably find that they complement one other. It is all a matter of interconnectedness.

26

HUMANOID: MAN VS ROBOTS

Nadine Thalmann
Nanyang Technology University

FROM MYTHOLOGY TO A.I., TO THE INTERNET OF THINGS

Fascination for automation is neither new nor modern. Living side-by-side with automated, mechanical beings which look like us and can do fantastic things or protect us is one of mankind's oldest dreams. In 400 BC, Greek mythology already featured the tale of Talos, a 10-meter giant automaton made of bronze. He was brought to life by the gods to ward off pirates and invaders and to keep watch to protect the island. In the late 15th century, Leonardo Da Vinci, always a visionary, created a mechanical humanoid automaton, a robotic knight which was capable of independent motion. It could stand, sit, raise its visor and maneuver its arms independently. The 19th century saw the emergence of automaton museums in Europe. For example, a Swiss museum features an automaton who can write. The only functionality for which she is programed is to write, but her behavior, her pose and look are all very natural. At the end of the 19th century, interest in this decreased with the emergence of the division of labor. Thanks to the dream of automated work, factory systems were established, which drastically revolutionized the way we work, and the world we lived in.

The development of automation did not only arise as a consequence of technological and mechanical progress. In the 18th century, French philosopher Denis Diderot reflected on the possibility of modelling intelligence. In his *Pensées Philosophiques*, he wrote "If they find a parrot who could answer everything, I would claim it to be an intelligent being without hesitation." As early as the 18th century, there was already a lot of discussion about what intelligence is and whether or not it could be modeled to be integrated within machines.

In 1950, Alan Turing developed the Turing Test, to test a machine's ability to exhibit intelligent behavior equivalent to, or indistinguishable from that of a human. The idea of this test is to put a machine and a human in a room and send in written questions. If it is impossible to tell which answers are from the machine and which are from the human, then this means the machine demonstrates intelligence. It led to the concrete proof that it was possible to model intelligence and actions, and therefore to create machines which could imitate us. The first program to successfully pass the Turing Test was ELIZA, a program written by American computer scientist Joseph Weizenbaum in 1976. ELZA was a natural language processing computer program which could simulate conversation by pattern matching. It was designed to analyze user input and engage in discourse following specific scripts. However, it was soon felt that the Turing Test was not sufficient. As we developed the notions of social and emotional intelligence in the 1980s and 1990s, human intelligence was understood not only as an ability to answer logical questions based on logical reasoning, but rather as an ability to take account of one's environment, the real world, social interactions, emotions, and this is something the Turing Test could not measure. This paved the way for new developments in computer science.

Alongside the evolutions in social sciences, computer science, too, evolved over time. Sixty years ago, computers were very large, and were very limited. Today, they are much faster, much more powerful and offer incredible possibilities of interfacing with people through sensors and actuators. Today, we have many software and hardware tools which can capture, understand and analyze a lot of signals and meaning. We can capture speech, sounds, gestures, shapes, etc. But most importantly, we can analyze all this data. Through the emergence of big data, we can analyze and model tremendous amounts of data, and predict future patterns. For example, we can have thousands of millions of items of data on walking patterns, and a computer can track any new walking pattern among all the existing patterns in its database and compare them. This is what is referred to as deep learning, i.e. the ability to store a lot of data and compare each new item to the main, organized data, and give an appropriate answer.

One of the many potential applications of this could be in the medical field. For instance, my lab has conducted a lot of work on joints and joint movements, namely through the analysis of the movements of dancers. We analyzed their motions, the movements of their joints, ligaments, and soft tissue in three dimensions. Thanks to algorithms, we can predict how this will change over time. This means that in the future, with specific indicators, we will be able to predict the evolution of certain medical conditions or bad habits.

Thanks to these advances, we have never been closer to achieving the dream of having robots as companions. We can have tremendous amounts of data, but most importantly, we have developed systems which can link this data analytically. This is what has enabled us to develop the Internet of Things (IoT), a set of smart, connected objects embedded with electronics software, sensors, actuators, which have network connectivity that enable these objects to collect and exchange data. The IoT offers tremendous possibilities, because just about anything can become part of a connected network with simple sensors. A glass of water, for example, could have sensors indicating when it reaches a certain temperature, or when it is nearly empty. We have also developed the internet of media, through the interconnection of different media. With this, we were able to offer dramatic visits for the visitors to an archaeological site. Thanks to a connected jacket, 3D glasses and multimedia information, visitors can experience ancient life and interact with virtual humans in Pompeii in Italy.

FROM DREAM TO REALITY, TO ASSISTIVE TECHNOLOGY

Contrary to popular misconceptions, robots are not only humanoids. Wikipedia defines a robot as "a machine — especially one programmable by a computer — capable of carrying out a complex series of actions automatically."[1] The key difference between automatons and robots therefore lies in the word "programmable." Automatons are based on mechanical actions, whereas robots are any object which can perform a series of actions automatically, as is the case with self-driving cars, drones, or cranes, for example. They have to be aware of the environment around

---

[1] *Source*: https://en.wikipedia.org/wiki/Robot.

them. Therefore, today, robots *per se* are already a big part of our lives. As for humanoids, over the past decade, extensive work has been conducted to build the perfect humanoid.

RobotCub, a European Commission funded project in Italy, developed a small robot which is 1m tall and weighs 22 kilos — i.e. the size of a toddler — to study human cognition processes. To date, it is one of the most advanced robotics programs as it can recognize objects and pick them up. This is extremely complex because it involves an ability to assess shapes, locate shapes in space, assess their weight, and understand meaning. In 2000, Honda manufactured ASIMO, a commercial robot which can hop, walk, play football, carry trays, and go up and down stairs, reproducing human movement in a fairly natural way. Boston Dynamics developed Atlas, a U.S. DOD funded project, a high mobility humanoid robot designed to negotiate outdoor, rough terrain.

A social robot is defined as "an autonomous robot that interacts and communicates with humans or other autonomous physical agents by following social behaviors and rules attached to its role",[2] in other words, robots which can take into account social, emotional and communicational aspects. With the combined effect of increasing lifespans, reduced mortality rates and declining birth rates, the world is growing older. Therefore, the need for social or assistive robots will become more pressing than ever before. A report published by the World Economic Forum states that "Current projections already estimate that by 2050, Japan will have 72 dependent people over 65 for every 100 workers. For Spain, Italy, Germany these numbers range between 60–70%."[3] In such a context, technology will become a necessary and vital ally in managing our ageing society in a sustainable way.

In 1993, a research institute in Japan presented Paro, a therapeutic robot designed to look like a baby harp seal, which can move its tail and show emotion. It responds to petting thanks to tactile sensors, it responds to sounds and can learn a name. It can also show emotions such as surprise, happiness and anger. RIKEN and Tokai Rubber Industries, Ltd. (TRI) jointly developed a nursing-care assistant robot named RIBA (Robot for Interactive Body Assistance). While not specifically a social robot, this

---

[2] *Source*: https://en.wikipedia.org/wiki/Social_robot.
[3] *Source*: https://www.weforum.org/agenda/2015/06/the-untapped-potential-of-the-elderly/.

robot is designed to assist the elderly by helping lift or set down a person from or onto a bed or a wheelchair. Nao, an autonomous, programmable humanoid robot developed by Aldebaran Robotics, a French robotics company, is used as a teaching-aid tool for autistic children. They offer psychic support, reduce stress, simulate interaction, improve relaxation and motivation. The Care-o-bot robot is a mobile robot assistant used to support humans in their everyday lives. It is currently being used in nursing homes in Germany. It monitors people, offers drinks, stays with patients and sings to them. It is equipped with the latest state-of-the-art industrial components, range and image sensors for objects learning and detection in a real-time 3D environment.

These technologies can be used to support the sick and the elderly, but they can also become an active part of increasingly connected lives to bring people together. A research center in NTU is developing 3D telepresence, a technology whereby real and virtual humans, social robots, real and virtual objects can simultaneously interact in the space which is a geometrically consistent blend of different remote real spaces and synthetic environments. For example, a working mother on a business trip can check in on her children thanks to 3D glasses, while a social robot is with children, and the mother can interact with her children through 3D imagery. The social robot can help monitor and entertain the children and inform parents. This is a tremendous undertaking, because it involves a combination of 3D imagery, telepresence, virtual reality and social robots.

THE CHALLENGES OF BECOMING SOCIAL

Social robots interact with people in social contexts. Therefore, they must understand the social context, i.e. understand users' behaviors, emotions, and respond with the appropriate gestures, facial expressions and gaze. Therefore, social robots must analyze and categorize behavior in order to identify the appropriate response. The challenge, then, is to program the robot to be able to sense and analyze situations and intentions, and make decisions appropriate to the social situation based on partial sensory input, and render synchronized and timely multi-modal behaviors.

In order for a robot to be truly social, it also needs episodic memory, i.e. "the memory of autobiographical events (times, places; associated emotions; and other contextual who, what, when, where, why knowledge) that can be explicitly stated. It is the collection of past personal experiences that occurred at a particular time and place."[4] Episodic memory is what enables us to keep the course of dialogue, plan long-term goals, explain reasons for actions, learn from past experiences, remember interactions, etc.

MIRALab's research with social robots focuses on several aspects of social interaction, such as affective computing, dialogue management and decision making, expressive behavior generation and facial expression recognition. More particularly, MIRALab is working on long-term inter-action with a social robot that can interact with users multiple times over a long period of time and that can establish engaging interpersonal relation-ships with them. This research involves modeling memory so as to enable a robot to remember people, their names and important past exchanges. Creating such a system requires an interdisciplinary approach at the inter-section point of several fields such as human–computer and human–robot interaction, computer vision and animation, artificial intelligence, robotics and social sciences.

This learning process of these robots is closely linked to social sciences and psychology. Based on the findings of these disciplines, computational engineers need to know what to encode and what to include in the mem-ory of the robot, so how the robot can retrieve the data, and how to pro-gram this so that the robot can filter this data according to the situation, and so behave more like a human.

The lab's first social robot project was EVA (2008–2012), a robotic tutor. The overall goal of this project was to develop a long-term social inter-action framework with a human-like robot or Virtual Human, modeling emotions, episodic memory and expressive behavior. More specifically, we wanted EVA to be able to remember individuals (faces and names) as well as past exchanges over multiple interactions. EVA can interact with users by recognizing and remembering their names and can understand user's emotional states through facial expression recognition and speech. Based on user input and her personality, Eva produces appropriate emotional responses and keeps a model of the long-term interpersonal relationships between her and the user. The project was such a success that EVA even played in a play with real actors in Zurich.

---

[4] *Source*: https://en.wikipedia.org/wiki/Episodic_memory.

Taking this one step further, in 2013, NTU started working on Nadine, a socially intelligent robot with a strong human-likeness, with a natural-looking skin and hair and realistic hands. Nadine is a socially intelligent robot. She is 35 kilos and 131 centimeters. She is small, but extremely realistic. The robot was developed in Japan, based on my physical traits, simply because it was easier for our research to compare my behavior and her behavior. Nadine is equipped with a black box of sorts which enables her to log and keep a trace of past interactions. Thanks to a Microsoft Kinects camera and a microphone she can recognize people, gestures and clues of social situations of emotion and behavior as well as speech, which enables her to "read" and understand social situations. She is equipped with an emotional model, a memory model and a social attention model as well as a chatbox, which means that depending on the input, she will generate the appropriate emotional response, remember interactions. Robot controllers control lip synchronization and her gaze, and enable her to adapt her facial expressions to emotions. She can respond positively to positive interactions, but can also become mean or angry in negative interactions, adapting her tone of voice and vocabulary. She has a personality, a mood, and depending on her relationship with any one user, her response will vary and adapt to each situation.

When Nadine was presented to the press it was the most-cited press event in the entire history of NTU. Nadine is truly ground-breaking. The public and the scientific community were aware of the technological aspects computational scientists had been working on to develop robots, but little work had been done on the social, emotional and behavioral aspect. This came as a great surprise to the media, and generated great interest. You may wonder what is next and what awaits us. Our on-going research focuses on how autonomous virtual humans and real humans can mix and interrelate. Tomorrow's mixed society will no longer only be a matter of mixed races and cultures, but also of virtual and non-virtual people. In our ever-more global society and lifestyle, we will rely increasingly on such robots for our interactions and our lives in general. The dream of living with robots is deeply-rooted in the history of mankind, and you, the younger generations will have the privilege of seeing that become a reality.

SEEING WITH OUR MIND'S EYE

27

Bridget Polk
Rock Balancing Artist

When I was younger, I often heard two things: "Oh that's just your imagination," and, "I'll believe THAT when I see it with my own two eyes." The words were powerful. They stopped me in my tracks.

Over the years, I have begun to understand the unlimited power hidden within those seemingly limiting phrases.

Imagination: seeing an image with our mind's eye. Seeing is believing.

When we believe in an image, we see with our mind's eye with the certainty we have when seeing something with our "own two eyes," the energy of our belief will summon the creativity we need to blast through the obstacles and make it real. Then it is for others to see and believe.

WELCOME TO SPACE

Jean-Loup Chrétien

Cosmonaut

ON BEING AN EXPLORER

Men are tireless and insatiable explorers. Not only those who travel through space, but each and every one of us. A new-born baby is an explorer, as is a student, the person stuck in a nine-to-five job, or people reaching the end of their life: we all explore out of a desire to fight for survival. This facet of our personality is one of the reasons we have traveled and continue to explore space: because life on earth is a constant fight for survival and it is in our genes.

I joined the French Air Force academy in Salon-de-Provence in 1959, and from that moment on, I had my heart set on space. The program started with an intensive 18-month training period which included traditional coursework and preparation for flying, in a very international context, bringing together people from all over the world.

In 1961, while still at the Air Force academy, I saw Yuri Gagarin accomplish the feat of being the first man to go into space, and that is when really I decided that one way or another I, too, would go travel to space. After a long selection process for the CNES[1] space program, I was selected, along with Patrick Baudry, to join the program in Star City in Moscow in the context of the cooperation agreement for manned flights signed between the French and Soviet governments. On June 23, 1982, after 2 years of training, simulations and preparation for emergency landings, I was on board the Soyouz T-6 to accomplish the "First Manned Flight", a ten-day mission

---

[1] *Centre National d'Études Spatiales*, the French government space agency.

along with Patrick Baudry and Soviet cosmonauts Vladimir Dzhanibekov and Alexander Ivanchenko.

This spaceflight involved a complex program of scientific experiments, which encompassed life sciences, astronomy, medicine, neurosciences, and research on materials. Studies were undertaken on the blood vessels of the brain, the acuity and depth of vision in space, the effects of cosmic radiation on biological specimens, and the threshold of color sensitivity, whilst observations of the night sky and investigations in infrared astronomy were made.

In 1984, Patrick Baudry and I moved to NASA, Houston, for our second spaceflight. We spent 10 days in space on the Discovery mission. One of the major differences we experienced between working with the Soviets and working with NASA was that the active and operational population of latter were primarily made up of pilots, air force engineers and aeronautical engineers. This probably explains why the US very quickly decided to send an airplane to space, i.e. the space shuttle.

Between 1986 and 1988, I was given the opportunity to go back to Russia for a long duration flight. Initially, this opportunity might not have been open to me because at the time, Russia never worked with the same country twice. But I was not ready to give up. On one of Gorbachev's official visits to France during which our paths crossed four or five times, I was invited to an event organized by the Russian embassy on Gorbachev's last night on French soil. None of the French dignitaries present that day spoke Russian, so I seized the opportunity. We had a short conversation in Russian, and I was able to tell him that I wanted to go back to Moscow to train for a long space flight. He simply turned to Mitterand who was listening through an interpreter, and told him that I could go. I nearly fainted! This only goes to show that you should never give up, and fight for what you really want right to the end. Recognize an opportunity when it presents itself, and seize it.

The long Russian flight was originally scheduled to last three months. However, one of the modules on Mir space station was not ready, and so the flight was shortened to one month. During this flight, I completed my first EVA,[2] for which I had been preparing for a long time, spending

---

[2] Extravehicular activity.

approximately 10 times in water the time I was to spend in space. This was a much anticipated and wonderful experience.

Between 1994 and 1998, I moved to NASA in Houston as a CNES attaché. During my first trip to NASA in 1984–1985, I had met George Abbey, who would later become the head of the Johnson Space Center of Houston, and a good friend of mine. At that point in time, the CNES wanted to initiate discussions with NASA authorities in order to set up an agreement for sending French astronauts to Houston to start training. I suggested I go first to initiate talks with him. The meeting was scheduled for one hour, but we talked shop for no more than a minute. By minute two, he asked me when I was ready to come, and said that I would come first to coordinate the arrival of the other team members. Three days later, I was on a plane to Houston, and never left.

There, I joined the Astronaut class of '95, a one-and-a-half year preparation course, with 22 astronaut candidates. I flew in 1997 on space flight STS-86 on a mission to Mir, during the time US and Russia decided to cooperate in space. This particular space flight on the shuttle to the MIR space station lasted 20 days, and was fully technological, with very few scientific experiments.

In 1998, due to the political climate in France, I was invited to retire from the CNES. NASA had already invited me to stay on as an official member of the NASA team, and so that is what I did. Two years later, I got dual citizenship, thereby becoming a US NASA astronaut, and was appointed as Assistant to the Director of the Johnson Space Center for ISS international operations.

In 2001, I was training for the force of the spaceflight in preparation for a flight scheduled in 2002. Unfortunately, an unhappy accident at Home Depot forced me to leave training, and I could not be on that flight. At that point, I joined Tietronix, a company under the auspices of NASA.

THE PAST, THE PRESENT, THE FUTURE ... AND BEYOND

From the door of our prehistoric caves to the gates of eternity, where do we stand today? This is an interesting question: are we still at the door of our caves or have we traveled most of our journey and reached the limits of what our civilization can achieve? What characterizes us is our constant quest to understand the mysteries surrounding us. Today, many questions remain. Why is life so short? Why do we die? Why is the universe so big? Is the speed of light the limit? And of course, one of the most debated about questions is whether or not we are alone.

The presence of men in what can be referred to as the "third dimension" is a very recent reality. Our exploration of the third dimension started just before World War I, in 1910, with the development of aviation. In 1961, 50 years later, Yuri Gagarin was assigned to space, and 50 years after that, the International Space Station was almost completed, which was a tremendous accomplishment given its complexity and the means and resources available at the time. Tomorrow, our gaze will be on Mars. But when exactly is tomorrow? In 10, 20, 50 years' time? At present, we are unable to know this with certainty.

Until the 60s and 70s, there was a genuine race to space. Everybody wanted to be the first to go to space, to break records. Less than 10 years after the flight of Gagarin, the focus shifted back to Low Earth Orbit (LEO), i.e. to space stations. Commercial aviation reached 40,000 feet in the 1950s and, with the exception of the Concorde which demonstrated commercial aviation could go higher and faster, this is still the standard used today. In other terms, both the aeronautical and space programs experienced an inflexion: after reaching the moon in the 50s–60s, the focus shifted back to LEO, and commercial aviation has not experienced any significant evolutions since the Concorde.

Over that period, many plans were made. There were plans to go to Mars right after reaching the moon, and in the field of aviation, there had been plans of establishing suborbital airports, which would, of course, have been significant accomplishments. However, these projects were never acted on.

Between Sputnik in 1957, and then Apollo 11, the level of technological development of the spacecraft could be compared to that of a modern-day cell phone. For example, the five computers on the International Space Station were installed in the 70s and were in operation for 30 years. Today, thanks to digital sciences and the exponential increase of data flow, we have experienced spectacular progress over the last 50 years, which could portend wonderful achievements in the future.

There has been a significant shift since Barack Obama was elected as President of the United States. One of the most significant changes is the participation of private funding, as opposed to solely public funding. This new approach came as an attempt to transfer certain duties to private corporations so that NASA could concentrate on focus on its real mission: exploring, inventing and innovating. For the last 20–30 years, the space program has not progressed. NASA has focused on making space stations which is not its original mission. Some of the missions the space program has set itself include going to Mars, of course, which we hope to achieve in the 2040s, although there is no evidence to affirm this will effectively happen. Another goal for the NASA space program is to reach an asteroid and maybe destroy it. Such a mission could only be accomplished through the collaboration between robots and humans, the former carrying out the deep space capture of asteroid and the latter the low orbital return.

LIMITING FACTORS IN SPACE EXPLORATION

Traveling at the speed of light, which we are still a long way away from achieving, means traveling approximately 300,000 kilometer per second. In fact, at the scale of the universe, this is very slow. At such a speed, it would take a 10th of a second to go round earth; one second to reach the moon; 4 years to reach our closest neighbor, i.e. a star; 300,000 years to cross the galaxy; and possibly 15 billion to travel across the universe. At the scale of the universe, which is 15 billion years old, several hundred thousand years is little more than a fleeting second.

Our universe has billions of exoplanets. Today there is much discussion about what may be happening on them. At the speed of light, it would take 10 lives to reach one of them. This would require a specific space vehicle designed to host new generations being born and growing on board, which, of course, is impossible. If we are not alone, we are certainly not ready to go and visit our neighbors.

Space is a very hostile environment, requiring specific and rigorous tools, selection processes and preparation. Once you leave Earth's orbit, you are faced with cruel loneliness, issues of self-confidence and mutual trust, individual and collective performance, task distribution, behavioral control, relationships, resource management, etc. In addition to these, there are key parameters: influence, authority and responsibility. The further away you are from earth, the less you will get information and decisions from the ground.

Today, priorities have changed. While 30 years ago, the priority was to complete the mission, mitigate risks and bring back the crew safely, today, bringing back the crew safely is the topmost priority, and the success of the mission only comes in second position. There have been too many accidents, and that is one of the reasons that the space shuttle program was discontinued by the Obama administration in 2011. Instead, NASA has chosen to focus on Orion, the next vehicle able to travel not only around the earth but also to travel to deep space, and capable of doing the heavy lifting, but also explore a wide range of destinations. NASA's mission is to explore and to keep exploring, to keep inventing and to keep going further.

The issue of communication is critical for the future of human–robotic combined exploration. The further you are from Earth, the less contact you have with the drone, and the longer it takes to receive data from a drone. For example, on Mars today, it can take anywhere from 10 to 25 minutes depending on the relative position of Mars with regards to Earth. When working with drones, over the years, the system becomes antiquated. And so, for missions taking place over many years, we will need evolutive artificial intelligence. Exploring space without such artificial intelligence could be compared to exploring the ocean like the crew of Christopher Columbus. Should we send a new voyager-automated system to capture images of a given planet, it would take 300 years to send back those images. This would be like receiving Leonardo Da Vinci's drawings today. They would serve no scientific purpose and would be stored in a museum. What we know now today, or are seeking to know, may not be of any interest or relevance to anybody in the next two or three centuries.

The need for innovation is ahead of us, as is the future of space exploration. This future is in your hands and your imagination: we need scientists, innovators and inventors. Right now, we are trapped in our world. Our civilization still has a long journey ahead of it to reach its goals. We need the involvement of all, to innovate and spread the results of our discoveries in accordance with the needs of people on Earth, their health, safety, and desire for a peaceful, long life. Our long journey through progress can only become a reality if future generations continue innovating, and taking care of our space keepers. A day will come when we will reach the new cradle of mankind. So, see you on Earth!

29

WORK: ALWAYS SOUGHT-AFTER, OFTEN ENDURED

Dominique Méda

Philosopher and Sociologist, Paris Dauphine University

THE VALUE OF WORK, AT THE HEART OF PUBLIC DEBATE

The question of work is increasingly present in the public debate, even though, paradoxically, it was never constructed as such. It manifests itself through issues of professional harassment, suicides in the work place or psychosocial risk. The two last French presidential campaigns, in 1997 and 2012, made work a core issue of their proposals, with the underlying denunciation of the erosion of "the work ethic." It was argued that the latter deserved to be "rehabilitated", with the aim of reaffirming the true meaning of work.

This statement conceals a kaleidoscope of explanations and perspectives.

For some, the deterioration of work values is ascribed to a particularly French penchant for leisure, as attested, for example, by the taste for early retirement — which has, admittedly, become less common — the 35 hour week, or social benefits, recharacterized in public discourse as social "handouts." All of which is further compounded by a low level of commitment to work on behalf of the youth, who are seen as being driven by individualism, nomadism and a refusal to make an effort.

Others, however, argue that it is the working conditions which have declined, with the simultaneous increasing imbalance between capital and work, leading to a reduction of the share of salaries as part of the added value.

The concern regarding the erosion of work values is, in any case, shared by both sides of the political spectrum. By way of illustration, this is what Nicolas Sarkozy stated during his Bercy speech in 2007: "*The Left has given up on merit and effort. It has ceased to speak to the workers, to feel concerned by their fate, to love the workers. Deep down, it does not address workers because it rejects their work values, because work values are no longer part of its values, because its ideology is not the ideology of Jaurès, the ideology of Blum, those who respected work, loved the workers, spoke about the workers. Today, the left talks about statuses, assistantship, egalitarianism, levelling, about the 35 hour week. It has turned its back on our country's workers. I say to the Left: I want to rehabilitate work and to talk about the workers.*"

As for Manuel Valls, he announced on December 14, 2015: "*I want to get the country out of this dependency on benefits. I want work values to be shared by all.*"

Before exploring the expectations which Europeans place on the concept of work, and considering possible scenarios to address them, I propose a retracing of the history of values associated with work over time.

FROM "TREPALIUM" TO WORK-AS-FULFILMENT

The concept of work has evolved over the course of time. What we refer to today is the result of a sedimentation of "layers of meaning" accumulated throughout the centuries without ever really combining and which, in some respects, contradict each other. Jean-Pierre Vernant, a specialist on Ancient Greece, summarizes the modernity of our understanding of work: "*In the same way that we do not have the right to apply modern capitalistic economic categories to ancient Greece, we cannot project on the citizen of the ancient City the psychological function of work as it is conceived of today.*"

Let us delve into the origins of what is known today as work.

BEFORE THE 18TH CENTURY: ABSENCE OF THE CONCEPT OF WORK

The vague notion of work which existed before the 18th century has nothing in common with the concept we have of it today. Anthropologist Marie-Noëlle Chamoux observes that it is impossible to find an identical meaning for the term "work" amongst the different primitive societies she studied. Some do not even have a specific word to distinguish productive activity from other human behavior, nor a term or notion which would synthesize the general idea of work. Jean-Pierre Vernant explains that whilst jobs, activities and tasks were present in ancient Greece, we would be hard-pressed to find an equivalent of "work."

In the Middle Ages, St. Augustine uses the word *opus* to refer both to divine and to human work. There followed, with St. Thomas in particular, the slow recognition of work as something that would contribute to the common good. Throughout the Middle Ages, manual labor was progressively valued, while at the same time, "forbidden" jobs begin to be identified.

FROM THE 18TH CENTURY: THE POLYSEMOUS EMERGENCE OF "WORK"

Amongst the various layers of meaning applied to the notion of work from the 18th century onwards, let me put forward the three main ones.

Firstly, the development of Western capitalism gave rise to the "invention" of work. To use a neologism, we might say that Adam Smith theorizes work as a production factor, that is, a means to another end, i.e. wealth creation. The work in question is market-oriented, detachable and abstract, thereby enabling men to sell their activity — what Marx will later refer to as "Labour power" — to earn a living. This act lays the foundation of his freedom and autonomy. Work is henceforth seen as something which gives value to things, hence the expression "the labour theory of value." Adam Smith places work at the heart of the social machinery: it is what assembles and unties individuals. Nevertheless, and this will be criticized by Marx, he sees work as a sentence and a sacrifice.

A radically new layer of meaning emerged in the 19th century, whereby work is seen as a creative freedom for mankind. This idea is promoted by French, English and German authors. For Hegel, for example, work enables man to transform the world and to transform himself. Marx brought this idea to its pinnacle, nevertheless specifying that it is in and of itself that work constitutes a formidable power. It, therefore, follows that it must be set free, and to do so, he saw no other solution than the abolition of the salary ties.

I cannot help but succumb to the pleasure of sharing with you this excellent quote by Marx, drawn from the *Manuscripts of 1844*.

Let us suppose that we had carried out production as human beings. Each of us would have in two ways affirmed himself and the other person. (1) In my production I would have objectified my individuality, its specific character, and therefore enjoyed not only an individual manifestation of my life during the activity, but also when looking at the object I would have the individual pleasure of knowing my personality to be objective, visible to the senses and hence a power beyond all doubt. (2) In your enjoyment or use of my product I would have the direct enjoyment both of being conscious of having satisfied a human need by my work, that is, of having objectified man's essential nature, and of having thus created an object corresponding to the need of another man's essential nature. (3) I would have been for you the mediator between you and the species, and therefore would become recognised and felt by you yourself as a completion of your own essential nature and as a necessary part of yourself, and consequently would know myself to be confirmed both in your thought and your love. (4) In the individual expression of my life I would have directly created your expression of your life, and therefore in my individual activity I would have directly confirmed and realised my true nature, my human nature, my communal nature. Our products would be so many mirrors in which we saw reflected our essential nature.

To be able to say that we are thanks to our work, and to make work an affirmation rather than a source of alienation, is an eminently modern idea advanced by Marx.

At the end of the 19th century, contrary to Marx's aspirations, wage ties establish themselves and become the cornerstone for the distribution of income, rights and protections. This too is a radically new idea. At the same time, the salaried condition becomes the ultimate desirable status. This salaried society places employment at the heart of its processes. Jürgen Habermas observed in 1990 that work is appreciated not for the pleasure it provides in its execution, but for the rights to which it grants access, the income it generates, and which enables consumerism: *The citizen is compensated for the onerousness which remains associated with the salaried status, even if this status is more comfortable; he is compensated by rights in his role as a user in the bureaucracy of the welfare state, and by purchasing power, in his role of consumer.*

Permeated by this legacy, the modern concept of work encompasses three aspects: a factor of production, a mode of expression for human uniqueness, and finally, a system for the distribution of rights, status and protection. These three dimensions contradict each other. And so, when work is viewed as a factor of production, wealth creation takes precedence over the quality of the activity and the pleasure an employee can find in it. But if work is the essence of human affirmation, above and beyond wealth creation, what counts is the activity *per se.*

AT THE END OF THE 20TH CENTURY: TOWARDS AN ETHICS OF FULFILMENT

By the end of the 20th century, in western societies, work is no longer perceived as a duty but as the "primary vital need." The standard of work-as-fulfilment gradually gains ground. Man no longer works only to make a living but, as Marx anticipated, as a pleasurable affirmation of his identity.

This new stage has to be put in perspective with the work of German sociologist Stefan Voswinkel, who demonstrated that recognition is now founded on admiration. Work is precisely a means of obtaining the latter, since it has become the site of self-actualization, a space where the individual can define his whole value and prove his greatness.

We can therefore see the significant transformations which the concept of work has undergone over the centuries.

GREAT EXPECTATIONS RELATIVE TO WORK

A number of international studies have questioned the expectations which citizens project onto work. As part of the European Values Study in 1999, the following question was asked: "How is work important in your life?" Whilst the vast majority of Europeans responded positively, significant differences appeared from one country to another. In Denmark, the UK and the Netherlands, 40% of those surveyed declared that work occupied a very important place in their lives. This is against 70–80% in Poland, Malta, Romania, Lithuania or, indeed, in France. We can question the meaning of France's alignment with these countries with which it has little else in common.

Another French specificity revealed by the CREDOC report, *The society of the leisure activities in the shadow of the value of work*, attachment to work is unanimously expressed by all social categories including individuals in full-time and part-time employment, entrepreneurs, unemployed retirees, students and home-makers. This attachment is, moreover, much more pronounced in France than in Germany or in the UK for all of these categories.

How should this specifically French phenomenon be interpreted? First of all, it is widely known that there is a very strong link between the rate of unemployment and the importance given to work. The high levels of unemployment in France would explain, in part, this unanimous conviction of its citizens.

Nonetheless, other factors need to be taken into account, distinguishing between the instrumental dimension of work (as a means of making a living), and its expressive dimension (as a mode of self-affirmation). Most European countries refuse to reduce work to the income it generates, without however negating its instrumental dimension. Over the past 30 years the expectations in Europe with regards to the content of work — expectations regarding the inherent, or post-materialist, nature of work — and the relationships it enables have been reinforced. Such expectations are even more pronounced in France than in other European countries: 65% of its citizens declared their attachment to the inherent value of work in 1997, and again in 2005.

Europeans also acclaim the idea that work is a means to fully develop one's capabilities. This is a major trend which is important to stress. The statement that "work is a duty towards society" was subscribed to by over two-thirds of those surveyed (71% in France). However, the French do not significantly stand out in terms of value judgements like "people who do not work tend to become lazy", or "it is humiliating to receive money without having worked for it" [1], which 55% and 45%, respectively subscribed to.

Beyond this quantitative data, interviews provide a clearer view on French aspirations regarding the intrinsic dimensions of work. The atmosphere in the workplace is unanimously important, as is the purpose of work — a concept which refers both to the content of the activity and to people's abilities. And so, above all, workers appreciate being intellectually stimulated and taking up challenges. It should also be noted that the importance of the relational dimension of work, with a particular attachment to the little team with which one works on a daily basis.

And what of the so-called lack of interest in work on behalf of the youth? Studies belie this prejudice. The under-30s, in higher proportions than their elders, demand the triple conditions of a pleasant working atmosphere, a good salary and an interesting job [2].

It is important to note that the value given by the French to family supersedes that given to work [3]. The family remains the pillar of identity-formation.

In sum, what can be deduced of French expectations with regards to work? First of all, it is granted a high importance, but still less than that given to family values. While its expressive dimension is widely valued, its instrumental dimension remains significant. Belying Ronald Inglehart's thesis, the post-materialist dimension, has therefore not completely replaced materialistic dimensions. In Europe, French expectations regarding work are among the most intense, particularly on behalf of young people. The higher the socio-professional category, the stronger these expectations become. However, the intensity of these expectations does not vary much based on gender.

The French therefore aspire to expressive work, which would bring fulfilment, self-actualization and self-expression, and allow them to demonstrate their uniqueness — with the added imperative of a pleasant working atmosphere. They demand meaning in work, social utility but also, and this is a new factor, its harmonious integration with the other dimensions of their lives.

These dimensions of expression, interrelations and balance seem at first glance mainly carried by young people and women in particular, but are in fact strongly correlated to levels of education.

EXPECTATIONS CONFRONTED WITH THE UPHEAVAL OF WORK

To what extent are these significant expectations taken into account by the productive system and its organization?

A TWO-FOLD TRANSFORMATION AT THE HEART OF COMPANIES

Since the end of the 1980s, companies have been undergoing a two-fold change.

On the one hand, new forms of work organization have been developed, with processes of overall quality or "just in time", admittedly, but also with a call for the engagement of subjectivity, for involvement, initiative-taking and responsibility. This leads to an exaltation of individual performance, supported by incentives, namely relative to wages. From this point of view, then, a congruence between individual expectations — revealing one's value by the mediation of work — and the professed promises of companies, in the framework of post-Taylorism, would be conceivable.

On the other hand, a new instrumentation of the monitoring of professional activity by means of multiple indicators and reporting tools, or of the new public management, has been implemented. A certain autonomy has certainly been granted to individuals, but in a tightly controlled way, accompanied by individual performance assessment.

This double phenomenon emerged in the context of rising unemployment, an intensification of constraints linked to globalization, reinforcement of competition and the delocalization of dirty and offensive productions. This context is also marked by the dissemination of dictates by international organizations which marked a turning point away from the Philadelphia Declaration of 1944. The latter, it must be reminded, stated that work was not merchandise and that the condition for sustainable peace was social justice — which was at risk of being compromised by poor working conditions. These principles have been replaced by the logic of reducing work protections and activating social protection. The injunction became to "make work pay" [4].

We must add to this landscape an accelerated financialization and heightened pressure weighing on companies in terms of profitability.

A DETERIORATION OF WORKING CONDITIONS

This context is at the source of a deterioration of working conditions and disappointed expectations in this regard, particularly in France. A study led by the Dublin Foundation in 2010 illustrates this: 27% of French salaried employees, a higher percentage than in other European countries, say that they are stressed. 54% of them admit to suffering from generalized fatigue, and 59% report working at a very sustained pace at least a quarter of the time. Barely over half of French salaried employees stated that they were consulted in the event that their work was reorganized, and a third said that they were able to influence important decisions in their professional activity. Finally, only 21% report being very satisfied with their working conditions (against 25% on average in Europe).

The French study *Conditions de travail* [5] confirms a deterioration between 2005 and 2013, as a result of heightened constraints regarding the pace of work, the frequency of organizational changes and a significant rate of employment insecurity reported by salaried employees. As a result, a percentage of salaried workers are suffering from a loss of meaning in their work, a lack of recognition and the feeling of not being able to carry out quality work.

It is interesting to note that this deterioration of work conditions is particularly felt in the civil service sector, especially in hospitals. A study by DARES shows 61.7% of hospital orderlies say they always or often have to hurry, against 46% in the private sector. A significant proportion of these agents also state they always or often have to carry out tasks which would require more care too quickly, do not feel proud of their work, and sometimes are even led to carry out acts they disapprove of. Interviews with civil servants reveal a radical calling into question of the new public management, management logics and the importation of methods from the private sector.

According to a particularly worrying statistic drawn from the DARES study, 52% of salaried employees between 35 and 55 years old would not feel capable of carrying out the same work up to 60 years of age. If the ambition of politicians is to push back the full-pension retirement age, it would then seem essential to address the issue of working conditions.

Is it possible to satisfy the great expectations of the French and of Europeans with regards to work? And is this something we should do? Or should we rather consider these aspirations as excessive? How can we place the quality of work, and decent work, at the heart of the concerns of France and Europe?

On what building blocks can we reinvent work?

On what bases can we reinvent work? In order to fuel your reflections on this, let us discuss three more or less plausible scenarios.

1ST SCENARIO: THE END OF THE SALARY SYSTEM

A first scenario, which is currently very much in fashion and subject to numerous variations, is based on evolutions of the productive system and seems likely to satisfy individual expectations. It relies on a wide-scale automation of tasks in the years to come, which would, in turn, lead to an increasing scarcity of employment and a transformation of the very nature of work. In this scenario, the salaried model is destined to disappear, giving way to "self- entrepreneurship" and informality.

This scenario is supported by seminal works such as *The Future of Work* [6], bringing together testimonies by CEOs and consultants, or the very renowned "The Future of Employment" [7] (2013) in which Carl Benedickt Frey and Michael Osborne argue that 47% of American jobs will disappear in 10–20 years due to automation.

If we follow all of these authors, emerging technologies will irreversibly destroy employment, which, following the thesis put forward by Jeremy Rifkin announcing the end of work, should be seen as a cause for celebration. Work, they add, will become increasingly collaborative, abolishing hierarchical structures. Henceforth, the creation of value would then come from platforms where consumers play an active role in constructing the products, following logics of co-working and crowdsourcing.

This perspective may prove congruent with expectations regarding work, insofar as it considers the latter as a passion. There would, incidentally, be little distinction between work and non-work. We would no longer need specialized skills, but would need to develop our aptitudes: how to communicate, exercise leadership, be mobile and adaptable, be on the cutting edge, be involved 24/7. In short, everyone would become their own manager and their own employer, entirely responsible for their own career. From this perspective, the salaried system amounts to nothing more than an archaic model to be abandoned.

This scenario resonates with the growing aspirations of individuals to perform and affirm themselves through work. Moreover, the recommendations of international organizations, since the end of the 1990s, tend towards a reduction of protection through employment and a reduction of workers' rights, considered as being an impediment to employment.

As far as I am concerned, this scenario seems not only rather unlikely, but also dangerous. It is based on an automated and dematerialized vision of production, whereas the consumption of raw materials has never been higher throughout the world. It essentially consists of a revival of an enchanted vision of the "new economy" which flourished in the 90s, whose formidable productive gains were supposed to revolutionize the world of work. Yet work remains largely human, Taylorian and hierarchical. Maybe this will change in one or two decades, but it would necessitate a giant leap. Moreover, a number of sectors are not meant for automation: agriculture, care, education, craftsmanship, repairs, etc. To summarize, the technological determinism of this scenario seems to require further questioning.

We must beware of the consequences of such a vision of work. The abandonment of the wage system and its protections in favor of an "Uberization" of work would not be without social risks. Equally implied is a less than palatable perspective of society's polarization, with a handful of individuals being totally invested in work that captivates them, but with the majority remaining slaves to the social machine or living on the margins thanks to paltry benefits.

Another major risk is the return of "free labour" which Eugene Buret criticized as early as 1840. A liberal, he wrote about the misery of the working classes in the UK and in France and denounced the English theory of "merchant labour" which, he argued, inexorably led to the reduction of salaries and generalized poverty.

Finally, this scenario radically omits consideration of rising costs of raw materials and energy, as well as of the imperative of engaging our societies in ecological reconversion. It completely skips over the ambivalent character of growth, which undeniably brings with it great benefits but also great ills.

2ND SCENARIO: THE SEARCH FOR QUALITY WORK

A second scenario is based not on the development of the productive system, but of people's expectations with regards to work: a search for meaning and recognition, and the desire to accomplish a work of some quality.

Matthew Crawford, a philosopher and motorbike mechanic, describes in *Shop Class as Soulcraft: An Inquiry Into the Value of Work* [8] the joys of re-establishing work as a meaningful and useful pursuit. He calls for the emergence of a community of makers and repairers, integrated inside a community of users. It would consist in returning to an age prior to the "drift" represented by Taylorism, capitalism, the wage system, manufacturing or indeed "free labor." I personally maintain some reservations concerning the probability of such a perspective.

3RD SCENARIO: AN ECOLOGICAL TRANSITION

A third scenario is being elaborated around taking into account of ecological constraints and the necessity of preserving natural and human resources. It implies reviewing the organization of work, the definition of companies and finally the role of institutions, which would conceive of social and ecological norms and ensure that they are respected. Let us go through these three aspects.

In terms of work organization, a number of modes can be found throughout European states [9]. Northern countries in particular know how to include salaried workers in decisions which affect their work. This condition is fundamentally tied to the strength of the unions.

For a new definition of companies, we might look to researchers such as Armand Hatchuel and Blanche Segrestin [10], Isabelle Ferreras [11] or Jean-Philippe Robé, who call for a break with company objectives which can be summed up by profit generation. Jean-Philippe Robé, a legal practitioner, thus contends that "neither the conception of 'companies-as-the-sum-of-their-contracts', nor that of 'community companies' are satisfactory", and that "nothing in today's world guarantees that the aggregated effect of company choices will be conform with the common good [12]." Furthermore, he reminds us, companies as legal entities are not the property of shareholders. Belgian philosopher Isabelle Ferreras, for her part, proposes an economic bicameralism, that is, a board of directors nominated by a chamber of labor and a chamber of capital.

This scenario includes one of the most provocative ideas for French society: the sharing and dis-intensification of work. Amongst them are calls for the substitution of current unchecked sharing by a more "civilized" kind.

To this, a number of economists counter that work is not shareable, and that such a logic is even dangerous. Yet it is undeniable that the volume of work is already shared between individuals at every moment. Nevertheless, this distribution is unequal, with some being full-time employees and others on part-time contracts. In this respect, it is important to dispel allegations that France is the country in Europe that works the least. In weekly and yearly work hours, and taking into account full-time and part-time positions, the Germans, Dutch and Danish work less than the French. One might add that France continues to create jobs, in proportions greater than those observed in the UK, the US or in Denmark. Above all, in these international comparisons, it is essential to factor in, more than rates of employment, the quality of the work.

REFERENCES

[1] Translations are our own.

[2] European Values Study 2008, France.

[3] *Histoire de vie, construction des identités* study, INSEE, 2003.

[4] Jobs Study, OCDE, 1994.

[5] "*Conditions de travail*" translates as "*working conditions.*"

[6] The Future of Work (The Aspen Institute, 2011).

[7] Carl Benedickt Frey & Michael A. Osborne, *The Future of Employment: How Susceptible are Jobs to Computerization*, Oxford University Programme on the Impacts of Future Technology, 2013.

[8] Matthew B. Crawford, *Shop Class as Soulcraft: An Inquiry into the Value of Work*, Penguin Books; Reprint Edition (April 27, 2010).

[9] Gallie and Zhou, 2013.

[10] Blanche Segrestin and Armand Hatchuel, *Refonder l'entreprise*, Editions du Seuil, 2012.

[11] Isabelle Ferreras, *Gouverner le capitalisme? Pour le bicamérisme économique*, Presses Universitaires de France, 2012.

[12] Translations are our own.

30

LEADING YOUR WORK AND YOUR LIFE

Desmond Kuek

President and Group CEO of SMRT Corporation Ltd.

You all have a future ahead of you filled with immense and exciting opportunities. It is easy to be bewildered by the massive array of ideas on offer, and often very convenient to simply follow in the road which is already well traveled and tested by others before you. But life is not just about making a living; it is about making a difference. Making a difference is founded on the way that we work and live, and on our individual and collective service to the community through our life and leadership.

At the age of 18, I joined the Singapore army and won a scholarship to study at Oxford University. At the time I would never have known that I would go on to lead Singapore's armed forces many years later. What I do know now, however, is that what you are and what you become is a product of all the seemingly small, everyday actions, decisions and choices you make as you step your way through life.

I found deep meaning in leading the Singapore army and being involved in the collective mission of ensuring Singapore's national security and wellbeing. More than a job, it was an amazing journey of opportunity and adventure. In 28 years, I had the privilege of commanding tens of thousands of people in major army formations. I organized the biggest National Day to celebrate Singapore's Independence of the millennium, and conducted the largest humanitarian relief mission in 2004 after the Indian Ocean tsunami. In my time as Director of Joint Intelligence, I worked with intelligence chiefs around the world as the specter of transnational terrorism reared its ugly head following the attack on the World Trade Center in the US in 2001.

Working in the military in Singapore often meant braving physical discomfort and inconvenience, out in the rain, in the sun, in the cold, in the dark, sometimes facing life-threatening situations even when all necessary precautions had been taken. In many ways, I would say that my life was colored by my work. Operational deployments brought me to troubled spots across the world. I celebrated my 19th birthday on patrol training in the tropical jungles in Brunei. By the time I was 21, I had traveled across seven time zones through Siberia and Mongolia. At 28, I was exploring the Maasai Mara in Kenya with the British army officers. I met with people from all walks of life, had the opportunity to lunch in regal style with Queen Elizabeth II, I partnered with the Sultan of Brunei for pistol shooting; and I learned a lesson or two about life from my 20 year old tank driver, and from a young trooper who had spent time in remand for gang fighting.

My career in the military culminated with 4 years as Chief of Army, another 3 years as the Chief of Defense Force, before I retired from active military service. I then joined the civil service to head a government ministry in environment and water resources as its permanent secretary. It was a challenging time in more ways than one. We undertook major works to re-invent water utilities, turning drains and canals into active, beautiful waterways so they could be used by the community and enjoyed as common public spaces. I particularly enjoyed the work of promoting and enabling a cleaner, more sustainable environment that would make for a more liveable, sustainable home for all of us now and for future generations.

Three years ago I decided to leave the government to grapple with new leadership challenges in the corporate world. My friends thought I was either very brave or crazy, especially when they found out I had agreed to become the CEO of SMRT Corporation, Singapore's public transport operator. This is arguably the "hottest seat" in town, because the ageing rail network was experiencing frequent disruptions, deteriorating reliability and increasing congestion problems. Every year, SMRT carries 1 billion passengers, so, as you can imagine, the company is under a great deal of scrutiny. Only three weeks after I had joined the company a power outage caused the entire circle line to come to a halt and my very first appearance was to apologize for the breakdown which had been caused by deficiencies during its construction. Shortly after, an unexpected downturn in labor relations led a number of our Chinese bus drivers to go on an illegal strike. Strikes may be commonplace in many other countries, but it was the first time this had happened in Singapore in 26 years, making international news headlines.

What my professional career has taught me is that every job you do, every task you take on, irrespective of the sector you choose to work in, will bring its own share of crises and opportunities. What truly matters is how you carry out your work, the mark you make and how you lead your teams. In my experience, being a good leader all comes down to the following 10 points.

1. Believe in what you do

You must lead with passion and conviction. Ask yourself what you believe in and what you stand for, what motivates you and fires you up. You cannot inspire anyone if you yourself are not inspired. That passion should be contagious, touch others around you so that every opportunity is used to influence the lives of those you lead in a more positive and powerful way. Believe in what you do and why you do it. Do not simply go through the motions. When others see you believe in what you do, they will be more inspired and more likely to share in your commitment, your dedication and your passion.

2. Set your goals high

You must lead with vision and high standards. This is what makes the real difference between being mediocre and being outstanding. Resist the temptation to look for the easiest way or the minimum you can get away with. You will not have stretched yourself and you will have nothing to feel proud about at the end of the day. Your team members may initially like the idea that you are easy going in terms of standards or discipline but they will not respect you for it. What they want is a leader with a vision, forging a collective goal that sets a direction and on which they can set their sights. As the saying goes, you cannot score if you do not have a goal. Simple goals will do, but set them with high standards. If there is something worth doing, I would urge that it is worth doing well, and to the best of your ability. Always strive for excellence; always reach for the stars. When you reach for the stars, you might not quite get one, but you won't end up with a handful of mud.

3. Know your job well

You must lead with professionalism and with competence. To be a leader, your team will expect you to be technically and professionally competent. Know your job, and know theirs, too. Know it well enough to be able to guide them, and even to show them how. Believe in yourself because you have been schooled and trained well. However, you must always continue to learn and hone your skills so that you can be excellent in whatever field you have chosen. Be confident that you have what it takes to do your job well, and always be willing and eager to learn in the areas where you may have shortcomings. When I was in the military, there was a saying that commanders would offer to their soldiers: "follow me and do as I do." That is a much more powerful way to inspire your people than simply saying "do as I say." But you can only say and do so with confidence and lead by example if first you know your job well.

4. Learn from others

This may seem like an easy thing to say, but in whatever position you perform in the future, you must lead with humility. Even as you show confidence, you must also be humble, ready and willing to learn from others. At one point or another, you will find yourself inexperienced in the face of more experienced and more knowledgeable specialists in whatever field of work you choose. Take the opportunity to learn from them with a humble heart and an earnest mind. There is nothing to be embarrassed about in not knowing, but there is something to be embarrassed about by not asking, and there is everything to be embarrassed about by not learning. In every situation, there is something to learn if you have the humility to learn it, if you show interest and have an open mind. Those more experienced than you will be more forthcoming with their advice and support; and those below you more patient and trusting of your leadership.

5. Make things happen

You must lead with decision and action. Your team members, your followers will expect you to make things happen, and not just wait for things to happen, or wait for somebody to take the initiative, or worse still, as a leader not even know what has happened. The first is the mark of a leader, the second the mark of a follower, and the third the mark of a loser. Make things happen, and make sure the things that happen are the right things to the best of your judgement. Those whom you lead expect that you make decisions and take action wisely and in a sound and timely manner because they are most likely and most often those affected by the consequences if you do not. Often, not making a decision is in itself the wrong decision, and no action is in itself the wrong action. So, be proactive, take initiative and make the right things happen for yourself and for everyone in your team.

6.   Take responsibility when you are wrong

Lead with courage and with integrity. It is very easy to stand tall and take credit whenever your team has done well or when praise and compliments go round. It is not so easy to stand up to take the blame when things do not go so well. Resist the urge to pass the buck to someone else or to blame your subordinates. There could be many times when things may go wrong. Your people will expect you to have the integrity and the courage to take responsibility for your actions and your decisions when you are wrong, and even when sometimes you are not personally to blame, but happen to be the team leader. Everybody makes mistakes, especially when you are doing something for the first time. Refrain from passing the blame on to those beneath you. Quietly accept responsibility as the leader and learn from that mistake. I have found in my own time that making the mistake is not the issue, in fact my experience has taught me that your maturity and your integrity will earn you greater respect than your wrongdoing had gained you criticism.

7.   Keep going, even when the going gets tough

You must lead with determination. It is not enough to set a goal or have an action planned if you cannot last the distance. In a navigation exercise, for example, to get to the endpoint you must first set the direction with your compass and then pace out the distance until you get there, regardless of whether there is a thorn bush, a hill, a river or a swamp in your way. Over, around, under the obstacle: do not let anything get in your way. To accomplish your goal will require physical fitness as well as mental toughness. Your team members, your followers will expect you to have the stamina, the discipline and determination to go on because they will give up if you do. As a leader you must keep going, even when and especially when the going gets tough.

8.   Care for your people

You must lead with your heart, not just with your head. Nobody cares how much you know until they know how much you care. Even as you push for high standards of excellence, your followers will expect you to know them well, to understand their strengths and their limitations, to recognize when they put in the extra effort and to look out for their wellbeing. Well-being is not the same as welfare, which is also important, but welfare does not always lead to well-being in the long run. Ensuring high performance standards is important, but it is imperative this is balanced with care for your people. This is even more pertinent when your followers are entrusting their lives or their livelihood into your hands. Your care must be genuine and selfless because, make no mistake, your followers will see right through you if you are insincere. No extent of lessons, case studies on leadership and management and no amount of discussion on mission, vision, and core values can ever be enough to make you a good leader if you do not feel passionately for the people who do good work for you. So take the time, take the trouble, to find out what concerns your followers or your team, and what their concerns, their fears, their motivations, and their aspirations might be. Show them that you do care.

9.   Keep your communication lines open

You must lead through mutual trust and understanding. Never assume your people or your followers do not or cannot understand what is happening. Keep them informed about the reasons for your actions and decisions. Communicate. The morale in a team is low when its members have no clue what is going on. It is lower still if they have reason to believe their leader is not telling them the 'what' or 'why', and it is lowest when they know their leader will not listen. Only if you keep your lines open can you build trust and confidence. So tell your followers 'why' whenever you have time so that they will trust you and not question 'why' when you clearly do not have the time to explain, such as in the heat of a crisis, in business or otherwise. Keep those lines of communication open so you know what is going on in their hearts and in their minds, so that they, in turn, also know what is going on in yours.

10. Build a strong team

You must lead through teamwork. One of your key priorities as a leader must be to get the people in your team to work together. When you succeed in building a strong team, people will find ways to work together and will want to do more rather than fight with each other over who should do less. Your followers want you to make them work together as a team, to build them up and to forge them into a team. They want you to help them gain confidence in themselves, in you and in the people around them. This sense of cohesion, bonding, esprit de corps, a spirit of not wanting to let the team down is a basic feeling for all human beings. This is the kind of team spirit that will help win over any difficulty or adversity.

As I underlined earlier, life is not just about making a living. It is not about high-paying jobs and glamourous careers. Of course, that is to what most people aspire, but life is first and foremost about finding yourself and making a difference through your work, to the betterment of the community and the lives of the people around you. Leading is not something that comes automatically, and being a good leader is certainly not simply a matter of holding a high job title or a senior rank or because you are armed with a prestigious academic degree like the one you are working towards at ESSEC. A leader is what you must be if you are to make a difference. Finding your gift is life's meaning. Giving it away through your leadership and your service in making that difference is life's purpose. I wish you all the very best leading in your work and in your life.

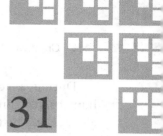

CRImagine

François Taddei

Director of the Center of Interdisciplinary Research (CRI)

HOW CAN WE STAY MORE INTELLIGENT THAN COMPUTERS?

When Garry Kasparov, chess world champion, lost a game against a computer, *The Economist* headline was: *If your job is like playing chess, get ready to change jobs.* At that point, I was doing research in genetics, a field which is somewhat similar to chess... And I could see why there was cause for concern. Understandably so. A couple of years later, the magazine *Nature* published an article entitled "The Robot Scientist", which presented a robot geneticist that was cheaper than a doctoral student. Today, a number of professions, from finance to journalism, have already been replaced by computers. However, humans are still capable of imagining things that robots cannot. And that is what means we will be able to keep our jobs, or at least temporarily, until robots catch up with us.

After having lost his game against the computer, Kasparov decided to get ready to play against the rest of the world. Anatoly Karpov had already done something similar a couple of years earlier, and had crushed his competition: the expert was infinitely superior to collective ignorance. In order to make the game more interesting, Garry Kasparov asked four teenagers to catalyze collective intelligence, namely by eliminating illogical moves. Thanks to a specialized software for mapping possibilities, this team completed its mission. For Kasparov, this match was fascinating because he had been challenged by collective intelligence. This goes to show that not much is necessary to go from collective ignorance to collective intelligence...

During a competition where teams were alternately made up of humans, machines or both, it was demonstrated that the human/machine alliance was better than machines alone, which in turn were better than humans alone. And what is interesting is that the winning team was not necessarily made up of the best human with the best machine, but rather of the humans who best knew how to use the machines. This then begs the question: why did schools ban the use of machines by students for such a long time?

To extend the metaphor further, I was selected by an educational system which is similar to chess, i.e. based on my ability to memorize and calculate. Today, any computer can carry out these tasks much faster than any human possibly could. I hope to be able to illustrate today that this weakness in our education system is a central problem in today's world.

Technology, Science and Education: Contrasting Evolutions

a. *Rapid technological advances*

The computer used to send men to the moon was small enough to fit in this room. Today, every mobile phone has more computer power than the computer used by NASA back then. Each and every one of you could conquer the moon! But technology was not the only key to achieving this incredible feat. It required teams, energy, and knowledge, and most importantly, an ability to bring them together in a collective effort.

The technological tools available to us in this, the beginning of the 21st Century, are much more powerful than those used by research laboratories of the 20th Century. Mobile phones have become a vital scientific object. By adding a microscope lens to a phone, it can measure the infinitely small. A phone can also locate you, and even measure your mood. For example, the Mappiness app maps people's happiness across space, and can identify areas or moments where people are happiest.

Another type of microscope is the one invented by Manuel Prakash. It looks just like a sheet of paper and costs 1 dollar. This researcher gave out 10,000 of these microscopes to individuals in Indian villages, to see what it would help them invent.

The first complete DNA sequencing was only concluded recently. In the past, it cost billions of dollars, it now only costs 100 dollars. This means it experienced an even faster evolution than the rhythm of Moore's law.

In a couple of years, it will be possible to get your genome and your friends' genomes for a couple of dollars, or maybe even less. Technology is increasingly affordable and compact; DNA sequencing is like a simple USB drive.

What will we do with these increasingly available technologies? You are here to imagine new possibilities; possibilities which were unthinkable just 10 or 15 years ago.

b. *Science is progressing*

Science evolves a little slower than technology, but it still evolves very quickly.

Printing revolutionized the world, particularly in its scientific dimension. But it took time. The first book which was ever printed, *the Bible*, was also quickly followed by erotic books. It took several hundred years for scientific books to appear. The dissemination of these books enabled science to literally take off in the 18th century, but in the following century, this growth became exponential: 100 times more scientific articles were written every 100 years.

c. *Education is lagging behind*

Science in the 21st century is practiced in very different ways than it was in previous centuries, partly due to the Internet. And, as discussed previously, technology is evolving rapidly. However, the physics program of scientific *classes préparatoires* haven't changed since 1905… This is one of the countless signs of just how slowly education is evolving. The room in which we are standing is not very different from what could be seen in the Middle Ages. The only difference is the clothes we are wearing and that we have a microphone. Major educational inventions! The Massive Online Open Courses (MOOCs), described by some as a revolution, are only a fairly relative innovation: they are simply very powerful microphones which can reach students worldwide.

HOW CAN EDUCATION BE MODERNIZED?

Our Dreams for Higher Education

Until mental barriers actually come down, it can sometimes be difficult to be aware that they exist. How many of these barriers are holding back our education system?

The Enlightenment hoped to transform universities, which had been founded in the Middle Ages. For Wilhelm von Humboldt, a liberal education reformer, universities have to offer the freedom to learn, the freedom to teach and the freedom to do research all in one place. Not many universities nowadays offer these characteristics, be it for professors or students. Yet our top universities today are the ones which come closest to this ideal, which proves the relevance of this proposal.

Wilhelm von Humboldt's vision is becoming a reality thanks to the Internet. In the Web, we have is a tool whereby all can learn freely and produce content so that others too can learn. *De facto,* you are free to share whatever you want and to use the knowledge available to carry out your own research.

Wilhelm von Humboldt also stated that a university professor should not be a teacher, and that students should not be pupils. On the contrary, students should be able to show initiative, imagine new possibilities. In which case professors should take on the role of mentors, capable of guiding students in this necessarily demanding venture.

Opening up to Different Levels of Intelligence

Geoff Mulgan, former adviser to Tony Blair, who is now the Chief Executive Officer of a foundation worth nearly 1 billion pounds sterling in the UK, tried to imagine new ways of thinking and developing intelligence. He differentiates three levels of intelligence: individual, collective and global, which all mirror one another.

For him, individual intelligence is made up of three levels of thought. Firstly, the ability to solve classic problems. The selection process of the French *École Polytechnique* is based on this form of intelligence. Then, the ability to solve new problems. In our current education system, this ability is only valued from Research MA-level onwards. And the third and final level of thought is the ability to define new problems and solve them. In spite of its appealing nature, this ability is often banned from our education system.

Machines can mobilize these forms of thought. They fully master the first level insofar as they can solve classic problems. In certain cases, they can even solve new problems when they are similar enough to previous ones.

Collectively, a company solves traditional problems (selling its products), but can find solutions to new problems (inventing products) but also define and solve new problems.

Finally, in auto-emerging systems, where decision processes are more bottom up than in traditional hierarchical systems, there are always forms of global intelligence. Wikipedia is a perfect example of this. It addresses a fairly traditional problem: defining the words of a dictionary.

For the moment, there are hardly any places where we can collectively discuss and solve new problems. The firm InnoCentive, however, succeeded in this: it publishes unresolved problems that companies bring to them on-line, and invites the entire planet to solve them. Multiplying these types of spaces would be extremely beneficial, especially given the proliferation of crises we are experiencing — financial, ecological, etc. However, who can we trust to find solutions in a new way? Without a doubt, the answer to this is: the younger generations.

d. *Wagering on collective intelligence*

We are all innate researchers. How can this innate ability, which is seldom developed by our system, be reactivated? All babies make observations, formulate hypotheses to try and understand the world, carry out experiments, analyze data and tell their peers what they have done to invite them to do the same and obtain the same results. We were all scientists in our early childhood, but only some of us preserved this ability.

That being said, many ordinary citizens carry out scientific processes and share them. For example, as well as Wikipedia, the growing popularity of the Do It Yourself (DIY) "movement" encourages people to tinker with programs, in network, with open source formats, without any patents. Originally confined to the field of electronics, this movement is now open to biology, with *OpenWetWare* which performs genetic constructions and shares them on-line. A group of students from the CRI (*Centre de Recherches Interdisciplinaires* [Center for Interdisciplinary Research] ... also known as the *Carrefour de Recherches Intéressantes* [Crossroads of Interesting Research]) became the synthetic biology world champion in November 2013, by using this type of technology to develop new drugs against tuberculosis.

Via the Kickstarter platform, anybody can post a wonderful idea, and ask the rest of the world to help them finance it. This has led to the establishment of a significant number of companies. One of them imagined a computer which costs 100$ and that can be assembled by children.

Another example, a mathematician who was awarded the Fields medal, equivalent to the Nobel Prize, published a problem on his blog which he could not solve. It was solved in three months, thanks to collective intelligence.

BECOMING A RESEARCHER IS ACCESSIBLE TO ALL

Anybody can become a researcher. In the field of medicine, this is the case of "impatient patients", who are mobilized by a pathology which affects them. For example, Sharon Terry, whose two children suffer from the same genetic disorder, has authored hundreds of scientific articles on the subject.

An American doctor tried to create a system using collective intelligence in order to break down the barriers between fields and laboratories which characterize traditional medical research. He refused to work within the limits of the traditional system, the shortcomings of which he was already aware of. For example, only 25 new drugs are marketed every year, yet there are still 5,000 pathologies for which we have no cure. This doctor invited his patients to share their medical records (anonymously) with communities which solve problems through *open innovation*.

Video game players can also become researchers and solve new problems, for example, unfolding a protein linked to AIDS. The International Game Competition for Education and Research (iGam4ER), organized in December 2013, brought together 20 teams of gamers from around the world. They had to invent games to offer new ways of learning or doing research. The winning team invented a sensor-accelerometer which informs us of our movements and those of our relatives.

At the *Centre de Recherche Interdisciplinaire*, we built an Open Lab, where we use open technologies to invite individuals to carry out projects together that they could not carry out alone. A young doctor collaborated with a physicist and an electronics engineer to design a sensor which measures heart frequencies. Sensors with a similar level of resolution would cost hospitals around 5,000 euros. In this case, it costs 200 times less, for a nearly identical result. This type of device offers a variety of medical applications, but can also enrich video games, giving players the opportunity to control their avatar's heart rate.

Guiding Children through Knowledge

In a TED conference, Céline Alvarez explained that all the pupils from her class in Gennevilliers, a disadvantaged area, can all read and count in pre-school. How did she achieve this? She observes her pupils and tries to understand how she can guide them. She understood that in order to progress, children have to be faced with obstacles they can cope with, that are adapted to their level. This is actually the principle adopted by video games, which offer progressive stages of difficulty.

Unfortunately, Wikipedia, does not follow this logic. It has a Platonic vision which seeks to get as close as possible to the world of ideas, and gives little credit to practical aspects. In an opposite logic, philosopher John Dewey, who strove to redesign education in the US, developed a "pragmatic" philosophy, based on the principle that one same object can be seen in different ways, and from different points of view, depending on the direction we are heading. For example, Wikipedia could offer different pages dedicated to Napoléon, which respectively reflect the French vision, the German, or English vision of this historical character. If students in history were invited to work on varied points of view, they would probably gain a deeper understanding of the subject.

We could invite young people to improve Wikipedia pages dedicated to the subjects on which they have to write assignments. University students could do it for high-school students, high-school students could do it for secondary-school students, thereby creating cascading knowledge.

Wikipedia could also include mind maps, in order to identify pages with different levels of difficulty on one same subject. By recommending specific contents for specific users, Wikipedia could educate communities and allow people who are interested in one given subject to work together.

Above and beyond anything else, it is crucial to encourage children to express their questions and their talents, which is not a priority in the

French education system today. In Israel on the contrary, as demonstrated in *Start-up nation*, challenging children to think is seen as something vital.

At the beginning of the 1970s, MIT professor Seymour Papert invited children to play with robots and program them. And it turns out they managed. Taking this experiment further, with *Scratch* children were given a place where they could program easily. Children have tremendous potential! Young Sylvia Todd — 11 years old (!) — animates *Sylvia's Super-Awesome Maker Show* on YouTube, where she talks about her scientific inventions: a piece of jewelry which blinks following your heart rate, an interface to draw on iPad and print in pastel. President Barack Obama even invited her to the White House to meet her.

Our world could be full of Sylvias if only we encouraged children: maybe they will know how to solve problems for which we are unable to find solutions.

Some of the youngest authors of scientific publications are barely 8 years old. This demonstrates that the ability to ask questions and solve new problems appears at an early stage in life, and does not require lengthy studies. These young authors took an interest in science, thereby overcoming their initial reluctance, thanks to an academic, Beau Lotto, who invited them to see this discipline as a game. He invited them to work on bees. What games do they play? Do they do Sudokus? Probably not. But if you look at Sudokus as a pattern, can we know if bees are able to recognize different patterns? These children were the first people who manage to demonstrate that they do.

School as a Place of Research

Ange Ansour, who is a primary school teacher in a ZEP ÉCLAIR, a priority education area, from Bagneux (in the Île-de-France region), invited her nine-year-old pupils from disadvantaged areas to study ants. Researchers installed an *ad hoc* lab in their classroom. Quite quickly, children noticed phenomena that researchers had not even observed. In particular, they observed that ants build walls in front of the entrance to the anthill. Researchers thought this was due to the earth they dug out from constructing the interior. But these children proved that these insects actually used "bricks" from outside.

This helped children understand that books do not always have all the answers, that articles on the Internet weren't always reliable, and that experts do not know everything, and that it was important to experiment and experience things by themselves. They made progress in science, but also in French and English because they tweeted in both languages and certainly in their ability to work as a group. They understood that none of them was more intelligent than all of them together, and that to see further, they had to "climb atop the shoulders of giants", as Newton once said.

The experiment was a success, and had massive media coverage. It was even published in the *New York Times*. The Paris City Hall asked for the experiment to be carried out in 20 more schools in Paris, and offered to provide a 6,000 m² venue in the famous *Marais* district, to all those who wanted to change the way in which we learn, the way we teach and do research, and to anybody interested in *Open Science, Open Technology, Open Education.*

Finally, it supports our *Open FIESTA Program* (acronym for *faculté pour l'innovation, l'éducation, la science, la technologie, les arts* [University for Innovation, Education, Science, Technology and Arts]) where students can define their project themselves, and achieve things together that they could never have managed on their own.

32

GLOBAL WARMING AT THE HEART OF OUR DEVELOPMENT — FROM THE POLAR REGIONS TO PUBLIC LIFE

Jean Jouzel

Geochemist, Climatologist, Glaciologist
Research Professor Emeritus at the AEC
Nobel Peace Prize in 2007

What career path will lead a glaciologist and polar region researcher to influence public life? How does he get involved in the city? After a presentation of my career, I will speak on the core subject of my research: the climate, with a focus on global warming and its links with human activity.

ICE IN THE ANTARCTIC AND GREENLAND, EXCEPTIONAL ARCHIVES ON THE CLIMATE AND THE ENVIRONMENT

My career can be explained in the simplest of ways, because I entered the AEC 48 years ago, never to leave.

Isotopic and Geochemical Analyses of Hail and Polar Ice

After graduating as a chemical engineer from the Lyon Higher School of Chemistry in 1968, I joined the AEC, where I had been offered a research post on the formation of hail. At this point, I should clarify that ice is not made up simply of water. Hydrogen and oxygen, its components, both contain heavy isotopes — deuterium and oxygen 18, respectively. The colder the weather, the lower the number of heavy isotopes, due to isotopic divisions. This means that heavy hydrogen and oxygen contents in the steam will never produce the same result from one day to the next, because these quantities depend on the history of the air mass.

In my research for a thesis on the isotopic analysis of large hail stones (5–6 centimeters), I demonstrated that hail forms when there are rising winds of over 150 kilometers an hour, and that the more successive rising winds there are, the longer the hailstones stay in cloud formation and grow (up to the maximum dimension of 6 centimeters). In other words, the colder the temperature, the higher the altitude of the successive layers of hailstones that form and the less deuterium and oxygen 18 they contain. Isotopic analysis, therefore, provides access to the altitude where these layers form.

During the 1980s, I stopped my research into hail in order to study the link between the isotopic content of precipitation and the climate in polar regions, where the same phenomenon may be observed everywhere: from the coastal regions (Dumont d'Urville) to the center (Dôme Concordia C) in the Antarctic, deuterium and oxygen 18 content varies according to prevailing temperatures. The lower the temperature, the lower the quantities of deuterium and oxygen 18. These variations, highlighted using isotopic geochemistry, enable us to reconstruct past climates in these regions.

At the time I was working in the Saclay isotopic geochemical laboratory, where Claude Lorius came to do his isotopic analyses. He had already done brilliant work on the Antarctic station of Charcot in 1957–1958, during the International Geophysics Year campaigns, before creating a polar glaciology branch in Grenoble, with the aim of reconstructing past climates in the polar regions.

Climate Change During the Last 800 000 Years

The study of glaciers in the polar regions has shown that the present Holocene, or postglacial, period began about 12,000 years ago. The last glacial maximum dates from 20,000 years ago. As for the previous warm period, it began 120,000 years ago.

We were able to reconstruct the climate of the last 45,000 years (the last glacial period) from the end of the 1970s onwards.

The first drilling to be done by a Frenchman was led by Claude Lorius, reaching a depth of 900 meters at Dôme Concordia C in the Antarctic, which took us back approximately 40,000 years. Isotopic analysis of the different layers of ice demonstrated that 20,000 years ago (the last glacial maximum), the Antarctic was around 10 degrees colder than it is today.

Our disciplines really came together and became the center of attention again after five successive drillings on the Russian base Vostok during the 1980s. This adventure led us to the discovery in 1999, not of the basement rock, but a lake as big as two French departments and 600 meters deep.

In 1970, the Soviet Union had already drilled for the first time. A joint Franco–Soviet venture was later born in 1983–1984, with logistics support provided by the Americans from the South Pole, because American C130s were essential for transporting the ice cores drilled out by the Soviet Union at Vostok to Dôme C. This support was all the more remarkable because we were right in the middle of the Cold War. It proves that the Antarctic was considered real scientific territory. In 1999, we reached a depth of more than 3 km, where geothermal flows cause the ice to melt.

This drilling enabled us to go further back than the last climate cycle for the first time, for both Greenland and the Antarctic region, using the analyses of the cores brought back by Claude Lorius to France — work for which Claude Lorius and myself received the CNRS (National Scientific Research Centre) gold medal in 2002.

For the first time, at least where polar ice is concerned, we were able to reconstruct the last period of global warming, which, as it has emerged and been clearly confirmed since then, was hotter than the current climate, for completely natural reasons.

Also, using trapped air bubbles from inside these samples, my colleagues from Grenoble, (I should specifically mention Jean-Marc Barnola, Jerome Chappellaz and Dominique Raynaud) and the entire team working with Claude Lorius, started to draw benefit from the complete analyses of the development of the greenhouse gas effect, which increased the value of this drilling expedition even more. The explanation for this is that only polar ice can be used to reconstruct climate change and the atmosphere as it was in the past with enough precision, thanks to the air bubbles that it contains. For the time being, we have no knowledge of other ways to achieve this.

Finally, thanks to the new drilling campaign in Dôme C as part of the European programme Epica,[1] we not only covered a period of 800 000 years, but we also highlighted, once again, a close link between greenhouse gas and the climate, for both methane and carbon gas, i.e. the two main greenhouse gases that our work focuses on.[2]

The ice cores from this drilling campaign were 3 meters long and a dozen centimeters in diameter.

We can learn so much from the ice that numerous laboratories are doing research work on it — and the same applies to hail — on the climate, the composition of the atmosphere or even the way the sun operates. Cosmogenic isotopes, such as beryllium 10 and carbon 14, but also volcanic dust and recent pollution are all completely exceptional archives in all areas of the environment.

Over and above this work on drilling campaigns in the Antarctic, I have had the good fortune to participate in several drilling campaigns in Greenland, particularly those that took place at the beginning of the 1990s, making it possible to highlight — which was a genuine surprise — that climate change in the North Atlantic took place extremely quickly, on a 10-year scale.

It is true that recorded oxygen 18 content in the ice shows a profile completely different from that of the Antarctic, with variations taking place extremely quickly and probably linked to changes in oceanic circulation and in any case to the Gulf Stream ceasing and starting to flow again. If this warm current runs more to the South and at the same time closer to the surface (when fresh water reaches the ocean's surface, for example), it subjects the North Atlantic to extremely cold periods.

Although they occur in the specific location of the North Atlantic, these rapid variations have repercussions on the whole planet.

Demonstration of the Link Between the Greenhouse Gas Effect and Climate Change

The link between greenhouse gas and the climate was discovered when air bubbles from samples taken during the first drilling campaigns at Vostok

---

[1] European Project for Ice Coring in Antarctica.
[2] European Project for Ice Coring in Antarctica.

were analyzed. This initial discovery played a not insignificant part in raising the awareness of policymakers on the effect of greenhouse gases on the climate in the middle of the 1980s. Modelers also demonstrated this link. It was therefore on the basis of results obtained from these models and to an even greater extent from the study of polar ice that the decision was made to set up an inter-governmental group on climate change (IPCC) in 1988.

Analysis of the last glacial sample from Vostok later made it possible to demonstrate extremely clearly and in a very visual way the link between the development of the greenhouse effect and climate change. During cold periods, for example, quantities of carbon gas are lower.

Our measurement of the development of the quantity of carbon gas is as follows: 200 parts per million (ppm) at the last glacial maximum, 280 ppm during the pre-industrial period (200 years ago) and more than 400 ppm today.

Similarly, we noted that the quantities of methane had doubled between the last glacial maximum and the pre-industrial period and had more than doubled since then.

It is essential to have these numbers in mind. They show that during the last four climate cycles, the link between climate and the greenhouse effect has been confirmed and has greatly increased.

It is important to specify here that it is, above all, the position of the Earth during its orbit which, like a metronome, provides the rhythm for the great glacial/interglacial cycles. Indeed, the elliptical shape of this orbit changes over time, as does the inclination of the Earth's rotation axis, which causes variations in the amount of energy received at a given location. These insolation variations have caused the great glacial/interglacial cycles. In this case, we have shown — and this is now accepted — that natural variations in greenhouse gases amplified these insolation changes and allowed these great cycles to occur during the Quaternary period.

ON THE RELEVANCE OF PAST CLIMATES FOR THE FUTURE

The future evolution of the climate can only be visualized through models. In fact, in the past, no climate existed that was exactly the same as that towards which we seem to be moving. Even if, during the last interglacial period, 125,000 years ago, the climate was warmer than it is today, this was for reasons different from those we foresee for tomorrow.

Knowledge of past climates is relevant in many ways to help us understand and anticipate the development of the current climate.

As we have shown above, the climates of the past are, above all, of interest to help us understand the mechanisms of climate change and to inform us about the effective role of greenhouse gases on the climate.

Rapid Climate Change

Until 200 years ago, it was generally believed that the climate did not change. Even in the 19th century, scientists who pointed out the existence of the ice ages were considered "wacky." Acceptance of a changing climate has been gradual. When I started my career, it was felt that the climate was necessarily changing slowly. But the rapid climate changes observed unexpectedly in the North Atlantic during the 1990s must be taken into account.

Reasons for Attributing Current Warming to Human Activities

Human activities began to have an effect on our atmosphere 200 years ago and probably began to affect our climate in the middle of the 20th century. But if we really want to show that the period in which we live is exceptional in that it is directly influenced by human activities, it is not enough to study data on temperatures (which has existed for only 150 years, with some exceptions). It is also essential to be able to reconstruct the climate of the last millennium, so as to place recent years in a historical context long enough to express its exceptional character. Attribution of the current warming is thus also based on the data on the past.

Rising Sea Level

125,000 years ago, when the average climate was only two degrees warmer on a global scale than it is today, the sea level was already 6–10 meters higher. Thus, past climates teach us that, in the long term (on a millennial scale), relatively small changes in temperature and climates, similar to those towards which we are moving today, can cause extremely large increases in sea level.

STATE OF PLAY OF THE RECENT AND CURRENT CLIMATE

We live in a climate which is getting warmer. The year 2016 features in the line-up of four "record" years.

This evolution is explained, in particular, by the fact that we are experiencing, as we did in 1998, an exceptional El Nino phenomenon. But beyond this quite natural phenomenon, which results in a temperature higher than the normal temperature of the majority of the equatorial and tropical Pacific Ocean, the warming trend is unequivocal, and is really attributed to human activities.

The reason for this, as we know with considerable certainty on the basis of thorough documentation, is that for 200 years we have been modifying the composition of the atmosphere through our activities. It should be noted here that when they speak of the "composition of the atmosphere", climatologists are referring mainly to greenhouse gas compounds. This means, first and foremost, water vapor, which changes without any direct link with our activities; secondly carbon dioxide, which has grown by 40% over the last 200 years, largely through the use of fossil fuels, deforestation and cement manufacturing; and finally methane, or nitrous oxide, which has more than doubled over the last 200 years and is linked to agricultural practices — including ruminants, which contribute to 30% of global methane emissions.

The Greenhouse Effect

On a clear day, solar radiation reaches the surface of the planet without much difficulty. It is then reflected and changes wavelength. As a result of this change, some of the reflected radiation is absorbed by the greenhouse gases. Thus, by increasing the amount of greenhouse gases, we increase the "heating" available to the planet.

For 200 years, the amount of heat available for components of the climate system has increased by just over 1% due to human activities. To understand the magnitude of this apparently moderate increase, it should be noted that 93% of this additional heat goes into the ocean (compared with 1% into the atmosphere).

Since the rise in sea level (combined with the decrease in ice surfaces) is one of the clearest indicators of global warming, the diagnosis is unfortunately very clear. In this case, sea level is rising at a rate of 3 millimeters per year (1 millimeter is linked to the expansion of the ocean due to melting ice, especially ice caps) — or 30 centimeters per century and this pace is likely to accelerate. For about 20years, Greenland and West Antarctica have contributed to the rise of sea level by 1 millimeter a year. Moreover, in the Arctic — and exceptionally this year, also in the Antarctic — there is 10–15% less sea ice than a normal year, both in the North and the South.

Global Warming Mainly Linked to Human Activities

Most of the climate changes observed since the mid-20th century are linked to our activities, and since this period we have observed climate warming of up to two-thirds of a degree.

Greenhouse gases alone could account for nearly one degree of warming. It is clear, however, that other human activities — namely pollution — counteract almost 20% of the effect of these gases. The role of pollution, which is so much the issue today, especially from sulfate aerosols, is rather one of cooling. As for the natural causes of climatic changes — variations in solar activity following 11-year cycles and volcanoes — they can influence warming only to the order of a 10th of a degree.

Here again, the diagnosis is clear: we are in a world where we have already changed the climate, to a considerable extent. In this respect, the future holds no secrets.

THE FIGHT AGAINST CLIMATE CHANGE AT THE HEART OF DEVELOPMENT

The latest IPCC report, which dates from 2015, uses models based on two major scenarios of the future: firstly, the emission scenario, i.e. what will happen if nothing is done to fight against global warming; and secondly, the low-carbon scenario.

All the Warning Lights are Red

The emission scenario takes us towards global warming of 4–5 degrees at the end of this century, i.e. the equivalent of the difference between the last glacial maximum and today. Global warming could even be 10 degrees in the polar regions, due to melting ice in the Far North, and it would be more significant on the continent than in the ocean. In addition, in this hypothesis, the climate is, at this time, not yet stabilized.

It is important to understand that this would be a climate totally different from the one we live in today. This would already be the case with "only" two additional degrees.

We classify the consequences of this warming into five categories. However, whatever the category observed, all the warning lights are red. The risks are high, or even very high. And this is not at all surprising.

The following describes just some of the risks of this climate change, in categories.

- Category 1: Ocean acidification, which is already 30% higher than at the beginning of the last century, is expected to increase by another 30% by the end of this century. This acidity remains very weak, but it has consequences on all elements made of calcite and limestone (shells, coral reefs and fishing resources).

- Category 2: Extreme weather (droughts, heat waves, floods and cyclones) may become more extreme. The scorching summer of 2003 in France resulted in 15,000 additional deaths, according to epidemiologists. But this summer was only three degrees warmer than a normal 20th century summer. In the Paris region of the future, summers could be 6–8 degrees warmer on average than the scorching summers of the late 20th century. This would be a completely different world.

- Category 3: This concerns the risks that would directly affect the populations. The notion of "climate refugees" will become increasingly important. An additional rise in sea level of 1 meter would result in almost 15% of Bangladesh being covered, to quote just this one example. Water resources will become problematic in many regions, with consequences for safety, whether this be food safety or security. Some people believe that the unrest in Syria may be partly due to droughts at the beginning of the century, which led one million Syrians to migrate to the cities from the countryside, where agriculture was no longer possible.

- Category 4: This focuses more on environmental issues, which are already causing problems in themselves, and which will be exacerbated by global warming (e.g. the loss of biodiversity). As half of the fauna and flora categories are less mobile than climate zones, global warming would increase this loss of biodiversity. The same would be true for the modification of natural ecosystems, pollution and health.
- Category 5: The risks covered by this category will cause irreversible phenomena to develop, such as rising sea levels or the melting of permafrost, i.e. ice in the Far North.

Moreover, global warming will appear everywhere, albeit with slight differences from one region to another. Its consequences will affect the entire planet.

Even in the low-carbon scenario, sea level will have increased by 40–50 centimeters by the end of this century and probably by another one meter at the end of the next century.

Not to mention the risk of Greenland melting, well-illustrated by data from the past. This would result in the sea-level rising by seven meters on a millennial scale. There is even a risk of complete melting if the rate of global warming is maintained beyond two or three degrees over very long periods. This is what the future holds if we do not react.

THE FIGHT AGAINST GLOBAL WARMING: A POLITICAL IMPERATIVE AND A PRIORITY FOR CIVILIZATION

The Kyoto and Copenhagen Agreements

Everything must be done to prevent the IPCC emission scenario from becoming a greater reality, because this has actually begun to happen, despite the alerts sounded for the last 20 years. Already, in its first report, the IPCC envisaged warming by three degrees in the middle of the 21st century and a rise in sea level of up to 65 centimeters in the second half of the 21st century.

We have, at least, succeeded in convincing policymakers of the seriousness of the problem. For example, the UN Framework Convention on Climate Change was launched at the Rio Earth Summit in 1992, 4 years after the creation of the IPCC. Then, following the meetings of the Conference of the Parties (COP) in Berlin in 1995 (COP1) and Kyoto in 1997 (COP 3), the Kyoto Protocol covering the period 2008–2012 recorded the reduction of greenhouse gas emissions as the main objective of the Convention to stabilize global warming. This solution was well-dimensioned to the problem, at the time. However, the main emitting country in the early 2000s — the United States — never ratified it, even though Al Gore signed it in Kyoto. It is not outrageous to think that the George Bush era had extremely dramatic consequences for the fight against global warming: we lost 10 years.

A second agreement was signed in Copenhagen in 2009 at COP 15 for the period 2013–2020. It has also failed, as only Europe and a few other countries, accounting for less than 15% of global greenhouse gas emissions, committed to it. However, these emissions have never increased as quickly as they have done since the beginning of the 2000s. China overtook the United States in 2005 and currently, its carbon dioxide emissions are twice as high as those of the United States.

However, COP 15 resulted in the inclusion of two quantified targets in the agreement. The qualitative objective of the initial climate agreement was to stabilize global warming, but without defining the level of this stabilization. It was not until Copenhagen that it was decided to limit global warming to below two degrees and to study the possibility of limiting it to below one and a half degrees compared with pre-industrial levels (i.e. between 1 and 1.5 degrees compared with the current climate). It was also in Copenhagen that the agreement announced that developed countries would make $100 billion a year available to developing countries from 2020, so as to help them in the fight against global warming and accompany them in their adaptation.

The goal of limiting global warming to below two degrees is essential.

If this goal were to be achieved, the effects of global warming would be less significant — allowing adaptation to the new climate, at least for the most part (with the understanding that the rise in sea-level would continue to be less significant but would not cease).

However, the conditions for stabilizing global warming below two degrees are drastic, since the level of long-term stabilization largely depends on the cumulative amount of carbon dioxide. This does not mean that other greenhouse gases play no role — assuming they do not increase. But, as we have seen above, the role of carbon dioxide accounts for three quarters of the increase in the greenhouse effect each year and stays longer in the atmosphere. As for methane gas, it has a lifespan of about 10 years. Its role can therefore be extremely important, but only in the short term.

In this situation, to stabilize global warming below two degrees we must limit carbon dioxide emissions to around 800 billion tons of CO_2 linked to human activities in the future. This represents about 20 years of use of CO_2 at the current rate, and nearly 15% of easily accessible resources (conventional and unconventional oil and gas and coal).

What is required, therefore, is a complete change in our mode of civilization — and this needs to be done quickly, right away, not in 20 or 30 years' time. We have already waited too long. We must also completely transform our energy system, with all the difficulties that will entail.

The Paris Agreement (COP21)

France was the only country that applied to host COP21, and I had the chance to participate in the steering committee for this event.

The Paris Conference proved particularly important in the light of the timetable. Indeed, it had been noted by all countries that the post-2020 agreement should be set up in 2015. What is more, the agreement reached was a success: firstly, a diplomatic success (150 heads of state or government were present), next, an organizational success (less than a month after the terrorist attack against the Bataclan) and finally, above all, a success because of its universal character. The situation was turned around when the participating countries were asked to estimate their own contribution in terms of the fight against global warming and adaptation, rather than decreeing that the developed countries would make 100 billion dollars a year available to developing countries from 2020 onwards. Laurent Fabius, who, I really must say, was remarkable, did not believe that all countries would cooperate. And yet everyone put their contribution on the table.

Above and beyond the moral and verbal commitment made by each country, the agreement is open for signature until April 2017. For the Paris agreement to come into force from 2020, it must be ratified by more than 55% of the countries accounting for more than 55% of greenhouse gas emissions. Admittedly, Donald Trump was elected during the first week of COP22, which was held in Marrakech. Nevertheless, even if the United States withdrew, in accordance with the election promise of its new president, the agreement would remain valid, since more than 55% of the countries have ratified it, representing more than 70% of the greenhouse gas emissions.

The down side of the logic change that I just mentioned is that, although countries were asked to make a commitment, their commitments do not necessarily match the original goal. Thus, maintaining the commitments of countries at their current level would not achieve the goal of stabilizing global warming below two degrees. By 2030, there would still be 35–40% more emissions than this target or 55 billion tons of CO_2 equivalent, taking into account all greenhouse gases, whereas the figure achieved should be 40 billion tons. Be that as it may, this gap between 40 and 55 billion tons of CO_2 equivalent does not come from the Paris Agreement as such, but from the failure of the Kyoto and Copenhagen agreements.

With current commitments, we are therefore on course for 3 to 3.5 degrees of global warming at the end of this century. Adaptation to this climate will be very difficult.

However, the benefit gained by the Paris agreement is that it provides for a review clause, which created a lot of enthusiasm at the time — but the current position of the United States makes things difficult. It also contains many positive points. Its major weaknesses come mainly from a lack of precise details on the actions to be implemented before 2020, whereas it is essential to act immediately. Thus, no CO_2 price has yet been set. The form of the agreement is not binding, and no sanction is provided for if a country does not live up to its commitments. Finally, shipping and air transport have been exempted — which is at the very least inelegant.

AN EXCITING FUTURE!

There has been real media interest in our disciplines for the last 30 years. Many films are based on our work and on reports from the IPCC, such as Roland Emmerich's *The Day After Tomorrow*, Al Gore's *An Inconvenient Truth* or Fisher Stevens' *Before The Flood*, starring Leonardo di Caprio. Media reports are numerous. During this iMagination Week, you have had the opportunity to listen to Jean-Louis Etienne, a passionate communicator with a keen interest in the polar regions.

Media interest in all aspects of global warming is equally real. And I must admit that I have benefited from this media dynamic.

Vital Interactions between Civil Society, Researchers and Policymakers

I am one of those people who thinks that scientists must come out of their ivory towers and respond to policymakers when they ask them to do so. It's the least we can do. This happened to me when I was invited to participate in the Grenelle Environment Forum. On this occasion, we re-examined all the environmental problems, with very open discussions. Unfortunately, all of the proposed measures have not been implemented, but the Forum itself was an important moment for interaction between civil society, the research community and policymakers. At this event, I was in charge of the "climate-energy" component, along with the English economist Nicolas Stern. I was also involved in the development of the plan for adapting to global warming. I was responsible for the definition of scenarios for France: every year between 2010 and 2015, we produced a report on the consequences of global warming in France.

I have been involved in French climate policy for 20 years, during the presidential terms of office of Jacques Chirac, Nicolas Sarkozy and François Hollande, as rapporteur for the Economic, Social and Environmental Council (CESE) to prepare the law on energy efficiency, but also as a member of the steering committee of COP21. This law is ambitious, even if it covers only the energy aspect in France, with the objective of a reducing greenhouse gas emissions to a quarter of their current levels by 2050. We must make it work!

I have also been a member of the CESE for 6 years. I was rapporteur for an opinion on energy transition, as well as another on adapting to global warming.

Finally, I was rapporteur, with my colleague Agnès Michelot, for an opinion on climate justice. The risk of increasing global inequalities is, in my opinion, the primary consequence of global warming, as it reduces the number of good places to live on the planet. We are aware that some countries are more vulnerable than others, more sensitive to global warming. However, these countries often do not contribute to greenhouse gas emissions, and therefore to the increase of the greenhouse effect. What we are less aware of, although the IPCC has highlighted it, is that poor people in rich countries are also vulnerable. And they will be even more sensitive to the consequences of global warming than the well-to-do. The risk of increasing inequality is a real one. Our opinion "Climate justice: challenges and perspectives for France" aims to stimulate thinking about the measures that could be taken in different areas (education and legislation) so that, at least, global warming does not increase inequalities in a country like France.

Using Inventive Capacities to Serve a Sustainable Development Mode

If we want to see a low-carbon society with a development pattern different from that of my generation, it seems to me that your generation should not negatively interpret the outlook I have just presented. This evolution will be positive, bringing with it inventiveness, in terms of techniques and uses and also of social fabric. And I am convinced that it is more exciting for today's youth to take up the challenge of changing the world, rather than to see it continuing to develop the way that we have built it up — we must admit — without paying attention to resources.

To succeed, we must change the development model. It's exciting! There is so much to do, in terms of renewable energy, for example. Technically, it's possible. But a political decision is needed, and action must be taken immediately.

33

FOLLOW YOUR DREAMS, EVEN WHEN THE GOING GETS TOUGH!

Jean-Louis Etienne

Doctor and Explorer

THE CALL TO ADVENTURE

Let me start by confessing to my own first academic failure. Except for me, it was not failing to get into HEC, but rather not getting into secondary school! My grades simply were not good enough. So, with a primary school leaving certificate, I decided I would become a carpenter. However, the only place the vocational school could offer was in the metal working course. And so, I was destined to become a milling machine operator. Fortunately, I was able to prepare for the technical baccalaureate, a diploma which had recently been created although not without controversy. The prevailing thinking back then questioned how a young pupil could possibly earn a baccalaureate without having studied Latin or Greek?

Once I had my diploma, I decided to study medicine. In my second year, I wanted to sit in on surgeries as an observer. I spent hours in the OR, watching and observing. One day, an emergency operation came in. The intern was not available, so the department head ordered his team to "Get Etienne prepped for surgery!" This announcement will be forever etched in my memory. As I was assisting him during surgery, I reconnected with the pleasure of manual work. That is the day when my passion for surgery was born. I stayed at the hospital day and night, to make sure I was available whenever there was an interesting case.

After two years as a surgical intern, I found a new appetite burning within me: the longing to go on an expedition. As a child, I climbed the Pic de Nore — a modest summit in the Tarn — day in, day out, in the freezing cold winter, and I would picture myself conquering Everest one day. In those colonial days, France sent boatloads of people from different trades all over the world. I dreamed of being part of one of those ventures featured in the famous magazine *L'Illustration*. An idea came to me: why not put my medical skills at the service of these adventurers? And so, I accompanied Éric Tabarly as his doctor for his race around the world, I sailed with Father Michel Jaouen. Medicine had become my passport to adventure.

In those 12 years serving as partner to adventurers, I harbored the desire to have my very own personal adventures, to write my own story. I imagined how one day, I might be on a mission to help rescue five mountaineers who were trapped in high altitude on the north face of Mount Everest; I would be alone in a tent at Base 2, reveling in the howling wind and the rumbling of avalanches. My mind was made up: next time round, it would be my turn!

For my first solo adventure, at age 40, I chose the North Pole. A deliberate choice, because it was not particularly challenging. In order to become a navigator or seasoned mountaineer, you have to have practiced these disciplines from a very young age and have trained tirelessly. I did not have this experience. I had discovered the mountains when I was 25 years old, and was even older when I discovered the sea! However, I knew I had two very important things going for me: first, perseverance; and second, I was a great camper!

PERSEVERE, AND STICK TO YOUR DECISIONS!

The North Pole is in the heart of a frozen ocean. I camped in temperatures as low as −52°C. With such fearfully cold temperatures, nobody would have blamed me for giving up. But the reason I succeeded is because I did not yield to the temptation of giving up. This taught me a valuable lesson which I would like to share with you today: whatever you choose to do, persevere. If you have ever had a dream which motivated you above all else, if you have felt that "sacred fire", go for it, get as close as you can to your "dream reactor." No matter what, whatever the cost, follow the path to your dreams. People sometimes tell me that things come easy to those who are driven by passion. I argue that passion is a fire which must be kept burning — and sometimes, you have to go out of your way to find the fuel it needs.

How does a person become an explorer? This is a question I often get asked. First and foremost, learn a profession. Once you have mastered a trade or specific profession, you can explore all the fields it is connected to. However, you need a base from which you can explore, just as you need a strong knowledge base to let your imagination grow.

"Be imaginative!" Such an ominous order can make us anxious, and block any creativity we may have. We end up asking ourselves "what on earth am I going to imagine?." In practice, that is never how things happen. Imagination is nurtured through culture. Imagination arrives at that point when, after having acquired knowledge, you go down a different road, to explore new ways of doing things. Knowledge is the foundation on which you can build your freedom — on condition that this freedom does not hinder the freedom of others. In order to build this freedom for yourself, you have to find the boldness to go off the beaten track. These deliberate changes, of course, can very rightly raise a few concerns. In my case, deciding to leave the Faculty of Medicine, where I earned a salary as an assistant lecturer, with a whole career laid out before me, and which implied leaving surgery behind, was a very difficult decision. I do not regret it at all. When you invent your own life, moments of doubt are inevitable. I have had my "crossing of the desert" between expeditions. It is precisely in these moments that you have to persevere.

CONNECT TO THE WORLD

No matter how brilliant an idea is, it will be pointless if you keep it to yourself, without trying to "connect" it to the world.

When I prepare an expedition, I see myself as a sort of entrepreneur, sitting behind a mixing desk. First I test my idea, talk about it, and see what people say. Gradually, it becomes my project, one I am determined to see through to the end. In order to take it as far as possible, to bring my invention to life, I have to adjust and operate all the buttons on my mixing desk simultaneously: technology, scientific research, funding, defining a business plan and building a team. My determination, however, does not entirely make up for my shortcomings and weaknesses. At times, the task seems insurmountable. To keep that sacred fire alive, I do not let a day go by without throwing out a line. I study boxes and boxes of business cards which I have collected over the years, and throw bottles into the sea. To nurture my desire and my drive, I need to constantly meet the world, through books, films and discussions. Then, things often fall into place.

That is the journey I followed to invent my own life. Jean-Luc Petithuguenin offered a perfect illustration of his rather drastic life choices. He chose to leave behind a pre-defined path and to take the risk of defining his own existence by connecting it to the global challenges faced by the world. Judging by his enthusiasm, he made the right choice! Of course, such a path demands considerable effort. When I was the patron of an event for the PhD program of the French National Museum of Natural History, I remember the distress of one student who could not see how he was ever going to get a job with his thesis on the chromosome of the third leg of the *Cetonia aurata*. The truth is, I had to agree with him! So my advice to him was to learn to explain the topic to which he had dedicated several years of his life as simply as possible, in order to make it more easily understandable. Once he was able to identify the essence of his work, he would then be able to share it, and he would then be able to "connect" all the skills and knowledge he acquired to the world. Very seldom does this connection happen spontaneously, without needing any effort at adaptation.

Inventing your own life does not necessarily mean doing something extraordinary. When I came back from my race around the world with Éric Tabarly, filled with energy and sun, I had the opportunity to give a couple of conferences in front of hundreds of doctors. At the end of my first talk, a dozen of them came to congratulate me for making the right choice, and confessed that they regretted settling down, with a family, a house, and loans. After my second talk, the same thing happened. For my subsequent talks, I decided to change my talk. I felt it was unfair of me to destabilize them. When I was traveling around the world, they had been brave enough to stay, I explained that the bohemian lifestyle I had chosen for myself — I slept in my car, had no letter box — might be right for me, but my intention was not to promote it as a model others should follow. They were fortunate to practice a very rewarding and universal profession.

Rather than dreaming of a life like mine, I invited them to further explore certain aspects of their job. Maybe they would meet a Japanese, Russian or Korean researcher, who was working on the same topic as themselves, and they might invent something new together. I believe in the positivity of the unknown. You can only benefit from going off course, capitalizing on the knowledge and skills you have. Do not try to be randomly: imagination comes naturally with culture, experience — provided you know how to put it into perspective and connect it to the world. That is how talent and history come together.

You all have talent and skills. Ask yourself how you can connect them to a moment in history. Do not listen to those who describe the jobs of tomorrow: nobody knows what tomorrow will be made of! Do not listen to those who are stuck in the nostalgic past: when they say "back then", they often refer to their youth, i.e. precisely the time of your life you are living right now and when anything is possible. Your life is in your hands, your generation has many opportunities, which are just as enriching as that of your elders. Embrace the opportunity offered to you by ESSEC to acquire universal and open knowledge. I say this all the more genuinely considering I am a terrible manager. Build yourself a toolset which will enable you to imagine your existence. Put this background at the service of your passion, without forever forgetting that passion must be nurtured. You will experience doubts, moments of uncertainty, will be tempted to give up. Hang in there, and remain true to what is important to you!

34

THE AGE OF THE HUMMINGBIRDS

Pierre Rabhi
Farmer, Writer and Thinker, Pioneer of Organic Farming in France

FROM INTELLIGENCE TO CONSCIENCE

Today, society is at a dead end. We have turned our world into a doomed hell, where we are destroying nature by depleting its resources; by destroying nature, we destroy ourselves. The unintelligent and absurd logic which has prevailed until now is not working and can never work. Modern society has decided that earth is nothing more than a repository of resources which we must drain, down to the very last fish or tree. In doing so, we are destroying nature, and in destroying nature, we are destroying our future. I have always thought that we should see the planet as a beautiful oasis in the middle of a vast astral and sidereal desert. The first people on Earth understood this, and built their entire philosophy around a nurturing Mother Earth, of which they were the custodians, and which they therefore had to protect. Unfortunately, we have lost touch with this intuitive, natural intelligence. It has been overridden by a profit-driven logic, in which everything is a tool for making money, regardless of what the ultimate cost of this may be for humanity as a whole, and for the planet. As a result, we have destroyed the human and social fabric of the world, and are now faced with the consequences of this logic, with the North–South divide, the conflict of ideologies, and the emergence of murderous rivalries.

How has it come to this? Human beings are endowed with intelligence. This intelligence led us to science, thanks to which we have achieved great technological prowess. We have deciphered the human genome, we can make planes fly in thin air. Science, however, is also what enabled us to create weapons of mass destruction. Science, therefore, is capable of doing the best and the worst. Technological prowess or scientific progress has little to do with Intelligence. The human body, for example, is intelligent because it knows what it is supposed to do in order to sustain life. Take a seed and plant it, it has no brain, and yet it knows it exactly what to do. Intelligence is a matter of life itself. Intelligence lies in what we do with science, and time has come for us to be "intelligent." An intelligent practice of science can only be possible through conscience, otherwise it will continue to lead us down the path of mutual destruction while children throughout the world are starving to death. If we bring conscience back into the logic governing our societies, science can become positive, and will force us into action because our conscience will understand that we can longer allow this dichotomy to continue. If we choose to remain on the path of immorality, meaning devoid of conscience, our society will continue to view life as nothing more than a cycle of being born, learning, working, and dying. The question today is not so much whether or not there is life after death, but rather if there can be life before death: is life only a matter of having a transient existence before disappearing? Or can we reach self-fulfillment, make something beautiful and establish a peaceful relationship among humans, and between humans and nature. These are the questions which have driven my life's work.

FROM AN OASIS TO MODERNITY

I lost my mother when I was four and grew up with my father, a blacksmith and musician, in an oasis in the desert. Our land was colonized, or more accurately conquered, by the French who discovered coal they wanted to mine. This shook Algeria to its very core, because the country was suddenly forced into modernity, leaving behind its history and traditions. My father had to go and work in the mines to provide for his family. He understood that it was a "brave new world", and that Europe defined the rules of this new game. He wanted his children to succeed and to master the new rules of the game, so he wanted me to have a modern education. I was sent to live with a French couple in Paris, who had agreed to take me on and provide me with a "modern" education. So at a very young age, I went from one society to another: from Islam to a Christian world, from a world of traditions to a world of modernity. I was trapped in this dichotomy, and wondered who was right, and which world view I should adopt as my own. I wondered if a consensus between these apparently opposing world views was possible or if there could only be division.

The colonization of North Africa was carried out by the European people, in a very peculiar and rational process, the primary victim of which was Europe itself. When you look at the tales of the travelers from the 16th or 17th centuries, they described Europe as being a mosaic of different ethnic groups, each with their own language, customs and traditions, unified by Christianity. This ideology was exported to colonized countries, who were forced to adapt to this Western logic. This process systematically wiped out the history, traditions and culture of the colonized, in order to establish a European history and frame of reference. For example, at school, I was taught the history of "our ancestors the Gauls", and nothing could have been further from the truth. As a result of this process, colonized people live in this dual sense of belonging, where one world view dominates and denies the other. Today, nothing has changed except that science has instrumentalized human violence, making it more powerful so that we can dominate and destroy efficiently. This culminated in the paroxysm of inanity and collective ignorance: the atomic bomb.

Today, on the one hand, we have the society of overabundance, but which relies increasingly on anti-depressants because people are not happy or at peace, and on the other hand, the deprivation and material poverty of people who do not even have a bowl of rice to give to their children. The ideology on which society is currently built has to be called into question. Challenging and rebuilding this ideology cannot remain merely theoretical.

LIFE BEFORE DEATH AND LIFE AFTER DEATH

As I grew older, living and working in this modern and European society, I joined the workforce. Over time, I felt that what was asked of me was to trade in my entire life for a wage, and that this left no room in my life for me. I wondered if I would be able to enjoy the fullness of life; or if I, like all of us, would have to "do time" in the name of economic growth, and wait for retirement to discover Life. But I did not want to be held hostage in my own life. Modern society has condemned us to live a life of incarceration, in which the only space where we can be free is during our annual leave. The rest of our time (and therefore our life) must be dedicated to contributing, to generating wealth, and to being at the service of the growth of the GDB. But a GDP will not fill your life with love, compassion and happiness. The pressure of relentless economic growth has led nations to compete against one another. Globalized, universal competitiveness has divided human society. This need for competitiveness is so entrenched in our culture that it has become a vital skill for survival, just as fire was for humanity so many years ago. From a very young age, we are taught to be the best, and we are brought up in the anxiety of domination. So much so that this fear of domination is what structures society today, be it one country over another, the North and the South, men and women, minorities, etc.

In the 1960s, I was working for a company in Paris. I met a woman, as young men do. We both felt that we did not want to be held hostage in our own lives, and felt the need to disengage from this society with which we felt at odds, in order to reconnect with nature. We moved to the Ardèche region to become farm workers. I discovered that agriculture as we practice it today is damaging. An increasing number of natural seed varieties are being eliminated, and agriculture today relies on very aggressive chemical fertilizers and pesticides. What primitive, naturally intelligent, cultures honored, our society has viewed as a substrate which we can fill with chemical products, and that it is these chemical products which give us our sustenance. We have now destroyed our natural fauna and flora, and everything which makes up the life of the land.

Today, we live in an orchestrated error, initiated and perpetuated by the international petro-chemical industry. At the end of WW2, the remaining stocks of explosives and powder which had been stockpiled as part of the war effort were converted into fertilizers. From that point onward, the entire agronomic philosophy was structured around the use of fertilizers. This opened colossal opportunities for profit, and we are still entrenched in this philosophy. We have forsaken millennia of knowledge and traditions, now considered to be archaic and obscurantist, in the name of modernity, which must prevail at all cost, as if millions of years of human presence on earth had served no purpose. Society has completely disconnected itself from this extraordinary heritage, in favor of a system whose dogma, beliefs and credos are based solely on productivity and economic efficiency.

Just as our land has to be "productive" and "efficient", time has also become a commodity, to which the adage "time is money" bears testimony. We are experiencing this, and are starting to realize that this does not make us as happy as we thought it would, or were promised it would. In this world of abundance, our society relies increasingly on anxiolytics in our quest for escapism. Productivity and overconsumption have become the palliative to our lack of happiness. The economically rationalized logic of our modern society has converted us, human beings, into an entity which must consume in order to increase wealth. We have become subordinated to financial wealth. For that reason, I refuse to be called a "consumer." That is not a label I feel comfortable with: I am first and foremost a living being.

Our society has promoted the economy as the cornerstone of our society, and yet, in the name of the economy, we are destroying entire ecosystems, forests, we are enslaving men and women into this dynamic, we are producing weapons. In a system which is dominated by money, the economy has become the only way to interact with the system. This is the system against which I want to rebel, a system which has alienated human beings, and made them a disposable ingredient of exponential financial growth or competitiveness.

ON BECOMING A HUMMINGBIRD

When we look at nature, we talk of the "law of the jungle" as if the jungle were a place of gratuitous violence and chaos. Nothing could be further from the truth. Animals take what they need to live, but there is no aggressiveness. Aggressiveness is a human construct, which we built on something intangible. We fight for ideologies, ideas, religions, etc. And yet, we should understand that we are all alike. Human beings learned to capitalize on the resources of nature, first to survive, and then to live up to the ideology generated by the promotion of the economy in society, using nature as a means to achieve this, but without considering the consequences. It is time for us to understand that we are not merely a part of nature, we are nature. By thinking our species is more important than the rest of nature, we have become disconnected from all this natural intelligence, and today we are at a dead end. We do not know what will become of us. Food has become toxic, we have dried out our lands. We have assaulted our own habitat and organisms with chemical and toxic substances, which interfere with the natural logic of our body, and this promotes the emergence of diseases. This situation can either lead us to breaking point, or to a revolution, because today we are experiencing a transgression of life itself, and that is why we are calling for an uprising.

Simply analyzing and condoning the situation is not sufficient. Today we must take action. One fifth of humanity consumes four fifths of the resources of the planet. This has created a divide in the world population, with the uber-wealthy on the one hand and the destitute on the other. Hunger on earth should not be a fatality. Africa is incredibly rich, and is not overpopulated. The billions of people who lack the most basic necessities on earth today should not have to be in that position. A collective conscience must emerge in order to bring about basic human ethics, a deontology which pushes us to face up to this disruption of the natural order, which is one of the greatest problems humanity has yet to face.

This is the founding principle of the movement we founded: bring about change to eradicate hunger on earth. Can we do something about it? Yes. Can we do this based on the existing system, with fertilizers, pesticides and our modern agriculture? No. We taught agro-ecology to local farmers of the Sahel region. We had to "un-teach" what they had learned. They had been taught that in order to produce more, and therefore to earn more money, they had to use chemical fertilizers to improve their harvests. Since they had no money to buy these fertilizers, they were offered work with cooperatives which provided the fertilizers. After the harvest, the cooperatives took their share and gave the farmers the rest. The entire system made farmers indebted through fertilizers. There is always a gap in the ratio between the consumption of fertilizers and the actual production, and so farmers are perpetually in arrears because they can never repay their debt. They then send their children to the city so they can have a chance at a better life, so they and their family will not have to live a life of hardships and deprivation. The shift in farming practices has led to terrifying urban concentration, which, in turn, has meant that we take more and more out of nature, leaving us with bare and crusted soils.

Bare soils are lighter in color, which means they reflect sunlight, the atmosphere therefore heats up, there is no condensation, rainfall becomes more irregular or scant, and when it does occur, it is often in the form of devastating storms, which leads to soil erosion, which leads to the general impoverishment of the land. This is the agricultural disaster in which we are entrenched today, and to this we must add human suffering. This system has destabilized and displaced entire societies, who must renounce the only life they have ever known and are forced to migrate to the North to try and earn sustenance. We are today faced with a generalized disorganization of human society as a whole, simply because our modern logic is not based on a natural logic. Today, the world is faced with the refugees of violence, but also the refugees of shortages and hunger, i.e., of the economy.

AGRO-ECOLOGY

Theoretical analyses and considerations alone cannot save the world. Theory calls for action. A true insurrection against any given system must go hand-in-hand with solutions to mitigate the shortcomings of the social system.

The approach of our movement is to find ways to "rectify" all this. We want to re-introduce and embrace a natural, life-breathing logic, model our practices on natural systems, so that, in turn, society can draw inspiration from this. We called this "agro-ecology." This principle is modelled on a natural principle: "nothing is lost, nothing is created, everything is transformed." Forests, for example, have thrived for millennia without human intervention. The forest metabolism is a perpetual cycle of nourishment: trees grow, produce waste, this waste is transformed into a vital source of life for the trees, which helps them grow, and so on and so forth. We want to foster the emergence of an agriculture whereby people can live off the land, without depleting it but nourishing it, thereby creating a virtuous circle to counter the cycle of devastation and division our society has created.

Our agricultural proposal is based on the notion of humus, decomposed organic matter which nourishes the soil and acts as a natural fertilizer. Since farmers cannot wait for a natural cycle to run its course, we use agronomic techniques to create our own humus, which we can then use to let life bounce back, based on the logic of life. This is what I did on my farm, and what we exported to Africa. We have been gaining stature because people have understood that our approach is preferable. This technique regenerates the soil, enriches it. Fathers are working towards the future of their children. We are not depleting the land and its resources, we are increasing its potential, and by corollary, are improving the outlook for future generations. Instead of leaving behind a contaminated, impoverished land, we are offering future generations the gift of a fertile, sustainable land, the gift of sustenance and being able to provide for their families.

It is my belief that what humanity is lacking today is humanism. If humanity were humanistic, we could shift our attention back onto these issues. Our philosophy today is to foster the idea that humanism is a philosophy, but it is also a practical approach. Our society should not be modeled around the notions of wealth, competitiveness and domination: we must place "humanity" at the heart of our social organizations. Our movement established a number of structures where we teach these principles. We named them "Collibri" [hummingbird], after an Amerindian legend. One day, said the legend, there was a devastating forest fire. All of the animals were terrified, at a loss, as they watched the disaster, powerless. Only a tiny hummingbird was busy flying from a small pond to the fire, each time fetching a few drops with its beak to throw on the flames, again and again. After a moment, the armadillo, annoyed by this ridiculous agitation, said to him: "Hummingbird! Are you crazy? It is not with a few drops of water that you'll put out the fire!" To which the hummingbird answered: "I know, but I am doing my bit."

We realized that if everybody "did their bit", instead of simply lamenting the state of the world, we could quite literally change the world. This movement is gradually gaining momentum. We have also founded another movement which we called 'Une oasis en tout lieu' [Oasis in Any Place]. Today, our society faces an issue of social desertification. Losing your job means being banished to a social desert in countries where you can overcome this (social welfare programs, etc.). In countries where this is not possible, however, you fall into destitution. If the system has reached its limits, then it is up to us to come together and to recreate places for joint action. This will enable us to pool our knowledge and know-how, and save people from social and economic exclusion. This system involves no money. This social entity is based solely on solidarity, which gives everybody the opportunity to come together, and to contribute.

Today, it is paramount that we, as a society, unravel the stalemate of the north–south divide. In order for Northern countries to thrive, they need countries from the south to sacrifice their resources and their goods. Consequently, the countries in the south are now experiencing terrible food shortages. If we do not revolutionize the principles on which our society is built, this trend can only get worse over time, leading to global violence and destabilization. Today's society will very probably live on in history, but the heritage we are leaving for future generations is not viable. Is this really what we want for them? For them to find ways to "survive" in our mistakes? There is still time to turn the proverbial ship around. In order to achieve this, we must all take action, one hummingbird at a time.

A CHEMIST COOKING, IMAGINATION BROUGHT TO THE KITCHEN INTRODUCING NOTE-BY-NOTE CUISINE: THE IMPORTANCE OF LANGUAGE FOR IMAGINATION

Hervé This

*Physico-Chemist at the French National Institute
for Agronomic Research (INRA)
Director of the Foundation Science & Culture Alimentaire
from the French Academy of Sciences*

Can a chemist invent a new type of food? Would it be tasty, useful or even acceptable? Let's admit it, in the eyes of the general public, chemistry is often associated with unpleasant phenomena — pollution, explosions and other disasters — and seldom with the notion of pleasure, which is ultimately what cooking should be. I propose to demonstrate the contrary, that by reconciling chemistry, gastronomy, imagination, conviviality and love, one can achieve surprising and delicious creations, a *chantilly* of *foie gras*, for example. These are not so much the product of a vivid imagination but rather the result of hard work. For that reason, I do not define myself as a cook, but as a chemist. Chemistry is my backbone. It guides my research, everything I undertake and my discoveries. In other words, it is what guides my imagination.

ANCHORS AWEIGH! MAKE WAY FOR SCIENCE!

What if we were to analyze cooking? Don't worry, I am not asking you to follow me down a purely theoretical and intellectual path. Imagination also has its place in this analysis. Doesn't the Greek expression *analysis* originally refer to setting sail (breaking loose from moorings)? When we venture into analysis, we embark on a journey that will take us far from all known lands. Anything is possible.

To cook is first and foremost to use techniques to produce dishes. If cooking is a technique, it is one that requires attention, and most importantly, it must be filled with love. Every dish must become a proof of attention and love for the person who is going to taste it.

Deciphering a Scientific Approach

During the Middle Ages, scientists worked to decipher nature so as to understand the divine message. Centuries later, Albert Einstein stated that science's role was to "lift a corner of the great veil." In all events, its role is to unveil a mystery through science, which can give birth to innovation. What are the characteristics of this scientific approach? For me, there are four main characteristics: experience; calculations; language; and culture.

(a) Experience

Galileo maintained that experience was to be preferred above any arguments of authority. The highest dignitary can say that something is true as much as he wants to, scientists will answer that it is not the case and that an experiment should be carried out to prove it. That is the first step in science: to carry out experiments and to give them more credit than any idea.

(b) Calculations

Second step: calculations. For scientists, the world is written in a mathematical language. Place a scientist in front of a mountain, his first question will be: "why is there a mountain here?" Then, he will measure it, analyze it, collect a multitude of data, which he will synthesize and on the basis of which he will offer a theory. But careful: all theories are wrong! Science produces only erroneous theories that it then works tirelessly to improve. Scientists carry out experiments so as to produce theories that they want to see disproved. Let us add that by definition, there is no such thing as scientific demonstration. Nothing can be demonstrated, things can only be refuted. So do not be fooled by journalists who affirm that a property has been "scientifically proven"!

(c) The right word

To analyze a mountain, first we need the concept "mountain", and also the word "mountain." It is impossible to be a good scientist without having a good command of language. Lavoisier, the father of chemistry, quoted Condillac in his *Preliminary discourse to The Elements of Chemistry* to insist on the importance of appropriate language: *But, after all, the sciences have made progress, because philosophers have applied themselves with more attention to observe, and have communicated to their language that precision and accuracy which they have employed in their observations: In correcting their language they reason better..* For him, it is by using the right words that we can have the right ideas and that reasoning is possible and maybe innovation also.

Lavoisier added: *The impossibility of separating the nomenclature of a science from the science itself, is owing to this, that every branch of physical science must consist of three things; the series of facts which are the objects of the science, the ideas which represent these facts, and the words by which these ideas are expressed. [...] the word ought to produce the idea, and the idea to be a picture of the fact. And, as ideas are preserved and communicated by means of words, it necessarily follows that we cannot improve the language of any science without at the same time improving the science itself; neither can we, on the other hand improve a science, without improving the language or nomenclature which belongs to it. However certain the facts of any science may be, and, however just the ideas we may have formed of these facts, we can only communicate false impressions to others, while we want words by which these may be properly expressed.*

(d) Art and culture

It is impossible to innovate without culture. I would like to invite you to draw on art and culture as a source of inspiration for your innovations, no matter how technical they may be. Here are some illustrations of what this can lead to in a kitchen. I am passionate about the Iliad and the

Odyssey, so just imagine the interest with which I read the correspondence between Goethe and his friend Schiller on the work of Homer. They see in it a characteristic trait of epic tales, in which the hero must face many obstacles and is hindered in carrying out his endeavor. That is why Ulysses' return to Ithaca, after countless adventurous events, will take 20 years. Would it not be better then, more fun even, if when cooking, we delayed that pleasure of tasting? We have imagined a system which allows precisely that. First we present the guest with a plate hidden under a lid that the waiter lifts. But they cannot taste it just yet. Another waiter pours some sauce onto the plate. What the guest then realizes is that the plate that has been presented has a double bottom, so the guest can enjoy a second dish, using the sauce from the first one. It is a very complicated thing to do. It is team cooking!

Just as Escher's infinite loop of stairs, or as in certain musical pieces in which the suites seem to know limitless expansions, I imagined a sweet and sour taste that expands. It is very easy: you simply have to reproduce a musical pattern, and replace notes with the intensity of taste. It is easy to find inspiration for innovation in other arts.

Just painters from the beginning of the 20th century abandoned any representation of reality to explore abstract painting, so too it is possible to do "abstract" cooking. We offer dishes that the taster will find delicious, but in which it is impossible to detect known flavors The Chef Pierre Gagnaire, with whom I regularly collaborate, was the first to make "abstract cooking." In doing so, we borrowed concepts foreign to chemistry to integrate them in cooking and invent a new culinary trend.

Local or Global Technologies?

Technology is the field of engineers. They are the people with whom you will deal at work. Scientists, on the other hand, work outside the corporate world, in universities. Engineers are asked to improve their techniques, either by observation and without any scientific input (what I call local technology), or by exploiting works developed elsewhere by researchers (what I call global technology).

Let us see what these two approaches can produce when applied to a simple egg white. The day some genius had the idea of creating a whisk to beat egg whites that was not made of branches tied together (which had the inconvenient effect of repainting your kitchen wall every time you used it), but of folded over branches, he produced an improvement by means of local technology.

We can go even further. When you whisk, you introduce bubbles of air into the liquid to create foam. Why not invent machines that can have the same effect? That's what I did when I created the machine that makes it possible to whip egg whites in no time at all, but then if you inject air into an egg yolk, vinegar and oil, it makes the easiest mayonnaise in the world.

Another machine I invented can combine a multitude of flavors, consistencies, colors or even smells into the final product. It offers more than 500 million possibilities. This makes innovation really easy! It is no longer a matter of imagining an original association of flavors, but to select the best among all those to which you have ready access. In terms of cooking, the selection criteria should be love, then art, and finally technique.

Why love? Imagine that I make a wonderful Parmesan soufflé for you, but that I throw it on the table and order you to eat it: you will not enjoy it. If I explain that I prepared it just for you, with great care and with your Italian grandmother in mind, you will have an entirely different experience. The great secret of cooking is not technique, but love. That is why the food industry choses the dishes that are as close as possible to "home-made", those that remind you of your mother's cooking. Let us never forget that food is mainly a social activity.

MOLECULAR GASTRONOMY: A NEW SCIENCE

In my laboratory, entirely dedicated to cooking, we have invented a new science: molecular gastronomy. My goal, in doing so, was not to innovate. I couldn't care less about innovation, and what's more, I would even say I abhor it! Generally speaking, science should never aim for innovation. Its only goal should be to explain phenomena. It is perfectly erroneous to talk about "applied sciences." Science, by definition, is never applied. If it is, it becomes technology.

My goal then, is to find a treasure, not in hard cash, but in knowledge about molecular gastronomy. The applications of this science, and that is when innovation really starts, are found in pharmacy, cooking, cosmetics, metallurgy, etc.

Soufflés, Onions and Carrots Under the Microscope

Here is one example of how we worked on soufflés. When we began exploring this field, there was a theory that claimed that soufflés rose thanks to an expansion of the air bubbles, caused by heat. A mathematic law indicated this expansion was of about 30%. Clearly, this is false, because some soufflés double in volume. By measuring the pressure and the temperature of a soufflé, I discovered that in fact they rose under the effect of the evaporation of water. This led to a new theory. When we know that a gram of water produces a liter of steam, I can therefore create 40 liters of soufflé from 40 grams of matter. This is an innovation, because the result is different from the soufflés that we knew before that.

There is another field to which my laboratory dedicated 10 years of efforts: carrot broth. To analyze this beverage, we used an extremely sophisticated and expensive machine (remembering it takes five days to analyze one sample of broth). We now know that it is made up of water, sugar (glucose, fructose), malic acid and other amino acids. On the basis of these results, I can now produce a novel food, based on glucose, malic acid, fructose and water, for example.

One day, using one same carrot, we made two pots of broth. We used the same water, and the same temperature, for the same amount of time. The broth in one pot was orange, and the broth in the other pot was brown. It was "normally" impossible. I mobilized the whole laboratory to analyze the phenomenon: I saw this anomaly as a possible source of great discoveries. For three months, all our researchers dedicated all their energy to this matter. There was no reason for the broth to become orange, since the pigments of carrots are not soluble in water. So, how could this color possibly have been obtained? We had to understand the underlying chemical phenomenon. We finally understood that the only difference between the two samples was that one had been more exposed to light than the other. So if you project light onto a carrot broth, it becomes brown. This is an important discovery for chefs, who generally use fried onions when they want to obtain a brownish color. Yet the same can be obtained simply by shining light onto it. Working on a matter that seemed trivial and carrying out purely scientific research lead us to successfully identifying an application that could be useful immediately, and by chefs from all over the world.

I recently put an onion cut in quarters in an MRI scan. Yet another crazy idea? Not really. The image obtained demonstrated that it was made of layers, something we already know, but most importantly, that there was a white membrane between these layers. We had no explanation for it. The next day, we reproduced the experiment with another onion. We finally understood that when you cut an onion, the knife applies pressure on the tissue of the onions and makes them take on a slightly brown color, just like an apple, a banana or an avocado do once they have been cut in two. However, if we use a knife that is not in metal but a ceramic knife, which is what Japanese and Chinese chefs use, the tissues are not pressed but delicately separated. Thanks to these experiments, we can offer recommendations for chefs in their choice of equipment.

Another idea that opened new perspectives was when I had the feeling that the human body was gel, which is generically defined as "water captured in a solid." Are we not solids essentially made up of water? Following the same line of thought, food is also essentially gel. If you look at an onion under a microscope, you can see it is made up of small bags full of water: gel. Meat is also made up of fibers filled with water and proteins: more gel. What a source for a multitude of experiments!

A Brief Review of Molecular Inventions

Let us review some other inventions in the field of molecular gastronomy.

I imagined a clarification solution by means of filtration, using one of the machines in my laboratory. It is a fast and modern application that gets far better results than any chef in a kitchen.

With the system of decantation bubbles, it is very easy to multiply flavors and to give new flavors to a piece of food. For example, you can make the odorous molecules of wine impregnate the oil.

By means of ultrasonic vibrations, the machine creates an emulsion (a mayonnaise for example) in a couple of seconds. This is an ideal solution for manufacturers.

Another very popular device is the low temperature oven that cooks very tender, juicy and tasty meat. The result is the same if you place your roast (carefully protected in a plastic bag) in a dishwasher!

Essential oils, with their very strong odors, are not soluble in water. How can you inject oil into a food that is mainly liquid? For that I use ethanol that dissolves very easily in water. More specifically, I dissolve essential oil in ethanol, and then pour this liquid in water. I then get a cloudy solution that is a perfectly stable mix, like the *ouzo* you drink in Greece or *pastis* in France. Thanks to this technique, it becomes possible to inject any flavor into a food. Pierre Gagnaire prepared a whole dish based on this principle.

This Chef, who owns restaurants in Paris, Las Vegas, Dubai, Hong Kong, Moscow, London, and Berlin, came to me one day with the following problem: how could he ensure the grains of salt he spreads on a piece of meat stay crunchy until the waiter presents it to the guest, and the grains do not melt? Solution: all you need to do is inject salt into oil, which will protect the grains. For Pierre Gagnaire, this is my most important invention! Yet it is very simple. An innovation therefore is not necessarily the result of intense intellectual work, but rather an answer perfectly adapted to a specific need. In the same spirit, the *icy salt*, salt that has the same consistence as icing sugar, spreads evenly on your chips.

One last example: liquid nitrogen, which makes it possible to make ice-cream very easily, has seduced a large number of chefs throughout the world. This has made it possible to cook melting mouthfuls inside a layer of ice, or for example, dishes made of a multitude of layers, some liquid, others solid.

ARTIFICIAL FOOD: WHY NOT?

Let us now talk about note-by-note cooking, to which I now dedicate a large part of my research. It is not molecular gastronomy, or science or technology, but actual cooking.

The idea came to me from a habit that my grandfather had: when he made liqueur, he placed a piece of wood inside the bottle. When you mix wood (that contains lignin) and alcohol, you obtain many aromatic components, including the wonderful vanilline. I adopted this principle that consists in playing with components, as if playing with musical notes. That is how I can tint a whisky with a delicate taste of peat by using paramethylphenol.

I have now started generalizing this idea, and dream one day it will be possible to cook only with pure compounds, i.e. without meat, fish, vegetables, fruits, or any other traditional ingredient, but only with components that are manipulated note-by-note. Pierre Gagnaire was the first one to use this principle in a dish in 2001. Since then, chefs from Bangkok to Dublin have used this technique.

Meat is made of fibers, water and proteins. It is possible to make artificial meat by injecting water and proteins into fibers. The same principle applies for vegetable and for a multitude of other foods. Who knows if that might represent an interesting idea to feed the planet tomorrow? Is it dangerous? Not as long as you avoid using dangerous components. On the contrary, it rules certain techniques which are harmful such as barbecue cooking. Does it taste good? If you like it, it does. "Good" does not have a meaning *per se*. The important thing is the pleasure that the dish provides.

It is possible to imagine all sorts of products by all sorts of tastes, colors and consistencies. It is a new artistic proposition offered to all the individual imaginations throughout the world.

COMBINING LIFE AND TECHNOLOGY TO POSTPONE DEATH: HOW FAR ARE WE PREPARED TO GO?

Dr. Laurent Alexandre

President of DNAvision

On September 18, 2013, Google launched Calico, a subsidiary which aims at increasing human life expectancy by 20 years by 2035. Its involvement in the race to cure aging and the fight against death proves the extent to which medicine has become an industrial sector, and that the rules are changing. Technology is leading us to experience a societal change which will modify the way we relate to life and our identity in decades to come.

This new step taken by Google has three primary motivations.

The first motivation is political and ideological, and is based on the principles of transhumanism. Google founders, Sergueï Brin and Larry Page, are fervent transhumanists, for whom it is legitimate to use the full power of NBIC technologies (nanotechnology, biotechnology, information technology, and cognitive science) to postpone death, even if that means changing our biological and genetic identity. Ray Kurzweil, the Director of the famous search engine, is the world leader of transhumanist organizations. Vint Cerf, co-founder of the Web, argues that we have to hybridize with machines in order to increase our capabilities.

The second motivation lies in the explosion of the amount of medical data. Over a period of a decade, medical and genetic electronic technologies will increase the amount of data in our medical files by a factor of 1 million. DNA sequencing generates 10 terabytes of data, i.e. 10,000 billion pieces of information per patient. Who better than Google to process this massive amount of data?

The last motivation is technological: NBIC technologies are close to reaching maturity.

THE AMAZING RISE OF NBIC TECHNOLOGIES

What does "NBIC" Stand for?

The expression "NBIC technologies" refers to four scientific fields.

First, nanotechnologies, thanks to which we can operate at the level of a billionth of a meter, i.e. modify matter at the scale of what composes cells. Next, biotechnologies, which operate at the level of biological matter, namely our DNA. Then comes IT, followed by cognitive sciences, which explore artificial intelligence, algorithms, and the brain.

These different technology waves are coming together, and are leading us towards a true revolution, the first impact point of which will be medicine, and our fight against diseases and death.

Practical Achievements

NBIC technologies have already led to a number of achievements, which in turn have already affected our daily lives.

For example, at the crossroads between cognitive sciences and IT, electronic brain implants have been created to fight Parkinson's and other brain disorders. Another example could be the creation of the MOOC online courses.

At the crossroads between nanotechnologies and cognitive sciences, there are the nano implant technologies, initially developed in Singapore, which aim to modify the way our brain works.

At the interface between nanotechnologies and cognitive sciences and IT, we could for example, refer to the development of microprocessors.

At the interface between nanotechnologies, IT and biotechnology, we have DNA chips, which are simply revolutionizing medicine.

Finally, at the interface between nanotechnologies and biotechnologies we can find nanosensor systems and nanomotors, destined to change the way our cells work and to fight illnesses.

To list but a few of some of the remarkable achievements made possible thanks to these technologies, we could mention the democratization of DNA sequencing, the creation of tissue from stem cells, surgical microrobots, the first artificial cells, or even the possibility to manufacture sperm and ovules from skin cells, thanks to the technique developed by Professor Shinya Yamanaka, 2012 Nobel Prize in Medicine.

Booming Growth

NBIC technologies are experiencing very rapid growth. For example, the enzymes capable of breaking down DNA, and changing a section, are 1000 times cheaper than nine years ago. The cost of DNA sequencing is also significantly lower, and is 3 million times cheaper than 10 years ago.

Another example is the iPhone 5S, which has 15 million times more computing power than the Apollo 11 lunar module which sent two men to the moon in 1969.

IT servers are 1 billion times stronger than 30 years ago, and, following Moore's law, they will get 1 billion times stronger over the next 30 years. In 1965, Gordon Moore, co-founder of Intel, predicted that the number of microprocessors and integrated circuits would double every 18–24 months at a constant price. This prophecy has been confirmed. Today, the integrated circuits of microprocessors are barely a couple of nanometers, i.e. the size of a few atoms. Electronics therefore are an important part of NBIC technologies.

Our ability to listen to extraterrestrial civilizations thanks to antennas like the antenna from the SETI Institute (Search for Extra-Terrestrial Intelligence) has been multiplied by 100,000 billion in 20 years... but without any result so far.

NBIC technologies are revolutionizing the 21st century, just as aeronautics, the telephone, chemistry, electricity or the automotive industries did the 20th century. However, they are different in some respects.

First of all, most of them are not developed in France. France successfully mastered the technologies of the previous century. Today, it is far less powerful in the field of NBIC technologies, which are the monopoly of the countries in and around the Pacific Ocean.

Secondly, NBIC technologies no longer affect inanimate matter. Their goal is to change our cells, our chromosomes, to modify our neurons. The NBIC revolution affects humanity.

Finally, NBIC technologies have led to the birth of industries characterized by exponential growth. Unlike DNA sequencing, the automotive industry has not seen its costs divided by 3 billion in 10 years!

WHERE WILL NBIC TECHNOLOGIES LEAD MEDICINE?

The Challenges of the 21st Century

Driven by NBIC technologies, medicine will be faced with numerous challenges as follows:

First challenge: Unpredictability, the technological brand of the 21st century. In 1990, an international scientific consensus reached the conclusion that humanity would never be able to sequence every gene on every chromosome. Twenty years later, DNA sequencing has become something somewhat banal. These technological waves are so fast-paced that achievements long regarded as being impossible have become reality.

Second challenge: A shift in medical added value. Tomorrow, *data mining* will do more for us than a stethoscope. Medical power will shift in favor of people who master technology, and companies which control medical algorithms. New actors will appear in the world of medicine, and these will be based primarily in the Californian ecosystem.

Third challenge: Important economic upheavals. The Asia-Pacific region dominates NBIC technologies. That is where almost all of their potential is located. China represents 50% of the potential of DNA sequencing, whereas Europe represents approximately 0%.

Fourth challenge: Major externalities. Individual decisions made regarding NBIC technologies will have significant collective consequences. Ultimately, the changes made to our biological identity and our genome in decades to come will modify the human species.

Fifth challenge: A host of biopolitical issues. How can we control, master and regulate the power we have over our biological and genetic nature? These vertiginous changes will have significant political implications.

Sixth challenge: Medicine as an instrument of power. The avowed aim of the Chinese "precocious youth sequencing" is to identify the genetic variations specific to intelligence, in order to increase the IQ of Chinese population overall throughout the 21st century by means of embryo selection. Social democrats and humanists could find themselves on the losing side of the argument against governments who consider it legitimate to increase the IQ of an entire population through genetic modifications.

NBIC technologies will take us in a very different direction from the practice of medicine as I was taught it.

Three Major Technological Waves

Three major technological waves affect and will affect our lives all the way to the 2040s: electronics; biological engineering; and nanomedicine.

In the field of electronics, the hybridization of our bodies with electronic components has progressed through various phases: the pacemaker in the 1970s; cochlear implants, electric circuits which are placed in the brain of deaf children to help them hear; intracerebral implants, used in the treatment of Parkinson's disease from 2008, or of compulsive eating disorders and serious obsessional behaviors, as well as in an experimental treatment against Alzheimer; electronic implants in the retina of blind people, first authorized in 2012. At present, they only offer mediocre vision, but perfect vision should be achieved by 2030; or electronic organs, such as the Carmat heart which was recently implanted in Paris.

Moreover, surgical robotics are developing rapidly. The surgeons of 2030 will be specialists in biomechanics and IT, and will no longer touch their patients.

Biological engineering explores three fields: genetic engineering, modification of our DNA to correct mutations and pathogens; cellular engineering, regenerating tissues thanks to stem cell technologies; and tissue engineering, creating full organs — larunx, retina, and brain — from a polymer matrix with stem cells.

In this third major current of nanomedicine, the role of nanotechnologies is to help modify the way our cells work. Nanomedicine will have to face several major philosophical questions relating to our ability to manipulate our biological nature, and the limits that ought to be set on this.

AN UNFORESEEN AND UNPREDICTABLE TECHNOLOGICAL TSUNAMI

The future will bring with it a significant number of innovations and opportunities, but will be very difficult to predict, because of the explosive nature of the technologies of which it is composed.

By 2015, DNA sequencing will be routine. By 2020, stem cell technology and gene therapy will be fully mastered, and we will be able to regenerate our tissues and modify our DNA. From 2025, nanomedicine will be a part of everyday medicine.

The 21st century will see other technological waves. We cannot yet predict what most of these will be; we know only that these explosive technologies will lead to the emergence of unexpected technological innovations.

For example, nobody foresaw how quickly DNA sequencing would become the norm. For the most part, such inventions used to stay in closed laboratories. Scientists and doctors could not imagine the future as we see it now. In this respect, in 1970 in his essay *Chance and Necessity*, Jacques Monod, the founder of modern molecular biology, Nobel Prize in Medicine, stated that *"the size of our DNA means that it is probably forever impossible for us to modify our genes."* Yet in 1975, the first genetic manipulations on bacteria were carried out.

Extraordinary IT Power to Help Understand the Living

Immense computational power is necessary to understand and modify living matter. Today, we have that power. In 1950, servers generated 1000 kiloflops (1000 FLoating point Operations Per second); by 2007 they were capable of 1 petaflop, i.e. 1 million billion operations per second. Today, the fastest computer in the world operates at 33 petaflops. The hexaflop threshold, necessary to represent the 100 billion neurones of the human brain, will probably be reached by 2019, the zettaflop before 2030, and the yottaflop (1 million billion operations per second) around 2039.

One thousand billion billion operations per second are necessary to fully reproduce all the synapses of the human brain, i.e. the thousands of interfaces in each of our 100 billion neurones. In order to reproduce an intelligence which is more or less equivalent to human intelligence, i.e. to develop a genuine artificial intelligence, we would first have to achieve yottaflop computing power.

The growth of computing power has greatly enhanced our ability to understand the changes of the living.

Genomics and its Applications

NBIC technologies are going to spark a genuine revolution, of which next generation DNA sequencing technologies, the alliance of nanotechnologies, biotechnologies, IT and artificial intelligence are the first tangible traces of this.

Current sequencing technologies. The cost of sequencing has been divided by 3 million over the last 10 years, going from 3 billion dollars for the first sequencing (with 22,000 researchers from all over the world over a period of 13 years) to 1,000 dollars. Today, it only takes a couple of hours, and it only requires one technician to launch the program. In the past, in the span of a lifetime a geneticist might sequence approximately 1,000 of the 3 billion chemical messages carried by our chromosomes. Today, the latest generation of sequencers can sequence approximately 50 billion per hour, automatically. There really has been an explosion in the number of human beings who have been sequenced.

The study of origins. Sequencing can help us better understand our origins. Because DNA can be conserved for up to approximately 1 million years, it has been possible to sequence the DNA of Neanderthals and the *Homo denisova*. The DNA of the *Homo erectus*, a more distant ancestor, will soon be completed. Thanks to this, researchers have been able to establish that Neanderthals could speak.

Towards a more lucid health care. Genomics have helped us understand how our organisms work, and identify our predispositions toward certain illnesses, to define our health care path, and to develop medical innovations. There is often great confusion between heredity, genes, and genetic predisposition. Our genomes do not determine whether we will be affected by a given disease with certainty. Some of these predispositions are acquired in the course of our life, because of DNA modifications.

The fight against cancer. All cancers are genetic, but only 15% of them are hereditary, i.e. had a DNA anomaly inscribed in patient's genes from birth. One in three human beings develops a cancer. This is an important challenge. Medicine can help fight genetic disorders, and "bad" genetic variants. Cancerology has been radically transformed by genetics, which has demonstrated that cancer is an excessively complicated disease, which affects each and every one of us in a different way. Every cancer presents specific genetic mutations. Therefore, each patient has to be given specific treatment, adapted to his or her own specific mutations. This "personalized medicine" became possible with the sequencing of tumors, which helped demonstrate the extreme biological complexity of cancers.

THE CONSEQUENCES OF NBIC-MEDICINE

Demographic Impact

Life expectancy has been on the increase since 1750, and in the past 250 years has tripled. In France, it went from an average of under 25 in 1750, to more than 80 today. To what extent can medicine increase our life expectancy? Ultimately, four scenarios are possible.

The first possible scenario is a reduced life expectancy due to ultraliberal globalization, GMOs, or cell phone radiation, etc. A second possible scenario is pessimistic: the collapse of technology. The third possible scenario is technological progress: life expectancy would then be increased by three months every year, like today, i.e. a life expectancy of approximately 100 years by the end of the 21st century. The last possible scenario is the one anticipated by Google, in which thanks to NBIC technologies, starting in the 21st century, we will be able to increase life expectancy rapidly, and to postpone death at a much faster rate than before.

Since the 20th century, genetic alterations have the potential to increase human life expectancy considerably. This has already been proven with rats and mice. But what price might we have to pay in terms of our humanity to die later and age less quickly? To what extent would the modifications we could bring to our body alter our philosophical, religious and political beliefs?

Philosophical Questions

To do or not to do? The question therefore is not so much: "can we do it?" but rather "should we do it?" Should we embrace the transhumanist ideology and accept that the human race be biologically altered? The younger generations will have to answer these questions, and will probably respond positively, influenced by the deep desire to prevent death at any cost.

When NBIC technologies are used to personalize medicine, regenerate our organs or avoid cancer, they do not raise significant philosophical dilemmas. However, the same cannot be said when it comes to the selection of embryos, "designer babies" or preimplantation genetic diagnosis.

Designer babies, a sensitive question. The "designer babies" phenomenon is without a doubt one of the most important ethical dilemmas of this century. Today, it is possible to draft the complete sequence of the DNA of babies during pregnancy, thanks to a simple maternal blood test. We already know that certain genetic variations can explain low IQs, as is the case with Down syndrome, for example. The genes responsible for higher IQs were discovered in the 21st century, thereby presenting society with a moral dilemma.

We now stand on the precipice of the age of eugenics. The choice made by Western countries to screen for Down's syndrome through amniocentesis, with a 1% risk of miscarriage, seems to indicate that moral barriers of Westerners are relatively low: 97% of Down syndromes which are detected in Europe lead to an abortion. Only one child in 30 with trisomy disorder survives the screening, and today there are 30 times less children with Down syndrome than 25 years ago.

This eugenic choice was made without any real moral debate. Tomorrow, our society will be able to do the same for myopathic children, or for children with cystic fibrosis, or forms of mental handicap other than Down syndrome. We have already adopted eugenic practices, without even realizing it.

Sequencing and choosing your life partner. Tomorrow, we will be able to choose our life partner in terms of his or her genetic characteristics. If, thanks to DNA sequencing, we are able to know what genetic abnormalities and illnesses we carry, we can also choose to avoid partners with similar anomalies.

Advances in neurogenetics. The most troubling dilemma comes with neurogenetics, i.e. selecting children based on their future IQ. In an article published in the *Wall Street Journal*, the head of the precocious youth program in China explained that neurogenetic problems troubled Westerners, but not the Chinese. In his opinion, it is legitimate to use technologies to increase the IQ of the Chinese population of the 21st century. It is true that in the intelligence-dependent economic war in which we are currently immersed, being able to "mass produce" equivalents of Bill Gates would be more useful than multiplying agricultural workers...

The repercussions of biotechnology on maternity. In the 21st century, motherhood will be transformed. Following embryo sequencing, gene therapies on babies will be routine as early as 2020. From that point on, it will be possible to produce an unlimited number of ovaries for women. It will also be possible for men to produce ovules, and for women to produce sperm from their skin cells. This is something that is being advocated by some gay associations in the US. The same applies to developing artificial wombs, so parents would not have to resort to surrogate pregnancies.

The Social and Economic Consequences of NBIC Technologies

The medicine of tomorrow will no longer depend on human skill. Part of the added value of medicine will be held by those who master biological and genetic algorithms. DNA sequencing represents 10 terabytes of information per patient, i.e. 10,000 billion pieces of information, and 20,000 billion for patients with cancer. This mass of data will completely redistribute medical power. The power of patients could then be more limited: *Doctissimo*-like websites will never be able to analyze a gene. Expert systems, powerful computers will be necessary.

Consequently, doctors will probably be marginalized, impoverished, and avoided. Their power will be threatened by medical technologies.

The health system will also be transformed as a consequence of this deluge of data. Every day, 100,000 new genetic mutations are discovered. They cannot be learned off by heart. Ultimately, health professionals will have to outsource their brain through *cloud computing*.

We will enter a world of risks without hazard. These risks will be identified at very early stages, which will transform the organization of the health system overall.

Tomorrow, the DNA of the Directors of the National Institute of Health (NIH), the biomedical research center in the US, or the National Institute of Health and Medical Research (INSERM) in France, will have to be sequenced in order to verify that they are carrying out research without any ulterior motives ... just as we currently determine the genetic heritage of elected representatives who are candidates for the presidential election so too we will check the genes of those in charge of the research.

WHO WILL BE IN CHARGE OF CONTROLLING THIS RESEARCH?

Controlling Data Streams

Google, thanks to its financial power and its mastery of algorithms, might be the one to control medical algorithms and so would be at the heart of NBIC-medicine. The leaders of this company are betting on exactly this, which is why they are currently investing heavily in health care.

The medicine of tomorrow will be more like nuclear physics and astrophysics than the practice of medicine as taught in the 1970s–1980s. The image of the doctor as a heroic, unique, and inspirational genius, who is able to offer a diagnosis based on his own knowledge and intuition, with practically no IT, will no longer be relevant in the era of NBIC technologies. Medicine will become a collective activity, which is supported by expert systems.

Who will manage the billions of items of genetic information? The DNA of a human being, which is a language structured around four chemical elements — adenine, guanine, cytosine, thymine — represents a total of 3.1 billion letters, which constitute our genetic identity. In order to be able to deal with these genetic signals, we will have to prioritize, plan and accompany patients.

Weak Moral Prohibitions

As things stand, today we are sitting on top of what I call a "bio-transgressive slope." More and more, we readily give in to the moral consequences of technologies. Our limits are like the Maginot lines: they are not strong enough.

Norms which vary over time. In the 1950s, the Pope decided not to excommunicate doctors who practiced breathing exercises with women during labor to reduce their pain. At the time, these "painless childbirth" methods were seen as an intolerable moral transgression, just as the pill, abortion, or organ transplants were deemed unacceptable at one point. It is also interesting to remember that 80% of Americans were against the first *in vitro* fertilizations.

Similarly, technologies which were seen as totally unacceptable are becoming normal, desired and sometimes even a necessity. Tomorrow, we will probably welcome surrogate pregnancies, artificial wombs and gene therapies that reduce suffering, that help us age less and die less.

Norms which vary in space. Euthanasia, which is illegal in France, is also legal in Belgium: 1,432 cases were recorded in 2013. In Flanders, a young transsexual who underwent sex reassignment surgery which failed obtained the right to be euthanized. Recently, Belgium has also authorized euthanasia for minors. The need for the consent of both parents was only introduced into the text law at a later stage.

Why do norms evolve? This demonstrates that moral taboos vary. Tomorrow, in order to die later and age less, adjusting them will be acceptable. Our moral norms will shift even faster tomorrow: our generation, the Nintendo generation, the digital generation, is a generation which will not tolerate frustrations, and will accept biotechnological alterations, just as did the previous generation. Faced with the threat of Alzheimer's, the now aging baby-boomers will eagerly welcome the development of cerebral implants, stem cells, nanoparticles and gene therapies, abandoning current moral barriers. The succeeding generations will benefit from this progress within a couple of decades.

In the 21st century, a new power will be built around these technologies. Without realizing it, we are already transhuman, human beings who are modified thanks to glasses, contraception, pacemakers, hip prosthetic implants, artificial crystalline for cataracts, etc. In order not to be sick, we have accepted to enhance our body. Tomorrow, we will consider it is better to be transhuman, better to be genetically modified, than dead. This means that your generation is likely to accept a significant number of biotechnological modifications.

Shared Power, Not Without Conflict

The power of NBIC technologies is currently taking shape around four actors: NBIC technology industrials, primarily located in the Asia-Pacific region; patient associations, who consider it is better to be transhuman than dead of a myopathy; transhumanist intellectuals, of whom many can be found working with Google; and phil-entrepreneurs, who invest in NBIC research, such as Paul Allen, the second largest shareholder of Microsoft, who is building an extraordinary research center for research on brain genetics.

Google is at the center of this new power. The company finances the *Singularity University*, the largest university in the world dedicated to NBIC technologies which trains transhumanist leaders.

These changes will not take place without generating political conflicts. Bioconservatives, such as Francis Fukuyama, former counselor to George Bush, consider that NBIC technologies must not be used to change people and help them die older. They might well oppose transhumanists violently, since their vision is in stark contrast with their own.

Political systems will also have to face major contradictions: should we apply a precautionary principle and put a hold on gene therapies? Seeing the brain as a sanctuary also means accepting genetic disorders, and maintaining inequities. Are we the owners of our genetic heritage? Are we entitled to know everything straight away? For example, at the age of 18 should we be told that we might develop macular degeneration linked to age, a disease which causes blindness due to the destruction of the retina? This type of information could clearly be very frustrating, as this disease affects one in three people over 80.

Should we introduce a moratorium on NBIC technologies, even if this means putting Europe in a position in which it will be dominated by countries who already master these technologies? Should we impose our values on the rest of the world and explain to China why they have to stop pursuing neurogenetics?

HOW FAR WILL WE GO?

The 21st century will be inundated by an array of challenges. How can we arbitrate the conflict between conservatives and transhumanists? How can we develop sustainable and long-lasting ethics? Should we improve people, accept eugenics? To what extent are we entitled to change the future? In decades to come, as citizens and managers, you will have to face these questions.

Personally, I believe that life expectancy will be extended significantly. By 2100, it is highly likely that it will be much greater, because people in their 80's will have benefitted from many biotechnological innovations. The first person who will live until the age of 1,000 years old is not born yet, and will not be the child of the technology of 2014, but rather of decades to come.

However, we can ask whether there is a certain form of technological determinism which necessarily leads us toward the victory of NBIC technologies. Will the transhumanist prophecy, disseminated through the magazine *Wired*, which proclaims that death can be postponed as early as the 21st century prove true? There is no way to know. Between bioconservatives and transhumanists, the battle is far from over.

The "death of death" is probably the most mind-blowing subject of the 21st century. We are going to manage our DNA, generate artificial life, command our own brains and fight death more efficiently. This fusion of life and technology, to postpone death, will be extremely troubling. It will not be done without conflict, even if it is only moral and religious conflict. The detractors of technology may win, and the 21st century may not be the century of the all-powerful and all-mighty NBIC technologies. It could also be the return to obscurantism.

GENOMICS AND ITS IMPACT

Dr. Liu

*Deputy Director and the Senior Group Leader of the Human Genetics
Program of the Genome Institute of Singapore*

I studied marine biology in China, and went to Duke University in 1991 to complete my PhD in this field. However, once I was there, I found recent developments in genetics so interesting that I decided to switch my field of study. In 2002, I joined the Genome Institute of Singapore to head its research program on human genetics. When we talk about human genetics, one cannot help but look back at the futuristic sci-fi thriller Gattaca (1997), in which the social fabric is defined by individuals' genetic make-up, and where genetic manipulation in order to ensure every child inherits the best traits from each parent is common practice. Could this happen in real life? The real question today is not whether or not this will become reality, but rather how soon will this be a part of our reality?

The fact of inheriting one trait or another is a field called heredity. In the 19th century, Gregor Mendel, the father of genetics, was the first to understand this key concept. This Moravian Augustinian friar studied plants and flowers extensively, and how they either varied or were similar in color, shape and form from one generation to another. The leading theory in biology at the time was that inherited traits, be it of plants or of human beings, blended from generation to generation. Mendel, however, identified that certain traits were not found in offspring plants with intermediate forms. He observed that sometimes, phenotypes disappear and do not show up in the offspring, but are however present in the second generation. This meant that something in the plant controlled its phenotype, that this was passed on from generation to generation, and that it was unbreakable. This led him to the conclusion that both sets of information co-existed in one way or another, and were inherited as a unit. This unit is referred to as the "unit of inheritance", and what we know now is that this is, in fact, our genes and our DNA.

Let us now see how this process operates in humans. Humans start as a single, unique cell called 'zygote'. It is the product of a fertilization event between two gametes. This single cell starts dividing, and creates an entire organism. The most important and precious element within this zygote is the DNA, because it carries all the information required to make an organism from a single cell. This single cell provides all the instructions on how to "make" or "build" the organism and helps to control the development, functioning and reproduction of all its organs. Nobel Prize winners James D. Watson and Francis Crick identified that DNA molecules exist in a double-helix structure. When you take a closer look at the molecules, they are made of smaller units called nucleotides. There are four types of nucleotides: A, C, G and T, each holding specific coding. Put together these characters build a sequence. This sequence is the basic physical and functional unit of inheritance. Today we have not yet identified what every single coding refers to, but most of it has been identified.

Within a cell, DNA is organized and packaged into a structure called chromosomes. They contain the DNA as well as all associated protein complexes. The molecule itself is a very fragile structure. Therefore, this information must be protected or it can be damaged or 'broken'. In order to grow from a single cell into an entire, functioning organism made of millions of cells, the DNA needs to be intact for each and every cell. Each cell has to be able to use this structure so that, in turn, it is able to carry out its function within the organism. The genome is the complete set of DNA or chromosomes of a living organism. Humans have 23 unique pairs of chromosomes, one set coming from the father and the second set from the mother.

The replication process of a DNA molecule is very accurate yet not perfect. Sometimes during replication, a small mistake is made. This is commonly referred to as a mutation. When such a variance is introduced, a certain degree of mutation can be observed between the parental DNA and the DNA of the offspring. There are many types of mutations: point mutations, those affecting a small gene in one or a few nucleotides involving the insertion or deletion of the genetic material, or large-size mutations, where one part of a chromosome is lost or is split into two pieces (duplication). Another phenomenon which can occur is recombination, which is the production of offspring with combinations of traits that differ from those found in either parent. This recombination can lead to an exchange of information between the chromosomes of a chromosome pair. This creates a new chromosome which is a mixture, a combination of sorts, of the parental chromosomes. As a result, a recombinant chromosome will exist in the offspring, thereby creating sequences which would not otherwise be found in the genome.

Ever since it was understood that DNA held the key to the entire inheritance process, scientists have dreamt of being able to identify the entire human sequence. The human genome is made up of 6 billion base pairs, which make up what is commonly referred to as "the book of life." The entire human sequence, the key to the book of life, can only be obtained through sequencing. When our cells replicate the DNA molecule during cell division, they need to open up the chromosome and use one strain as a template in order to make a new strain. Sanger understood this process, and used this concept to develop a strategy to sequence DNA. He used a fragment of DNA as a template, and tried to make the fragment correspond to all possible fragments. The fragments are then separated by size, and the bases at the end are identified, recreating the original sequence of the DNA. The copies vary in length, and by analyzing these fragments, the original sequence can be read. Sanger applied this method to complete the sequence of all the amino acids in insulin, and it took him years to complete this. Later in time, technology automated this process. Thanks to a 384 format reaction, the sequencing by synthesis could reach up to a thousand base pairs. This marked the beginning of the 'industrial scale' of sequence production.

Thanks to this technological breakthrough, the scientific community started contemplating the idea of sequencing the entire human genome, and so started the human genome project. Scientists from all over the world came together with the goal of determining the sequence of all the base pairs which make up human DNA, and of identifying and mapping all of the genes of the human genome from both a physical and functional standpoint. It involved over 20 research groups, hundreds of scientists, from six countries (China, U.S., U.K., Germany, Japan and France) and billions of dollars. The project was launched in 1990, and the entire human genome was completed in 2000. In 1998, while this publicly-funded, collective effort was on-going, Craig Venter, the founder of Celera Genomics, started a private funding venture to sequence the human genome. He received no money from the government, but assured everyone he would be able to reach this goal faster. And indeed, he completed in 2 years' time what the other project achieved in 10. Vender's joining the race actually speeded up the process of the public effort as he had announced that should he complete the human genome first, his intention was to patent it. This, of course, generated great concern among the public community, which encouraged them to speed up the effort to ensure this discovery stayed part of the public domain so it could not be patented. In fact, both projects actually finished at roughly the same time.

To achieve in 2 years what had taken the other, massive, project 10 years, Craig Venter used novel technology. His strategy was to break the entire genome down to the smallest possible pieces, and then use random sequencing over this pool of millions of billions of small fragments. He relied on computer technology, and a sound team of computational scientists, and rumor has it that he borrowed data from competing project which had already become part of the public domain. From this moment onward, there has been a strong interrelationship between genomic science and computer science. The data to be processed represents such large volumes that it would simply not be possible to assemble the genome without computer technologies.

The completion of the human genome marked the beginning of a new journey. Scientists then moved on and started sequencing more organisms, and in so doing, the process became faster, more accurate and cheaper, meaning that the cost of sequencing a single genome reduced over time. The first sequencing cost $100 million. Following the principles set out by Moore's law, whereby speed and cost efficiency double approximately every 2 years, the cost of sequencing gradually decreased every 2 years, until 2007, when a dramatic acceleration of this decrease was observed. This was made possible by a technological breakthrough: new sequencing technology came onto the market, i.e. the second generation sequencer called SOLiD system, which enabled scientists to sequence 60 gigabases per run. This marked the trend until 2015, when the sequencing of a human genome cost approximately $1,500. Now, it would take less than a week to obtain the full sequencing of a genome, as opposed to the ten years at the outset. As you can see, we are not quite at the stage depicted in the film where people can buy a sequencing over the counter, but we are definitely not very far away from it!

Once the human genome project was completed, scientists started applying it to other species in order to understand their DNA sequences. To date, we have complete sequences for 100,000 bacterial, hundreds of plants, about 80 to 100 mammals, etc., which has helped us understand how they are related. While these achievements are nothing short of outstanding, sequencing the genome is only the starting point. What we need to understand is what instructions this coding is giving; we need the key to decipher the book of life. Several projects have been launched to achieve such an understanding. For example, the 1000 Genome Project (2008–2015) sequenced a total of 2,504 genomes, including 504 from East Asia, 489 from South Asia, 661 from Africa, 503 from Europe, and 347 from the Americas. This project was purposefully designed to obtain a map of the human population and world regions. Today, there are many more ambitious initiatives that have been launched throughout the world: Genomics England, UK, which aims to sequence up to 100 K individuals (with cancers and rare diseases); Precision Medicine Initiative, US, which aims to sequence up to 2 million individuals; Human Longevity Inc., founded by Craig Venter, which is planning to sequence up to 40 K human genomes per year, up to 100 K human genomes. Another interesting project is Mychael Synder's iPOP Project, in which he sequenced himself. He took 20 blood samples, approximately once every 2 months while healthy, and more frequently during periods of illness. He tracked about 20,000 distinct transcripts coding for approximately 12,000 genes, 6,000 proteins and 1,000 metabolites.

What can sequencing do? Why are governments around the world pouring so much money and effort into these projects? Above and beyond the desire of gaining a scientific understanding of the so-called 'book of life', sequencing can have more practical, medical applications from which we, as individuals, can benefit greatly. For example, Nicholas Volker was born in 2004. He was a healthy baby but as a toddler, he failed to gain weight and at the age of 2 he developed chronic intestinal inflammation, necessitating over 100 surgeries, including the removal of his colon. Despite their best efforts, doctors were unable to establish a clear diagnosis. In 2009, in a desperate attempt to understand the underlying cause of his symptoms, his doctors sequenced his DNA. They found a mutation known to lead to a fatal immune disease, not dissimilar to Leukemia. This hypothesis dictated treatment: if it acts like leukemia, then it should be treated the same way. And so, Nicholas received a bone marrow transplant, and he magically recovered. More recently, Angelina Jolie made the headlines for her medical issues. Her mother and a maternal aunt had both suffered breast cancer. She decided to get tested to see whether or not she carried a BRCA mutation. Women who carry a mutation in the BRCA1 present a 60–80% risk of developing breast cancer throughout their life, and a 40% risk of developing ovarian cancer. A BRCA2 mutation induces a 50% lifelong risk of developing either of these cancers. The tests showed that Angelina Jolie carried the mutation, and in an attempt to prevent both breast and ovarian cancer, she made the decision to undergo surgery. In 2013, she underwent a double mastectomy and in 2015 she completed the procedure with a hysterectomy.

Not all diseases follow as dramatic a pattern as the BRCA1 pattern. However, there are substantial genetic risks for most of them, which are then considered to have a very high level of heritability. This means 90% of the risk of contracting disease is controlled by our genes. This includes well-known diseases, such as Alzheimer's, celiac disease, diabetes and auto-immune disease. A company developed a commercial service based on this idea: it sold a sequencing service informing 'clients' of the risks they have of developing given genetic-controlled diseases. However, this service was subject to much debate, and the FDA decided to interrupt it. As it pertains to medical information and a disease control of sorts, the FDA considers this is a biomedical issue, and so should be controlled by the FDA. Others, however, argue that this is just a service sold to normal, healthy people who are simply curious about their genetic make-up. The issue of who should manage such services is still under debate. Providing this type of information freely, without any kind of consultation or support can be dangerous because some people may not be able to handle this information, and this may, in fact, be doing more harm than good.

Sequencing is being applied to numerous fields of study. For example, applied to history, it can help scientists understand more about the origins of our species, the evolution of man, and immigration patterns. Today, all humans are 99% identical. The remaining 1% difference is due to different mutations over time and generations. This has helped us identify a "genetic map" of the world: how similar and close we are genetically worldwide, and from one region to another. Such studies are fueling a reflection on human evolution and human migration over the ages. Of course, entrepreneurs were quick to capitalize on these findings, and genomics has left the realm of what is merely scientific, and has become a consumer business. For example, companies offer a service which consists in informing people on their ancestry thanks to their genetic information.

Now, scientific efforts are concentrating oñ identifying the functions of each individual gene in order to understand the 'instructions' they give. In order to do so, we must knock out one piece of DNA at a time to identify each individual function. This is called functional annotation. For example, we were able to identify the 'eyeless gene', the master gene of eye development. If this gene is removed, the organism in question does not develop any eyes. If overexpressed, a fully-functioning eye will be found on a different part of the body. This is remarkable because eyes, for example, are such a complex structure within an organism that it is astonishing that after 'turning on' one single gene, the body is able to develop an entire human eye. This means that the network already exists, and that the gene provides the instructions on how to 'activate' it, and once activated, the machinery sets itself in motion. In order to understand each individual gene function, we must adopt a gene-by-gene strategy. We have recently started using a more systematic computational strategy, in order to sequence which 'instructions', i.e. functions, each element provides. Gene function is important, of course, but where and when it is expressed are equally important. To this end, the National Human Genome Research Institute (NHGRI) launched a public research consortium named ENCODE, the Encyclopedia of DNA Elements, in September 2003.

Once we are able to identify gene function, then we should be able to replicate it, or at the least, manipulate it. Genetic engineering consists in modifying an organism's genetic composition by artificial means, often involving the transfer of specific traits, or genes, from one organism into a plant or animal of an entirely different species. This is what we did with GMO crops for example. We borrow a gene from a different species because it presents a desired trait, which is then introduced into the target plant or organism. With corn for example, crops were affected by insects. We borrowed a gene from a given bacteria which is known to kill these insects. We overexpressed it in the corn, so that the corn could become naturally resistant. This is a very common practice today, which is, however, subject to much debate. The general public is calling for tighter regulations and controls. At the same time, we should not forget that the process of crop domestication is, in fact, a process of natural genetic manipulation. Modern vegetables are the product of a genetic manipulation through slow, natural cross contamination and breeding processes.

Genome editing is slightly different. It does not consist in introducing a new gene into the genome, but rather editing the actual genome. DNA is inserted, deleted or replaced in the genome of an organism at desired locations. The induced double-strand breaks are repaired through a natural process, resulting in targeted mutations, or 'edits'. This technique is currently being applied for something unexpected: mosquitoes. Mosquitoes are a real danger in a number of regions of the world. In Singapore for example, they carry Dengue. More devastatingly, in Africa, they carry malaria. Every year, millions of people are infected, and half a million people die, most of whom are children. Over the years, in order to prevent this epidemic, scientists have focused their efforts primarily on vaccinating people. This process has proven somewhat slow and so far has been unsuccessful in preventing deaths. Scientists have therefore turned to genetic manipulation with two different strategies. The first consists in introducing a recessive mutation that causes infertility in female offspring, ultimately leading to a reduction of the mosquito population and the prevention of disease transmission. The downfall of this method is that the offspring only have a fifty-fifty chance of passing it on, and if this mutation were to become too rare, it would disappear altogether. The second, more recent, is called "Gene drive." A mutation is introduced which changes the sex-determining chromosome, the correcting mechanism cuts the gene and makes it become mutant, i.e. it becomes male. As a result, all progeny will become male. Infertility can spread rapidly throughout a population. While this can be considered very efficient, it does call for caution and raises a debate as to whether or not it is moral to decimate an entire species. The actual malaria virus is completed inside the mosquito's body. Instead of focusing on the carrier, some scientists have now started focusing on the disease. Therefore, instead of producing sterile mosquitoes, scientists are generating mosquitoes able to resist the virus. This would prevent the spread of the disease without destroying the species. The same process can be applied to humans, in what is called gene therapy. For example, the HIV virus relies on one cell surface receptor known as CCR5. By mutating the gene, the virus would not be able to get into the cell. This therapy has already proved very successful and patients have shown signs of recovery.

After identifying, understanding, replicating and editing, what is left? In 2010, scientists at the J. Craig Venter Institute designed, synthesized and assembled a bacteria genome starting from digitized genome sequence information. This complete, synthesized genome was transplanted into another bacteria recipient cell to create new bacteria cells controlled only by the synthetic chromosome. This process enabled them to get the best from each gene and synthesize a new one. While all these achievements are nothing short of astonishing, this is ethically very complicated territory, and caution is necessary. It is not only a matter of being able to do it, but also a matter of whether or not the uses that can be made of these achievements are dangerous, ethical and moral.

IN WHAT WORLD WILL WE BE LIVING IN 2030?

Joël de Rosnay

Special Advisor to the President of Universcience
(Cité des Sciences et de l'Industrie de la Villette et Palais de la découverte)
and President of Biotics International

I would like to encourage you to be guided by three keywords: creativity, trust and optimism.

Firstly, **creativity**, because nothing is more beautiful than what you can achieve yourself, by creating: a company, projects, etc. Then trust, i.e. trusting yourself, trusting your network, trusting your friends, your professors. And last but not least, optimism, or rather, a positive attitude toward the future, because it is better to build the future you hope for rather than the future others — industrialists, politicians, religions — have imagined for you. However, this is no easy task. As Jacques Monod, my mentor from the Pasteur Institute, once told me: in life, when you want to launch a project, you will come across three types of people: those who do the same thing, those who do the opposite, and those who do nothing, i.e. everybody! However, in no way should this discourage us from innovating.

To describe what the world will be like 15 years from now, let me describe a typical day in the life of an Engineer, Julien, who has invited his friends and family to celebrate his 60th birthday on October 23, 2030. His granddaughter Chloé takes this opportunity to ask him what life was like in 2015. Of course, this story will be filled with technological and digital innovations. However, this will not have taken anything away from the human dimension: people will still be baking birthday cakes, following rituals, people will be dressing as they do today.... With this story, I hope to reveal some of the positive evolutions that would have occurred. The media take pleasure in focusing on the dangerous and negative aspects of new technologies, but I much prefer to be bold enough to think positively.

A TYPICAL DAY IN 2030

Welcome to a day in Julien's life. He has invited his friends and family to celebrate his birthday. His energy-plus house generates more energy than it consumes thanks to its roof which is completely covered in solar tiles, all connected to each another. They receive satellite data and the Internet, which is then redistributed throughout the house. In the garden, the genetically engineered lawn stops growing before it needs mowed. Julien uses his communication room to contact his colleagues remotely, because he works from home. His house is connected to a "smart grid", which sends electricity to others. His hybrid car works on hydrogen and an electric battery, and sells on electricity to the neighborhood when it is not running. His car has become a "mobile societal battery" of sorts.

Julien has taken a "blue-sky day" (term coined by Google in the 2010s): a day where his employer, Transnational Instrumentation, pays him to "do nothing." This gives him an opportunity to think freely, come up with new ideas and discuss them with others in his communication room. It is covered in tactile and 3D screens. When he puts his smartphone (or Unitcom, designed in China and offering all the standards of yesteryear) on the table, the content of the phone is displayed on the screens and he can share it with the people on the other end of the line.

In 2030, "smart agents" are a part of everybody's daily lives and pro-actively act on their behalf. They do not need to wait for you to give them orders: they already know the things you do routinely, your calendar, your communication network, and act accordingly. When Julien organizes creative sessions in his communication room, these smart agents listen to the conversations and are able to produce detailed reports or summaries. They edit these digitally, and send a copy to Julien's Manager and his company's R&D department. These reports all contribute to building wonderful archives for the company, and are accessible to all through databases.

Julien invited his granddaughter Chloé, born in 2017, for his birthday celebration. At the young age of 13, she is already a project manager for a company of educative and entertaining products, which offers a range of pedagogical games created by children her age. She receives a salary, and young game designers can either earn royalties or give up their royalties for intangible benefits derived from their notoriety, enabling them to be remunerated in other networks, for other services.

A Connected Health Care

Chloé asks her grandfather how he manages to look so young. It is because biology has made considerable strides over the previous decades. One of the noticeable advances is "measurable prevention." The connected tools that people wear (bracelets, glasses, shoes, collar buttons, T-shirts, etc.) record a series of body parameters (blood pressure, heart rate, cholesterol, creatinine, phosphate, transaminases, blood sugar, etc.) and are connected to the PHCD, the Personalized Health Care Dashboard. The data from this dashboard is sent to a doctor who has become somewhat of a life advisor. Rather than prescribing medicine to treat his or her patients, he can help them adopt the best possible lifestyles in terms of nutrition, physical exercise, stress management and meditation. This system is based on the principle of "quantifiable prevention", which has had a significant impact on the pharmaceutical, cosmetic and food industry. The revolution of lifestyles brought with it a revolution of traditional industries.

One of Julien's favorite tools is his ARCLs, Augmented-reality contact lenses, formerly known as Google Glass. Let's remember how challenging the launch of this product proved to be in the early 2010s. It came up against strong opposition, for fear that this innovation might violate personal privacy — for example, by giving you the name of the people you came across in the street thanks to face recognition. Smart watches and other smart glasses did not have the expected success; however, Bio-Glasses — contact lenses that can measure people's biological features — are being used more and more. For example, lecturers use ARCLs to read a script on a teleprompter which scrolls down as they speak. With his ARCLs, Julien can take photos of his friends by simply blinking. He can then send this photo to his brother who is taking a walk in the woods, and who can see the photo with his own lenses.

With these "wearable" tools and new medical technologies, healthcare has made such progress that life expectancy now reaches 120, 130 or 140 years. Representatives from the transhumanist movement, in which Google invested significantly at the beginning of the 2010s, have taken a keen interest in NBICs, (*nanotechnologies, biotechnologies, information technologies & cognitive science technologies*). Google X and Calico (Californian Life Corporation), created by Google, no longer simply sell time-savings thanks to their search engines: they also sell a longer life expectancy and better health. Among the products they are developing is genetic screening to detect possible diseases. Because in 2030, for 100 Euros, you can order a full DNA screening, which will reveal possible pre-dispositions to certain diseases. Ray Kurzweil, one of the greatest thinkers of transhumanism, says he is convinced that thanks to the progress made by medicine, which has made him extremely fit at 60, he will never die. Laurent Alexandre, author of *La Mort de la mort* [1], thinks that among those born in 2014, some will live up to the age of 1,000.

In 2030, embryonic cells are programmed on demand to reproduce specific organs — like a lizard whose tail grows back when it is cut off — making it possible for people to re-grow damaged organs. Organs can also be built from scratch with 3D bioprinters, which place embryonic cells on collagen or other surfaces where they can connect with each another. With this system, medical teams can grow skin, parts of a heart, a liver, a muscle... By 2030, then, regenerative medicine has developed considerably.

Julien's father, Bernard, who is 98 years old, joins the party. He is wearing bio-chips which correct any metabolic mistakes in his body, and has had several organ transplants which were all successful. He regularly runs marathons. He does not need to worry about nutrition, because his smart agents, who know everything about him, automatically suggest specific diets or exercises. He has also had some implants in his brain. Science has acquired a better understanding of the inner-circuits of the brain with the help of computer simulation. In 2014, the Human Brain Project was launched, involving some 50 laboratories throughout the world, with the aim of understanding the brain better and making a digital model of it, so that it can communicate with machines.

A Global Brain

Chloé asks her grandfather if one day, the "giga-computer" made up of all these inter-connected networks and systems, might start thinking. Julien tells her that in the 2000s, people already discussed the idea of a "global macro-organism." A researcher had even coined the term "cybiont", combining cybernetics and biology, to refer to global macro-organisms which people were building from the inside out — as if people were neurons and were building a brain from within. The idea of a global, worldwide brain grew from there. There is a certain point, which researchers refer to as "the point of technological singularity", which could happen somewhere between 2050 and 2060, when this system could become aware of its own existence. In other words, the system will become our own consciousness. We will become symbiotic men and women, in symbiosis with the system. This will lead us from the Era of Communication to the Era of Symbiosis. Over time, communication will no longer require keyboards, and will rely only on physical contact, voice or by impregnation within 3D images, with the support of proactive agents. This opens to the way to the possibility of simultaneous creative communication.

Emotion and Human Beings Before All Else

Chloé wants to go to the bakers to buy some wholemeal bread and a birthday cake for her grandfather. With a simple click on his phone, Julien calls his Electroyota, a connected car which comes to them automatically. Chloé asks if they can take the scenic route, which is much more pleasant than connected e-highways where cars travel at 200 kilometer/hour one meter apart from one another.

The next day, they decide to go to the former *Cité des sciences* [City of Sciences], which has been renamed the *Cité des Sens* [City of Senses] — which reflects just how much feelings and senses have overshadowed scientific knowledge. When they enter the museum, there are tools to prepare their visit, starting with augmented reality glasses to walk through the exhibition. A drone finds them by GPS and knows their names, and invites them to follow it, and to guide them to wherever they want to go. Such a scheme already existed in 2012 at MIT. Each visitor also receives an active badge, which transmits a halo of keywords within a 100-meter radius pointing out both things that match their interests and people who they are interested in meeting. This means that whenever you visit an exhibit, it recognizes you and adapts its content to your profile and tastes. With these tools, visitors can also receive Oled documents (*organic light emitting diodes*), on a support which is as flexible as paper, but where information is displayed in the same way as on a tablet. When you want to speak to a stranger, with Tradomat, an automatic translator, you can speak to him or her in your own language, and he/she will understand it in his or her own (Skype had tested this as early as 2014). Robots roam the corridors of the *Cité des Sens* to help visitors with limited mobility, or those who are blind or deaf.

To go back home, our friends call their car, which drives itself back from the parking lot where it had parked itself, and automatically takes the e-route. They can replay their visit on the car screen, and can talk to the people they met thanks to the active badge.

A GLOBAL DIGITAL ECOSYSTEM

In 2030, we will be living in a digital ecosystem. In the past, in 2014, we went *on*-line. Now each person lives *in*-line, in an omnipresent digital ecosystem that is controlled by their Unitcom. The real challenge is managing to disconnect. More and more, individuals have understood the importance of human contact, of personal ties. Social ties and lifestyles make up for the excessive digital presence and or over-connectedness. De-connecting is no longer a luxury but a need, to take time to live and think. Wisdom and common sense compensate for the excess of information.

People have become mutants equipped with an array of tools. In their symbiosis with the digital ecosystem, less and less people use screens to communicate: they use words, eye movements and *body language,* or even communicate directly from brain to machine thanks to *brain activated technology.* The human body has become a transmitter–receiver. Thanks to molecular electronics attached to skin like tattoos, people can communicate information from within the body to the outside world. Thanks to electromagnetic fields this data is transmitted toward these tattoos, and transmitted to the body to modify certain behaviors.

While this is a source of advances in terms of health care, education and business, it also involves a certain amount of risk. Because your body is constantly communicating, so too information about you is gathered constantly. What used to be referred to as *big data* in the 2000s–2010s now also comprises more and more genetic data.

One risk is that this could lead to the emergence of digital monopolies, those that, in 2014, were called the Gafama (Google, Apple, Facebook, Amazon, Microsoft, Alibaba). These are "State-businesses", platforms that use collective intelligence, and make individual people their slaves, a "pronetariat" of sorts. We must be aware that we are working for these Gafama. By going on Amazon, Google or Facebook, we actually generate added value for them, by informing them on trends, names, links — information that they subsequently sell to their clients. Such exchanges can be a win–win situation, as long as by 2030 we are able to control the risk of allowing the emergence of digital monopolies against which States would have no weapons. States are centralized, pyramidal, localized, whereas these State-companies are delocalized, horizontal and present throughout the world. They do not pay taxes to the territories in which they operate and are as rich as States. Gafamas alone has the financial capacity to buy out the entire French automotive Industry! That is why it is important that we, citizens, join forces to establish citizen co-regulation.

These State companies will increase their presence in two sectors in particular: the automotive industry, with electric cars becoming iPads on wheels; and the home, which will become an iPad with four walls. The *home cloud* is becoming the core focus of companies such as Google, Honda or Toshiba, which offer solar panels and other energy-producing devices, but mainly sell houses for 20% less than real estate agents. These *home clouds* will be one of their primary sources of profit. This system involves internal electronics which ensure the education of children, the safety of the elderly, protection of the house, etc. Between 2014 and 2030, these digital actors will have progressively taken over all the large traditional industries (banking, insurance, tourism, luxury, entertainment, real estate, automotive industry) from the inside, by operating digitally. Our political and economic elites do not seem to see this tidal wave coming, so focused are they on their own power pyramid and on being re-elected.

In summary, with all the connected tools that we will be wearing, because of our symbiotic connection with the global living organism that we will have built, we will evolve, and become mutants of sorts. This global, connected brain will change us, and we will co-evolve with it. We are already

HBGM, des "hybrid, biodigital, geolocalized mutants." By 2030, symbiotic people and the Symbionet will be a reality.

OLD TECHNOLOGY, FUTURE STUDIES AND A SYSTEMIC APPROACH

Old technologies, future studies and a systemic approach can help anticipate future evolutions, as I have just done. The first key to understanding future mutations is to step back from the analytical approach we are traditionally taught at school, subject by subject, and to try to adopt a global understanding of the interdependency of systems, a combinatorial approach which mobilizes assessment, follow-up, future studies, networking, and simulating cascade effects. Analytical (Cartesian) approaches and systemic (global) approaches are not opposed to each other but rather they are complementary. Systemic methodology can help organize knowledge so as to gain in efficiency.

This vigilance follows a sequence of steps: it means defining a need, identifying the strategic research axes and trend indicators, mobilizing research tools, analyzing by cross-comparing sources, sharing information and then, to complete the cycle, redefining needs.

As Gaston Berger, the founding father of this field of studies, once said: futures studies is about imagining oneself in the future, in order to see the effect of this future on the present. Consequently, it is not a case of making linear extrapolations. The most efficient method, which I developed at MIT with my students, is called *technological forecasting by analysis of converging trends*. Based on our observations from a technological watch, we are able to build possible scenarios (a technological innovation, for example); then, from among the trends already described, those which could lead towards this or that scenario are chosen. Relevance tests are then performed, retrospectively, to validate the soundness of these scenarios, taking into account the technologies involved for each of them. This then leads to adjusting the scenarios. It is a back-and-forth game between futures studies and retrospective, which ultimately helps define increasingly likely and credible trends.

This is the method I used to make up the story I just told you. In 2030, technological innovations aside, the human factor, human interrelationships and lifestyles will not have changed drastically. This makes me hope that the world will become what we make it, and not what some want to impose on us.

REFERENCE

[1] Laurent Alexandre, *La Mort de la mort, comment la technomédecine va bouleverser l'humanité*, Jean-Claude Lattès, 2011.

39

UPGRADING IMAGINATION

Kevin Warwick

University of Coventry

All things concerning a human being's imagination are controlled by that individual's brain. Most likely, a dog or spider may well have their own imagination. However, we can only speculate, as Kafka did in his metamorphosis, as to what those imaginations consist of. It is highly probable though that they would relate to that creature's experiences and life. Clearly though they would be directly dependent on the number of brain cells involved and the connectivity of those cells. Obviously, the different sensory inputs and motor outputs that the individual has will limit certain imaginations whilst enabling others. A water spider spends its life traveling up and down inside a bubble in water. What is its imagination like?

For humans, our experiences and life control what imagination we have. Our brains and bodies dictate and therefore severely limit what it is possible for us to imagine. A person who has lived all their life in a small remote village in Africa may well have a different imagination to that of a Theoretical Physicist living in New York City. So why don't we change things? Through neural implants, an individual human's brain can be plugged into the internet, thereby providing a multi-way communication via a network both with computers/machines and other humans whose brains are similarly plugged in.

Such a scheme opens up a plethora of possibilities, included amongst these are: Communication by thought alone; extended range of sensory inputs; the individual's body is extended over the network — so the brain can directly control technological body parts (possibly on another planet) and obtain feedback from them; upgraded mathematical and memory abilities due to the computer link — essentially memories can be outsourced and multi-dimensional perceptions. Maybe there will be more than these, but it is difficult for human's to imagine such until we have more experience of such implants.

Each of these upgrades, in its own way, brings about a distinct change in performance for the individual concerned. Thus far, rudimentary results have already been obtained on the first three of the upgrades — communication, sensory enhancement and remote feedback — however, it is the latter two that will be real life changers, particularly, the capability to conceive of, understand and imagine a multi-dimensional world. We do not mean here four or five dimensions but rather hundreds or thousands of dimensions.

There will always be those who grumble about such innovations, who say that they are not possible or the world is fine just as it is. There will also be those who are stuck in a limited, present day understanding of their environment and might say "But the world is 3D, there's no point in making it more complex, we will not gain anything." Let us be 100% clear on this, it is the human brains of today that impose a 3D understanding of the world around us, nothing more and nothing less. But in doing so we impose a multitude of restrictions as to what is possible and what not.

The world around us is not 3D, it is quite simply the world around us and that's it. In making sense of it, it is possible to consider our environment in terms of any number of dimensions. In fact, superstring theory posits that the universe exists in 10 dimensions. Other theories take this number up to 13, 14 dimensions and beyond. There is no 'final' dimension in reality, merely a limit to human imagination. So for theoretical physicists there is no problem in considering things to have such complexity. The difficulty is imagining such a reality when our present day brains have been restricted to a 3D existence.

Presently, we are faced with a limited outlook on what is possible for human achievement. A limited number of humans have been to earth's moon and back, but that is rather akin to merely popping to an outside toilet. When the first humans travel to Mars, as surely they will before long, it will be like visiting your next door neighbor. We need to be thinking about traveling much further afield — to other galaxies, to the distant reaches of the universe. Such thoughts are however merely dreams at present because we usually conceive of the world around us as consisting of merely 3D space.

We presently feel that travel, even to the edge of our solar system, will take a lifetime or even several lifetimes in order to return to earth. This could involve some people spending their entire life merely as part of a small unit traveling to or from a planet which contains no life form and no resources. Not a pleasant thought, a sort of prison existence when the individual has committed no wrong. It could be regarded as much worse than in previous centuries when prisoners were transported on a one way ticket from England to Australia because of past crimes.

However, as soon as we start imagining our universe as being multi-dimensional so space travel becomes an immediate possibility, wherever we wish to go. Just as taking to the air over 100 years ago meant that continental travel on earth later became an instant success using airplanes, so brain implants will subsequently mean that space travel is a similar success. In both cases, it requires thinking outside the box and merely looking to a future in which the present day understanding needs to change. Before the Wright Brothers got off the ground, Lord Kelvin and others claimed that it was not possible for heavier than air machines to fly, only a few years before they did so. Now there may well be those who claim that humans will never be able to imagine in 100 dimensions — do not listen to them!

So it's OK for you to imagine the future in which your main means of communication between yourself and other upgraded humans will be directly by thought, where your nervous system will be extended over the network so that your brain and body can be in different places, where you can have whichever sensory inputs you choose (try ultrasonic as a starter, it's cool!!), where you don't need to worry about remembering anything as your part-machine brain will do it for you, where your body will have technological parts such as buildings and vehicles and where you'll be able to travel around the universe in fractions of a second using dimensions that ordinary humans of today cannot even conceive of.

40

THE DISILLUSIONMENT OF SCIENCE

Jacques Testart

Biologist, INSERM

THE DEATH OF SCIENCE

Science is dead. This is the ominous conclusion I reached after 43 years as a researcher. I was not born a science critic. As a child, I was a naturalist. I was fascinated by insects, by mice and by the beauty of science in general. However, my career as a researcher taught me that science has gradually been dead and has been replaced by techno-science. Techno-science is a discipline whereby fundamental knowledge is applied with a view to creating a technological result. It capitalizes on the tools offered by science to do more science, which, in turn, will lead to the defining of better tools, and so on and so forth. This cycle has become an important element of the economy, but it is incompatible with making new discoveries. Today, innovation takes precedence over discoveries. When you hear about the great achievements of genetics, the invention of CRISPR–Cas9 to edit the genome, etc., these are all technological achievements, but they offer no understanding of how the human organism works.

Techno-science also hinders the freedom of researchers. Today, scientists are mere contractors. There is about one chance in 10 of being awarded a research contract, and then researchers are tied for several years to producing something designed to be useful to the economy. This means that it is the market which governs innovation. As such, it is an economic tool rather than a cultural one. The science philosophers talked about is dead.

Today's techno-science takes advantage of the prestige of this science, but only to favor patentability over truth. This has taken such proportions that today, reputable international journals have openly admitted that over half the papers submitted to them are falsified. The message the author(s) try to get across may be accurate, but charts, figures or results are edited so as to reach the desired result. This goes against the very principle of fundamental research, in its quest for knowledge, and is an extremely alarming trend. Young students and researchers are exposed to these practices and forced to do the same if they want to survive in the world of research.

Techno-science is in no way democratic. It takes advantage of how the people worship techno-science thinking it is science, but has no regard for the population which finances research. Who chooses what topics should be researched? How are they aligned with the common good?

THE BIRTH OF IVF

In 1964, I was hired by INRA as an agricultural engineer to find ways to improve milk production. There had already been some attempts with gonadotropin therapy, i.e. ovarian stimulation thanks to a gonadotropin-releasing hormone in order to increase ovule production. Because *in vitro* fertilization was not available, we had to use *in vivo* fertilization. This method, however, proved unsuitable, for two reasons. Multiple births are dangerous in cattle, and they lead to freemartinism, which causes infertility in female cattle born with a male twin. These outcomes were not compatible with the desired economic outcome of increasing milk production. I therefore developed a technique based on the same principle, i.e. ovarian hyper-stimulation, after which we inseminated the females with the semen of major milk breed bulls. A few days later, we retrieved the embryos by means of a uterine wash, and re-injected the embryos into desirable heifers, thereby developing gestational surrogacy for cows. The first calves were born from this technique in 1972. That same year, the European Union implemented milk quotas. While I was working on a way to increase milk production, the European Union, who had funded my contract, was also implementing commercial methods to prevent the overproduction of milk. I started questioning the organization and most importantly the legitimacy of science and research in Europe and in France. When I brought this up with the Director of INRA, he remonstrated with me, telling me that it was not simply a matter of increasing milk production but also a matter of having more competitive cows.

I felt increasingly guilty, and this was my first disillusion. During my research, I had met and worked with farmers, cattle ranchers, etc. Some of them expressed concerns that the results of my work could be a threat to their livelihood. This made me realize how my scientific work was destroying the place of farmers, an issue which is still relevant today. It became evident to me that the so-called research industry was not acting on behalf of society. Had anybody thought of the impact my work would have on these men and women? Had anybody even asked consumers if they needed more milk or if they preferred more local and varied production?

After this experience, and by the end of the 70s, I felt the need to move on to something new. I had acquired unique skills in reproductive research and hormonology, and had made a name for myself in the field. In 1977, Dr Emile Papiernik, the head of the maternity unit of the Antoine-Béclère Hospital, suggested we set up a research laboratory in his service to work on human infertility. After my first experience, I felt that helping people build a family and bringing them happiness was a noble cause, all the more so that our goal was not so much to create assisted procreative technology, i.e. to produce tools or techniques, but rather to understand the underlying mechanisms of human reproduction. One year later, a British team of researchers announced the birth of Louise Brown, the world's first test-tube baby. After the success of the British team, French gynecologists were putting a lot of pressure on me to achieve the same, which I was not opposed to. For me, this project the opportunity to help more couples, in ways we had been unable to until then.

IVF is a twofold undertaking. There are, on the one hand, obstetricians, who deal with the patients, prescribe the hormones; and then there are the labs, in which the gametes are fertilized. In the 1980s, there were two laboratories in Paris working on IVF, mine and another in Necker. Colleagues at Necker hospital were able to achieve IVF. I had succeeded in fertilizing the ovules, but when I transplanted the embryo it never led to a pregnancy. There was a lot of competition between gynecologists to "catch up" and to be the first in the country to achieve the same as the British team.

Gynecologist Jean Kohen came to me and proposed a scientific protocol to identify why we were failing. This protocol consisted in harvesting eggs in both hospitals, transporting them by taxi to the two laboratories which were doing IVF, and then returning the embryos, if there were any, back to the initial hospital so the patients could receive their embryos. To our great surprise, the first attempt succeeded. It was terrible for the gynecologist I worked with, Rene Frydman, who had not been involved in this process, and who was suddenly at the head of the first test tube pregnancy. This experience gave me the opportunity to get a behind-the-scenes look at the medical world, which is driven by personal interests and competitiveness.

It took us 2 more years to conceive our first test tube baby, Amandine, who was born in 1982. This achievement attracted significant media attention, to an extent that made me uncomfortable. This success also triggered exacerbated competition among gynecologists and biologists, who fought to receive the praise for this achievement. Not only was I not interested in this race for fame and glory, but I suddenly became aware that medical research and the medicine "industry" was no longer at the service of patients, but rather at the service of those who practice it. This scientific achievement sparked numerous debates, and led to the establishment of a national ethics committee. But most importantly, from that point forward I started questioning our success, and the possible abuses of medically assisted reproduction. At that point, I met a group people from social sciences with whom I worked for about 10 years: philosophers, sociologists and psychoanalysts. We met regularly for discussions, and this was a breath of fresh air. Researchers are surprisingly narrow-minded. There is an undeniable intellectual poverty in the scientific field, which is terrible when you consider the responsibilities entrusted to them. This was the opportunity for me to broaden my horizons, and to think beyond statistical results and scientific findings.

The media attention the birth of Amandine attracted was not a revolutionary scientific feat, our success came 4 years after the first test-tube baby. The Church and psychiatrists said we had separated sex from reproduction. But sex had long been separated from reproduction, ever since people started practicing *coitus interruptus*. We already had a number of very efficient birth control methods. I then understood that what we had done was actually bring about the conditions for the potential "lift the veil" on reproduction. When the embryo is under the microscope, it is in the spotlight, and we can therefore analyze it and foresee what type of embryo it is going to become. There are always multiple embryos with medically assisted procreation techniques. Therefore, what these new methods were offering was in fact the potential selection of specific embryos based on specific, genetic criteria. When I first raised this concern, gynecologists and geneticists thought it was ludicrous.

FROM BUILDING FAMILIES TO EUGENIC DETERMINISM

Four years later, in 1990, a team in the UK developed a technique called Pre-Implantation Diagnostics (PID). This method consists in harvesting one or two cells from the embryo in order to determine certain of their genetic characteristics, so as to choose the embryo which best suits the parents' project or health requirements. I felt the contribution I had made to helping infertile was already being abused. It was no longer a matter of helping couples who could not procreate to have a child, but to program a child for potentially fertile couples who desired a child which met specific, non-medical criteria. The difference between prenatal diagnosis and PID is that whereas the former gives a couple the opportunity to avoid the worst, based on their own personal ethics, the latter is applied to find the "best", without this being motivated by sound medical reasons. I grew increasingly concerned that this would turn children into a manufactured product, and that society would gradually move towards a more and more pronounced refusal of differences between people based on arbitrary, genetic criteria. I also feared that children born from this type of process would live a life of immense pressure, having to live up to the expectations their parents had placed on them.

I refused to take part in this and, of course, I was dismissed from the lab. I simply could not contribute to the development of research enabling the manufacturing of calibrated children. The media misinterpreted this refusal; one newspaper headlined its story: "Jacques Testart, at the threshold of the sacred." As a fervent agnostic, this title baffled me. The article said that I had chosen to retire permanently from research. Of course, this statement was unfounded, because I had clearly expressed my intention of continuing to find solutions to help infertile couples have a pregnancy that would lead to a naturally "random" child. And this is exactly what I did. In 1986, I developed a method for freezing embryos. This enabled couples to freeze the embryos they did not use for their initial IVF should they want to use them again at a later stage, thereby saving them the trauma of having to go through the entire treatment all over again. In 1994, we obtained the first baby from a new, revolutionary method developed by Belgian researchers: intracytoplasmic sperm injection (ICSI). Instead of having thousands of spermatozoids to enable the strongest to fertilize, the sperm is injected directly in the ovule, thereby enhancing the chances of success.

At this stage, I published extensively on the abuses of IVF. Today, IVF counts for 3% of all births in France. In one third of these, IVF is used with no medical justification, and in two thirds of these births, the embryos are fertilized with the ICSI method, even when it is not medically necessary. This method is most widespread because it is easier to have the same process applied to all, even when this process is not necessary. I personally believe this is a mistake. We do not yet have enough hindsight to be sure this method does not lead to epigenetic diseases, but it is too lucrative a business for clinics and hospitals to give up on. Assisted reproduction has opened up a very lucrative business opportunity. This also explains its success and the support it receives, as well as the extent to which it complies with societal criteria, which are neither medical, nor well-founded.

LIBERATING RESEARCH AND MAKING SCIENCE NOBLE AGAIN

These two experiences led me to the conclusion that there is always somebody pulling the strings behind research. Researchers have no independence in this business-driven environment. I felt the need to reconnect with Science and to rekindle my passion for it. At that point, I was in charge of the research laboratory at the American hospital of Neuilly, with younger gynecologists. I wanted to do real scientific experiments, engage in selfless science, the science which elevates people, the poetic science. I was interested in studying how human gametes recognized each other. All species have a mechanism enabling them to recognize gametes from their own species thanks to dedicated proteins which can be found in the ovule and the spermatozoid. The scientific commissions authorized to issue research licenses and credits asked me what financial or medical benefits could be expected. This meant that for them the knowledge I was offering had no intrinsic. The second question they asked me was why I wanted to conduct this research, since a technique which I had myself developed rendered this knowledge unnecessary. This criticism was fair, but still a little difficult to hear. It meant that the technology I had contributed to develop was hindering the development of knowledge. I applied a second time, but this time round, I had defined a technological project which would "justify" the research in the eyes of the commission. Given that the proteins on spermatozoids and ovules I wanted to study enabled fertilization, understanding the underlying mechanisms would enable us to develop a vaccine to inhibit these proteins, thereby creating a form of immune contraception. This would have been particularly relevant for third-world countries because it is very cost-effective solution. They accepted the principle I was defending, but they then asked me who my industrial partner would be. This meant that in order to be judged worthy, a research project has to serve economic growth. Of course, I was unable to find a partner for this project. The pill and other contraceptive methods are too lucrative a business to jeopardize it! Because the project had no commercial outcome, the commission did not authorize the project.

All these professional setbacks and scientific disillusions led me to become what I call a science critic. In 2002, I founded with fellow researchers *Sciences Citoyennes* [Citizen Science], an association designed to democratize and rehabilitate science. We apply for recurring credits for fundamental research, which are disappearing today. In the past, half of the budget of a research lab was dedicated to producing a contractual outcome, and the other to what we called "free research", i.e. on topics which researchers were curious about and which they themselves chose. I believe we should bring this back, even if only in the interest of those who want to commercialize the product of scientific research. Today we are building only on the heritage of past knowledge. Our failure to renew this knowledge base can only lead to the exhaustion of investment possibilities in the future. From a less financial point of view, it is paramount we continue developing our understanding of the human organism. Should we fail to do so, this would leave us exposed to the consequences of changes in our environment and climate.

I also believe that targeted research should be based on the needs and desires of the population, and no longer dictated solely by economic interests. With that in mind, our association has developed a system to enable the general population to give their point of view. A group of people is picked at random, and is given contrasting information on the research proposals. They are then invited to discuss the issue in question, and decide whether or not the research project we have offered is worthy of interest, is something that should be done, and whether or not it serves the greater good. In doing so, we are putting "humanity" back at the heart of research. We also work on the protection of whistleblowers, reforming expertise and the idea of re-enchanting research. Today, the research situation is quite bleak. Other scientists, just as I do, feel disenchanted or disillusioned with their work as scientists. Bringing back the pleasure and enchantment of science, by offering projects which are requested by or supported by society, would give researchers a renewed sense of purpose, and that is what we need if we are to preserve the future of research.

The environmental disasters which await us in years to come make it all the more vital for the future of humanity to mobilize the vital forces of science and technology to ensure the survival of the species. Climate change will present threats we cannot yet imagine. Not just because of climate change itself, but most importantly because of the parasites and bacteria that this will bring about. This could happen as early as within the next 30 years, leaving us biologically and medically powerless. I believe a different science is possible, but this can only emerge in a new political economic context, freed from mercantile concerns.

Printed in the United States
by Bookmasters

Printed in the United States
By Bookmasters